ABRAHAM HESCHEL'S IDEA OF REVELATION

Number 171
ABRAHAM HESCHEL'S IDEA OF REVELATION
by
Lawrence Perlman

ABRAHAM HESCHEL'S IDEA OF REVELATION

by
Lawrence Perlman

Scholars Press
Atlanta, Georgia

ABRAHAM HESCHEL'S IDEA OF REVELATION

Library of Congress Cataloging in Publication Data

Perlman, Lawrence
    Abraham Heschel's idea of Revelation / by Lawrence Perlman.
        p. cm. -- (Brown Judaic studies : no. 171)
    Includes index.
    ISBN 1-55540-350-6 (alk. paper)
    1. Heschel, Abraham Joshua, 1907-1972. 2. Revelation (Jewish
theology) I. Title. II. Series.
BM755. H37P47 1989
296.3'11--dc20   89-6191
                                                      CIP

Printed in the United States of America
on acid-free paper

Contents

Acknowledgements

The completion of this book is not only a result of my own energy and initiative. Throughout this quest for knowledge many people sustained me in different ways. My wife Sharyn has seen me through this process, which is no small feat, and brought our first child, Ariela, into the world. The satisfaction of completing this work, pales in comparison to the pleasure of the familial life Sharyn has provided. My parents, as always, have supported me thoroughly. There is no adequate expression for the patience and kindness they have extended to me.

I am deeply grateful to Professor Victor Nuovo of Middlebury College, with whom I read many of these books for the first time, for without his guidance I may never have chosen this path. His nobility, wisdom and compassion have remained as a vision in my mind of the essential qualities of learning, regardless of its context. Professors Joel Roth, Neil Gillman and Fritz Rothschild of The Jewish Theological Seminary, in various ways, have helped me formulate and clarify the issues that faced Heschel as a thinker whose concern spanned the horizons of all types of knowledge. I appreciate the remarks and encouragement of both Professors Kimelman and Johnson of Brandeis University. Professor Marvin Fox, my teacher, has provided exactly the right measure of gentle advice and good counsel. Without his help this work would never have achieved the form it needed.

Finally, I am most indebted to Professor Heschel himself. As a young student I made my way through the philosophical and religious classics of both western and eastern civilization. After coming into contact with Heschel's books I was convinced that until that time I had not really learned to read. Amidst the lines and words of his thoughts I have learned the most precious instruction of all. I hope I have adequately returned the favor.

Introduction

This book, while it explores several theological and philosophical themes, has one main purpose in mind. It intends to instruct the serious reader how to read the works of Abraham Heschel. It wants to delineate a phenomenological point of view from which one can continually and continuously return to the body of Heschel's theological and philosophical ideas that don't seem to cohere with any rigor.

With this aim in mind, one must realize that the usual historical and cultural comparisons found in intellectual histories are not paramount here. History or the study of history cannot supply a point of view. The selection of information is an interpretive and analytical function and this work is firmly committed to the interpretation and analysis of philosophical and theological ideas as Abraham Heschel presented them in his writing. In an important sense this book is a propadeutic to a set of religious problems in a profoundly Jewish and modern context that has not been recognized previously. It is my intention to outline the religious problems that Heschel had before him and to explicate the method and answers which he applied to those problems. Anything less would be philosophically unacceptable and anything more would be an infusion of cultural and historical opinion which has no priority here.

It should also be understood from the outset, that this book makes no attempt to explain each and every aspect of Heschel's thought. This book does not investigate the hasidic and kabbalistic influences on Heschel for instance, or Heschel's existentialism which is rooted in Kierkegaard, or his reliance on Dilthey, but claims, nonetheless, that the philosophical program of Heschel is the methodological ground from which everything else comes into a coherent existence. Heschel may use kabbalistic ideas and phrases, as he uses Maimonides, to indicate and signify what he means by revelation, but the problem to which these phrases and ideas point is consistently phenomenological in the strict sense of the term.

Another introductory remark about the manner of explication of Heschel's thought is in order. Since there is no discursive reasoning found in any of Heschel's work,[1] and since Heschel's texts have been so misunderstood, there is a profound need to incorporate the texts themselves into my explication, as much as necessary, assuring that Heschel speaks for himself. If Heschel is indeed investigating the idea of revelation phenomenologically, then the texts themselves must be read through again and again for their phenomenological depth and not for their logical coherence.

When I approached this subject matter for the first time, about sixteen years ago, I was convinced of its desire to function on a philosophical level. Between then and now I remain convinced that any reading of Heschel that ignores this aspect of his work, by necessity, misconstrues the ideas of that remarkable man. The passage of time has a way of highlighting the significant and of downplaying the incidental. Heschel's sensitivity and complexity in dealing with religious and philosophical problems will become more apparent as the phenomenological aspect of his thought is captured throughout his writings.

---

[1]"The roots of ultimate insights are found, as said above, not on the level of discursive thinking, but on the level of wonder and radical amazement, in the depth of awe, in our sensitivity to the mystery, in our awareness of the ineffable. It is on the level on which the great things happen to the soul, where the unique insights of art, religion, and philosophy come into being." *God in Search of Man*, p. 117.

Chapter One

Heschel's Place in the History of Philosophy

The theology and philosophical method of Abraham Joshua Heschel have received little serious attention since its 1936 appearance in Europe in a study on prophecy.[1] The publication of *Man Is Not Alone* – in the United States in 1951, and approximately ten other volumes and hundreds of articles on the philosophy of religion, the philosophy of Judaism, rabbinic theology and Hasidism – with one exception,[2] effected minimal change on the attitudes of philosophically knowledgeable critics.[3] At the time of Heschel's death in 1972, still little serious attention was given to the entire corpus of his work. His followers and colleagues produced testimonies of his noble character but hardly any independent evaluations of his work.[4] Similarly, Heschel's detractors have criticized different aspects of his thought without attempting to understand the underlying principles which guide the individual parts.

It is ironic that the most thorough evaluations of Heschel's theology have been written by Christian theologians.[5] Unlike many modern Jewish theologians, Heschel's thought is full of references to every conceivable facet of Judaism. Yet, an independent analysis of the totality of his work has never been attempted by a Jewish critic. To what may this neglect be attributed?

One reason is more prominent than all the others. Heschel's theology is radical. It is a total departure from the manner in which Jewish theologians have approached religious problems over the past twenty centuries.[6] Heschel's theology does not possess the slightest parallel of style or method to anything written by any Jewish theologian at any time. There is no greater paradox than this. Heschel, himself a product of eastern European Jewry, whose work constantly utilizes references to all kinds of Jewish theologies, produced a thoroughly Jewish theology which is unlike any other in style and method.

The precise idea which lies at the heart of this paradox is the starting point for this investigation. Heschel's radical break with the past is centered on his attempt to distinguish conventional theology from his own new concept of depth-theology.

> The theme of theology is the content of believing. The theme of the present study is the act of believing. Its purpose is to explore the depth of faith, the substratum out of which belief arises, and its method may be called depth-theology.[7]

It is the contention of this book that depth-theology is based on a serious philosophical doctrine – Husserlian phenomenology – and that it is focused primarily on one theological issue – the idea of revelation.[8] For this purpose, Heschel explicitly makes use of such Husserlian ideas as intentionality and the noetic-noematic correlation. Implicitly this requires Heschel to perform a phenomenological reduction that places the natural and scientific outlooks into a phenomenological context. Once Heschel establishes the connection between his phenomenological method and the idea of revelation, he extends phenomenological treatment to all of the content of depth-theology. The main theological topics he deals with, God, revelation, deeds, prayer, man, and the Sabbath are aspects that emerge from the comprehension of the prophetic act as a noetic-noematic correlation.

The method of depth-theology, its philosophical basis and the idea of revelation, which is the seminal aspect of Heschel's thought, have been overlooked by both Heschel's followers and detractors. Consequently, very little progress in understanding Heschel's work has been made. This method can be traced back to Heschel's first academic work, *Die Prophetie* and is the unifying factor of all his subsequent studies. The method is intimately intertwined with the structure of prophetic consciousness. As a result, depth-theology and its underlying phenomenological basis provide the only backdrop for a clear understanding of Heschel's central idea, the idea of revelation.

There is a second aspect of Heschel's thought which is presented here in a novel framework. Heschel's ideas about rabbinic theology, contained primarily in *Torah Min Hashamayim*, are usually regarded by those who have analyzed them,[9] as disconnected from his philosophical works and as lacking in any recognizable cohesion. It will be argued here that his ideas about rabbinic theology are the necessary elaboration of his phenomenological method. Heschel's phenomenological method requires a novel idea of content within the idea of revelation, because his method is not primarily concerned with the dogmatic content of belief[10] but rather with the act of believing. Without Heschel's unique approach to rabbinic theology, his phenomenology would be a method without roots, virtually unconnected to the body of Jewish tradition.

A thorough explanation of depth-theology that can explain the idea of revelation must account for two things – depth, which is at the root of human existence,[11] and theology. The depth is the philosophical dimension available through the use of the phenomenological method. Theology is the internal cohesiveness of Heschel's statements about God, revelation, and man et al. The first concern, the 'depth' or the phenomenological attitute of Heschel, has been totally neglected. Consequently the second concern, the theological issues, especially revelation, have been given less than adequate treatment by anyone who has analyzed Heschel's thought. Moreover, the connection between the phenomenological method and the idea of revelation has not been adequately explored.

Not incidentally, the phenomenological thesis advanced in this work, has a large impact on the location of Heschel's thought, in the history of modern philosophy. A pure explication of Heschel's phenomenological doctrine may indicate the philosophical complexity of Heschel's thought, but it will not demonstrate an understanding of Heschel's desire to use Husserl's method. In other words, why does Heschel use the phenomenological method at all? Why doesn't he use some other philosophical method? No doubt, the answer to this question will clarify Heschel's location in the history of religious and philosophical thought because it can only be contemplated if Heschel's own concern for these issues is itself brought to the fore. This issue is clearly conceived outside both the providence of Heschel's own scholarly work and his internal usage of the ideas of Maimonides and other medieval Jewish philosophers. Phenomenological method is applied absolutely even when Heschel uses a quote from another philosopher who had no bearing on this method. On the other hand, the everpresent phenomenological method does not discount the manner in which Heschel may utilize these medieval philosophical texts or incorporate their issues into his idea of depth-theology.

Even the casual reader of Heschel's works cannot help but be overwhelmed by the number of references Heschel makes to his religious and philosophical predecessors. Heschel's conceptual approach to classical Greek philosophy alone demands serious attention in relation to his biblical claims. But, even that treatment, while it may, in a significant way, help locate Heschel in the history of philosophy, it cannot address the issue of Heschel's adoption of Husserl's ideas. My assumption is, that there is a problem in the history of philosophy that Heschel believes only Husserl's method can deal with. Heschel's acute awareness of the philosophical climate at the time he wrote *The Prophets* and his succeeding philosophical works, is the response to that problem.

But, the serious reader is hard pressed to elicit these claims. Heschel never put this problem in sharp relief because he never wrote a systematic theology. Nonetheless, it hovers over all his work and comes to the surface in some discussions, which primarily concern the Bible. Clearly, Heschel presents a philosophy of religion and a philosophy of Judaism which is based on its biblical precedents. In his eyes, the Bible is absent in the history of philosophy.[12] Heschel's use of phenomenology and its analysis is directed at this absence. According to Heschel, a particular thinker at a particular time, began the onslaught against biblical thinking.

> There are two approaches to the Bible that prevail in philosophical thinking. The first approach claims that the Bible is a naive book, it is poetry or mythology. Beautiful as it is, it must not be taken seriously, for in its thinking it is primative and immature. How could you compare it with Hegel or Hobbes, John Locke or Schopenhauer? The father of the depreciation of the intellectual relevance of the Bible is Spinoza, who may be blamed for many distorted views of the Bible in subsequent philosophy and exegesis.[13]

Heschel's perception of Spinoza's distortion of biblical thinking is elaborated in another part of *God in Search of Man.* There, the general topic is religious behaviorism.[14] Oddly though, the terms Heschel uses to explain Spinoza's religious behaviorism, do not exactly address the topic at hand. There is an unannounced issue which leads to Heschel's position against religious behaviorism. This issue is latent in his reasoning and motivates his entire view of Spinoza's depreciation of biblical thinking. Heschel's view of Spinoza's religious behaviorism centers on Spinoza's claim that the religious knowledge of the prophets is without merit. It is worth citing Heschel's quotation of Spinoza in its entirety, because it illustrates the main philosophical issue to which Heschel is responding.

> Spinoza advanced the theory that the Israelites were distinguished from other nations neither in knowledge nor in piety. "Of God and nature they had only primitive ideas," above which not even the prophets were able to rise. "Scriptural doctrine contains no lofty speculations nor philosophic reasoning, but only very simple matters, such as could be understood by the slowest intelligence." "I should be surprised if I found [the prophets] teaching any new speculative doctrine which was not a commonplace to...Gentile philosophers." "It, therefore, follows that we must by no means go to the prophets for knowledge, either of natural or spiritual phenomena." "The Israelites knew scarcely anything of God, although he was revealed to them." It is hardly likely that they "should have held any sound notions about the Deity, or that Moses should have taught them anything beyond a rule of right living....Thus the rule of right living, the worship and the love of God, was to them rather a bondage than the true liberty, the

gift and grace of the Deity." What the Bible contains is not a religion but a law, the character of which was political rather than religious.[15]

Clearly Heschel views Spinoza's claims about the intellectual and spiritual irrelevance of the Bible from the point of view of knowledge. Moses' prophetic knowledge is behavioral at best because there is no natural or spiritual basis to it.[16] In other words, God has not *revealed* any knowledge to Moses and to the Jews. The Bible of the Jews is only a political compendium.[17] According to Spinoza, revelation, the transmitting of spiritual or natural knowledge from God to man, is an impossibility because of the nonspeculative character of scriptural doctrine.[18] Spinoza's criticism of Judaism in Heschel's eyes, both implicitly and explicitly, is based on the impossibilty of revelation as a relationship between a personal God and man. It follows quite directly, that Heschel's entire response to the depreciation of biblical thinking is rooted in his desire to indicate the possibility of revelation, i.e. the communication of a divine content to man.

This philosophical context established by Heschel, is not devoid of historical consequences either. Heschel claims that Kant, Fichte and Hegel adopted Spinoza's views about the Bible while they rejected his metaphysics.[19] The connection between these philosopher's attitudes to religion and the Bible is certainly diverse, but another prominent fact stands in bold relief. Kant's desire to place religion within the limits of reason alone, albeit transcendental, has the same effect in Heschel's eyes as Spinoza's metaphysics. The transcendental deduction is the basis of knowledge and according to Kant there cannot be any claim to knowledge made outside its realm.[20] As such, revelation of a divine content by a personal God is intellectually impossible and religiously irrelevant.[21] For Kant, this is especially true of Judaism.[22] The fact that Heschel is directly referring to Kant's opposition to knowledge through revelation, as asserted in *Religion Within the Limits of Reason Alone,* is evident at the beginning of *God in Search of Man.*

> We must therefore not judge religion exclusively from the viewpoint of reason. Religion is not within but beyond the limits of mere reason. Its task is not to compete with reason but to aid us where reason gives only partial aid. Its meaning must be understood in terms compatible with the sense of the ineffable.[23]

It is Heschel's expressed purpose to explain religious knowledge in terms which are intellectually compatible with the ineffable.[24] Revelation, is a prophetic event which has a positive content. Therefore, according to Heschel, there must be a method of conception and analysis which can open up that event to the modern mind.[25] A phenomenological analysis of the ineffable can indicate that positive content of revelation.[26] Experience, even that of the philosopher, is not closed to an incursion of the divine. Moreover, each of Heschel's philosophical works is predicated on this premise. The phenomenological method can redirect our attention to the possibility of prophecy and its ineffable content. Consequently, any adequate understanding of Heschel's philosophy must go through its phenomenological roots. It must begin with his methodological concerns, demonstrate their intregrity, locate them in the proper historical-philosophical context, spell out Heschel's own phenomenology and then explain how the idea of revelation employs this phenomenological analysis and content. These concerns are precisely those elaborated in this book. Heschel's adoption of Husserl's phenomenological method and his eidetic understanding of experience opens up a new realm of knowledge that both Spinoza and Kant, each in their own way, tried to close. It should be noted, that Heschel's philosophical concern does not stop with these two philosophers. He merely begins his prolegomena with their criticisms.

Heschel's perception of the problem of philosophy and the main problem of theology, revelation, lead him to confront the most basic modern philosophical judgment about religion. Heschel's perception of the impossibility of revelation from Spinoza's and Kant's points of view, lead him to consider revelation from the phenomenological perspective, which investigates and explicates any experience without prejudging its claims and allows for the possibility of revelation. To a lesser degree though, Heschel's perception of philosophical ontologies is a motivating factor in his choice of the phenomenological method.[27]

---

[1]*Die Prophetie*, [German], Cracow, The Polish Academy of Sciences (Memoires de la Commission Orientaliste No. 22), 1936.

[2]With the exception of Fritz Rothschild, no one has maintained the philosophical integrity of Heschel's work. Rothschild's introduction to *Between God and Man*, which appeared in 1959 and a seminar taught at the Jewish Theological Seminary in 1977 which I attended, employing Wisdom's, Wittgenstein's and Bambrough's analyses of religion, are the only attempts I know of that maintain the philosophical basis of Heschel's work.

[3] All of the criticisms of Heschel's work have one major fact in common. They do not identify and explicate both Heschel's major concepts and his method. Indeed, many of the criticisms assume, without demonstration, that Heschel's work is bereft of ideas and method. While the critics, may have achieved important insights into Heschel's work, they have totally overlooked its phenomenological method. As a result they have also neglected Heschel's central theological idea, revelation, which depends on his phenomenological

method. Several critics have asserted that Heschel presents nothing more than intuitions in a poetic style. These include Jacob Petuchowski, "Faith as a Leap of Action," *Commentary*, Vol. 25, No. 5. Marvin Fox, "Heschel, Intuition and the Halakhah," *Tradition*, Vol. 3, No. 1. Arthur Cohen, *The Natural and the Supernatural Jew*, (New York: Pantheon Books, 1962), pp. 234-259. Eliezer Berkovits, *Major Themes in Modern Philosophies of Judaism*, (New York: Ktav, 1974), pp. 192-224. These criticisms, especially that of Berkovits, may also be viewed in the light of their desire to use ideas and preconceptions which belong to the venerable past of Jewish theology, but which have nothing to do with Heschel. These positions are distinguished by the point at which they apply their objections. They each chose one idea without necessarily considering it in relation to Heschel's method or ontology. For example, Cohen chooses critical ideas, Fox chooses halacha, Berkovits chooses God's passibility and Petuchowski chooses action as a general category. Even Cohen, in what is perhaps the most profound work of Jewish theology to appear in this decade, *The Tremendum*, still did not achieve an understanding of Heschel's theology. Cohen's description of Torah and teoria [*The Tremendum*, (New York: Crossroad, 1981), p. 100], with some minor alterations, blindly approaches Heschel's idea of the corevelation of God and man. Another critic who has lamented Heschel's lack of rational argument, has claimed that Heschel is a process theologian whose claims are consistent with those of Hartshorne. Sol Tanenzaph, "Abraham Heschel and His Critics," *Judaism*, Vol. 23, No. 3, pp. 276-286. While there are some similarities between Heschel and Hartshorne, they quickly become inconsequential when Heschel's methodology is viewed in its proper perspective. This is based primarily on Heschel's distinction between process and event in *God in Search of Man*, pp. 209-217, and *Who Is Man?*, pp. 42-44. Two other critics have recognized the existentialist nature of Heschel's thought. Maurice Friedman, "Divine Need and Human Wonder, The Philosophy of Abraham Heschel," *Hagut Ivrit Ba-Amerika*, (Tel Aviv, Yavneh Publishing, 1973), pp. 400-425 and Edmond La B. Cherbonnier, "A.J. Heschel and the Philosophy of the Bible: Mystic or Rationalist," *Commentary*, Vol. 27, No. 1, pp. 23-29, and, "Heschel as a Religious Thinker," *Conservative Judaism*, Vol. 23, No. 1, pp. 25-39. Another critic has rendered an internal analysis of Heschel's biblical and rabbinic sources. David S. Shapiro, "The Prophets," *Hadoar*, Vol. 44, No. 36, pp. 665-666, and "A New View on the Systems of Rabbis Akiva and Ishmael," *Hadoar*, Vol. 53, No. 39, pp. 769-772. This textual analysis is totally bereft of any philosophical basis. The author even goes so far as to claim that Heschel's doctrine of pathos has a speculative counterpart, a position which Heschel himself vigorously denies, (*The Prophets*, pp. 221-231).

   Several other commentators stand in bold relief precisely because they offer absolutely no critical view of Heschel. Zalman Schacter, "Two Facets of Judaism," *Tradition*, Vol. 3, No. 2, pp. 191-202. Franklin Sherman, *The Promise of Heschel*, (Philadelphia: Lippencott, 1970). Harold Kasimow, *Divine-Human Encounter: A Study of Abraham Joshua Heschel*, (Washington: University

Press, 1979). They quote his insights and aphorisms and make general observations about his philosophy and theology, but these authors make little or no attempt to analyze the underlying methodological and philosophical issues with which Heschel is grappling.

Another critic, in a series of articles, attacks Heschel's position as being representative of neo-mysticism. Meir Ben-Horin, "The Ultimate and the Mystery," *Jewish Quarterly Review,* Vol. 51, No. 1, pp. 55-71. "Via Mystica," *JQR,* Vol. 45, No. 3, pp. 249-258. "The Ineffable: Critical Notes on Neo-Mysticism," *JQR,* Vol. 46, No. 4, pp. 321-354. In this series of articles, the author sets out to prove that Heschel's dependence on the ineffable involves serious contradictions which infuse all of his writing. This attack has the merit of citing the relevant passages in Heschel's work, which many others do not, but is ultimately a victim of its own zeal as it overlooks anything not included in its own point of view. It also makes no attempt to explicate and evaluate the phenomenological method that Heschel uses.

Two commentators have addressed the philosophical and theological issues with which Heschel is dealing. Nathan Rotenstreich "On Prophetic Consciousness," *The Journal of Religion,* Vol. 54, (July, 1954) No. 3, p. 185ff and Fritz Rothschild, "The Religious Thought of Abraham Heschel," *Conservative Judaism,* Vol. 23, No. 1, pp. 12-25, and *Between God and Man,* "Introduction," (New York: The Free Press, 1975), pp. 7-32 have rendered analyses of aspects of Heschel's thought from within the phenomenological viewpoint that Heschel claims as his own. Rotenstreich's essay, which is based on *The Prophets,* clarifies some of the substance and the limits of Heschel's phenomenological treatment of prophetic consciousness. Rothschild, while not carrying out a phenomenological study of Heschel, does suggest how phenomenology is part of Heschel's overall method. In addition, he suggests how this phenomenological structure might lead to several philosophical positions in Heschel's thought. In a general way, Rothschild also places these Heschelian positions against the backdrop of other traditional epistemological and psychological claims, (Rothschild, *Between God and Man,* pp. 12-23).

The most thorough treatment of Heschel's work belongs to Robert Earl Clarke and John Merkle. Clarke's dissertation was the first attempt to put Heschel's work into any philosophical perspective and is an attempt "to present an orderly content analysis of Heschel's philosophy of religion." (Clarke, p. iii). This strategy, while having the virtue of bringing an external order to Heschel's thought, cannot expose the underlying phenomenological structure of Heschel's thought precisely because that phenomenological structure resists exposition based on an orderly content analysis. Phenomenology can only examine a stream of consciousness. The attempt to place the focus of the investigation into fixed categories denies the fluidity of the content. The interrelationship of God and man is the main theme of Heschel's philosophy of religion (*The Prophets,* p. 231). It is dynamic in character. Ontology, epistemology and axiology create a surface order which obscures the most prominent character of Heschel's thought, the "depth."

With the possible exception of Rotenstreich and Rothschild, the uniform problem with all of these claims, whether they are correct or incorrect, is that not one approaches Heschel's work systematically by examining Heschel's methodological statements. Each critic makes assumptions about either the nature of Judaism or the nature of philosophy. Then, it 'analyzes' Heschel's position and dismisses it for not meeting its presupposed standards or overlooks the phenomenological basis of his theology. Not one study has approached Heschel from an independent point of view to see whether or not he has a consistent philosophical program and whether or not he manages to achieve understanding within his own parameters. A study of any other type cannot make a critical judgment about Heschel's ability to sustain philosophical analysis, nor can it claim to evaluate his theology which is essentially dependent on his philosophical method.

[4]*Conservative Judaism,* Vol. 28, No. 1 (Fall, 1973).

[5]John C. Merkle, *The Genesis of Faith: The Depth Theology of Abraham Heschel,* (New York: Macmillan, 1985). Robert Earl Clarke, *The Biblical Philosophy of Abraham Heschel,* [dissertation] (Southwestern Baptist Theological Seminary, Fort Worth, 1965). Merkle's book is a thorough and well written examination of the content of "depth-theology." However, it never breaks through to the phenomenological basis of the act of thought, that characterizes Heschel's method (God in Search of Man p. 17). It does not examine the meaning of consciousness in relation to depth-theology. Not until the conclusion of the book does Merkle lay out his own methodology: "Rather than foisting an alien system upon Heschel's mosaic of insights, I have attempted to explicate the inner coherence and consistency as well as the dynamic movement of his thought on the genesis of faith." (Genesis of Faith p. 218).

[6]The Christian theologians such as Clarke, Merkle and Cherbonnier ("A.J. Heschel and the Philosophy of the Bible: Mystic or Rationalist," *Commentary,* Vol. 27, No. 1, pp. 23-29. "Heschel as a Religious Thinker," *Conservative Judaism,* Vol. 23, No. 1, pp. 25-39), unburdened by the previous methods and contents of Jewish theology, have appreciated Heschel's radical nature. The Jewish commentators, for the most part, as I will show, have measured Heschel's thought against the backdrop of twenty centuries of theology. His completely novel approach, as Heschel himself explains, begins from a new perspective.

[7]*God in Search of Man,* (New York: Farrar, Straus and Giroux, 1976), p. 7.

[8]Merkle, Clarke and Rothschild cite biographical references to Heschel's attachment to Husserlian phenomenology. (Merkle, p. 32, Clarke, p. 20 and Fritz Rothschild, "The Religious Thought of Abraham Joshua Heschel," *Conservative Judaism,* Vol. 23, (Fall 1968), p. 22.

[9] Y. Levinger, "Remarks on A.J. Heschel's Torah min Hashamayim," [Hebrew], *Deot,* Jerusalem, No. 31, (Winter-Spring, 1965), pp. 45-48, and D.S. Shapiro, "A New View on the Systems of Rabbis Akiva and Ishmael," *Hadoar,* Vol. 53, No. 39, pp. 769-772.

[10]*God in Search of Man*, p. 330. "We deny the exclusive primacy of dogmas not because we think that Judaism has no beliefs or that Judaism is merely a system of laws and observances, but because we realize that what we believe in surpasses the power and range of human expression."

[11]*Who is Man?*, (Stanford: Stanford University Press, 1978), p. 31.

[12]"However we would look in vain for the Bible in the recesses of Western metaphysics. The prophets are absent when philosophers speak of God. What we mean by the absence of the Bible in the history of philosophy is not references or quotations; scriptural passages have occasionally found admittance. What we mean is the spirit, the way of thinking, the mode of looking at the world, at life; the basic premises of speculation about being, about values, about meaning. Open any history of philosophy. Thales or Parmenides is there; but is Isaiah or Elijah, Job or Ecclesiastes ever represented? The result of such omission is that the basic premises of Western philosophy are derived from the Greek rather than the Hebraic thinking." *God in Search of Man*, p. 24.

[13]*God in Search of Man*, p. 24.

[14]*Ibid.*, p. 320.

[15]*Ibid.*, pp. 321-322.

[16]*Theologico-Political Treatise*, trans. R. Elwes, (New York: Dover Publications, 1951), p. 27.

[17]*Ibid.*, pp. 46-47.

[18]"Prophecy or revelation, is sure knowledge revealed by God to man." *Ibid.*, p. 13.

[19]*God in Search of Man*, p. 322.

[20]I. Kant, *The Critique of Pure Reason*, trans. N.K. Smith, (New York: St. Martins Press, 1965), pp. 122-123.

[21]I. Kant, *Religion of Reason Within the Limits of Reason Alone*, trans. T. Greene and H. Hudson, (New York: Harper and Row, 1960), pp. 142-144.

[22]I. Kant, *Religion of Reason Within the Limits of Reason Alone*, p. 155.

[23]*God in Search of Man*, p. 20.

[24]See *Man is Not Alone*, pp. 3-34.

[25]*God in Search of Man*, pp. 6-9.

[26]*Man Is Not Alone*, p. 22.

[27]Many of these positions are briefly mentioned in Chapter Two. Heschel's major opposition to modern ontological commitments is directed at Heidegger. I hope to complete a discussion of Heschel's anti-Heideggerian arguments in the near future.

Chapter Two

The Methodology That Unifies Heschel's Thought

Without returning to Heschel's first methodological statements concerning revelation, the critics can, at best, only grasp unconnected elements of Heschel's work. Heschel's earliest major work, *Die Prophetie,* published in 1936, was revised and partially updated and published in English in 1962 as *The Prophets.* In the English work Heschel refers the reader to the introduction of the German edition for an elaboration of his methodology.[1] Unfortunately this introduction has been completely ignored, as it contains some of the most essential philosophical remarks Heschel has made.

Heschel's purpose in that introduction was to distinguish his own explanation of prophecy from the psychological, political, ethical and dogmatic explanations popular at that time. In so doing, Heschel lays the foundation necessary for an understanding of a prophetic self and a unique prophetic consciousness.[2] Heschel's characterization of his own undertaking is extremely revealing and more than any other reference, sets the tone of our inquiry.

> But the act of inspiration must also be adequately comprehended. Without the difficult problem of the limits of revelation ceasing to exist, the noetic character of the content of inspiration can be proven, that also inspiration itself leads into the general relation of consciousness, that also content, which is not original consciousness, that becomes a revelation to the enduring consciousness. The prophets had clear conceptions about the course of events of inspiration and a knowledge about the kind and structure of their experience.[3]

The meaning and essence of prophecy, according to Heschel, can only be considered from the point of view of its noetic character. The consciousness of the prophet, has an explicit noetic character and Heschel's explanation of prophecy is based partially on that phenomenological point. The completion of the explanation of the prophet's consciousness rests on another implicit, but no less significant point.

> It was already intimated that for the consciousness of the prophet the prophetic phenomenon possesses a real objective reality, to which a subjective emotional [intuitive] reality is attached....Both in the objective sphere as in the emotional [intuitive] sphere the two essential components may be distinguished, which may be defined as content and form. The basis for a division into inspiration and event on the one hand and in event-content and event-form on the other hand results in a specified relationship.[4]

The preceding reference to the noetic aspect of consciousness is not an isolated phenomenological remark. In this passage, Heschel clearly identifies another phenomenological aspect of prophetic consciousness. It is the objective, noematic aspect of consciousness (the prophetic phenomenon possesses a real objective reality). Any attempt to understand prophetic consciousness which cannot include an objective reality given in that experience, is less than satisfactory. It belies a total lack of authenticity, which from the outset will denigrate the prophetic experience.

> From a phenomenological point of view, we can do justice to the essence of the experience only when we include in our discussion the awareness of that which is given *to* experience We must, therefore, examine the structure of inspiration in its objectivity, which is a given fact for experience, in order that we may be in position to grasp the character of the experience which it initiates.[5]

This objectivity to which Heschel refers, is not an isolated reference to the prophet's consciousness. It typifies the very essence of prophetic consciousness and is integral to each and every aspect of it.

> To the consciousness of the prophet, the prophetic act is more than an experience; it is an objective event. This is its essential mode. Whatever be the mode in which inspiration is apprehended, there remains always its character as an event, not as a process.[6]

Twenty six years later the same reference to the objectivity of the prophetic event is fully intended by Heschel as part of his phenomenological treatment of the prophetic event and as part of the event itself.

> From a phenomenological point of view, we can do justice to the essence of the experience only when we include in our discussion the awareness of that which is given *to* experience. We must, therefore, examine the structure of the inspiration in its objectivity, which is a given fact for experience, in order that we may be in a position to grasp the character of the experience which it initiates.[7]

The objective aspect of the experience is responsible, just as the noetic aspect is, for a specified relationship in consciousness.[8] This relationship does not exist in a vacuum as an epistemological category because it is part of an event and it does have a basis capable of sustaining philosophical analysis.[9] It is the relationship between God and the prophet.[10] Moreover, this phenomenological characterization of consciousness is not without a particular theological purpose. As Heschel noted in his early study of prophecy,

> However the acts of inspiration and events become accepted as the starting point, they approach the pure religion in the midpoint of the inquiry. The political as well as the ethical is not considered here, as in many prophetic explanations, as the central, as the original motive, but rather as a derivation from the religious. Correspondingly we join to the re-presentation of the prophetic act a method of treatment of theology and religion of the prophets.[11]

This is the earliest and most explicit link in Heschel's work between the phenomenological treatment of prophecy and the theological and religious treatment that the act and content of the prophet receives. The phenomenological treatment of prophecy and Heschel's treatment are continually joined together. It should be minimally clear, without even explaining the noetic-noematic relationship of prophetic consciousness, that it forms the basis of Heschel's theological method.

Although there were considerable changes in *The Prophets*, as the title itself indicates,[12] the English edition that appeared twenty six years later contained the same basic methodological kernel.[13]

> Such an inquiry must suspend personal beliefs or even any attempt to inquire – e.g., whether the event happened in fact as it did to their minds. It is my claim that, regardless of whether or not their experience was of the real, it is possible to analyze the form and content of that experience. The process and result of such an inquiry represent the essential part of this book as composed a good many years ago. While I maintain the soundness of the method described above, which in important aspects reflects the method of phenomenology, I have long since become wary of impartiality, which is itself a way of being partial. The prophet's existence is either irrelevant or relevant. If irrelevant, I cannot be truly involved in it; if relevant, then my impartiality is but a pretense. Reflection may succeed in isolating an object; reflection itself cannot be isolated. Reflection is part of a situation.[14]

The differences between an earlier and later usage of the method pointed out by Heschel, is not given any methodological weight as we find the same categories used in both editions. At best, we may assume that in his own mind, Heschel was altering the emphasis of the method but not the method itself. The following statement concerning the structure of prophetic consciousness continues two seminal points made twenty six years earlier.

> The structure of prophetic consciousness as ascertained in the analysis was disclosed as consisting, on the transcendent level, of pathos (content of inspiration) and event (form), and on the personal level, of sympathy (content of inner experience) and the sense of being overpowered (form of inner experience).[15]

In the later version Heschel maintains the ideas of form and content that are used to convey the prophetic inspiration and event. The methodology remains as it was first conceived by him in 1936. Second, the theology of the prophets and their relationship to God, is placed in the same phenomenological context twenty-six years later. The noetic-noematic correlation is referred to implicitly as an object of human experience.

> Pathos means: God is never neutral, never beyond good and evil. He is always partial to justice. It is not a name for a human experience, but the name for an object of human experience. It is something the prophets meet with, something eventful, current, present in history as well as in nature.[16]

For our immediate purposes this means that revelation, the combined experiences of God and the prophet, is directly connected to Heschel's own methodology. The prophet's consciousness and Heschel's own method of explicating that consciousness, that is, the theology Heschel extrapolates from their experiences, are parallel considerations.

> Pure reflection may be sufficient for the clarification of what the prophet's consciousness asserts – but not for what his existence involves. For such understanding it is not enough to have the prophets in mind; we must think as if we were inside their minds....In probing their consciousness we are not interested only in the inward life, in emotion and reflection as such. We are interested in restoring the world of the prophets.[17]

In Heschel's eyes, method and content are inseparable.[18] The method he employs to uncover the depth of prophetic experience and the structure of prophetic consciousness must be open to each other. They must be capable of exploring each other's assumptions without corrupting the dialogue with any explicit or implicit prejudices or value judgments.

> My aim is therefore to attain an understanding of the prophet through an analysis and a description of his *consciousness*, to relate what came to pass in his life – facing man, being faced by God – as reflected and affirmed in his mind. By consciousness, in other words, I mean here

not only the perception of particular moments of inspiration but also the totality of impressions, thoughts and feelings which make up the prophet's being.[19]

For Heschel, the analysis of the prophet's consciousness is not a passing remark or secondary intention. The analysis of the prophet's consciousness is the phenomenological foundation upon which all of Heschel's thought is based because consciousness must include "the totality of impressions, thoughts and feelings which make up the prophet's being." As such, phenomenological consciousness is the key to understanding prophetic religion.

It may be assumed that this phenomenological inquiry begins and ends with Heschel's treatment of classical Jewish prophecy because it is impossible to find in any other of Heschel's writings explicit methodological statements such as those cited above. One might conclude that Heschel's modernism is absolutely disconnected from his treatment of classical Jewish theological issues including his work on medieval Jewish philosophers. If this were the case, then any elaboration in any of his own theological statements about a method of theology that is related to prophetic consciousness would have to be construed as an errant statement. Surely this is not the case.

In books of an entirely different and modern nature, Heschel makes similar remarks that are based upon this early method, which is closely intertwined with the structure of prophetic consciousness. In *God In Search Of Man*, Heschel describes the type of philosophy of religion that he is writing.

> Philosophy may be pursued as a process of thinking thought, of analyzing *the content of thinking,* such as principles, assumptions, doctrines. Or it may be pursued as thinking about thinking, as *radical self-understanding,* as a process of analyzing *the act of thinking,* as a process of introspection, of watching the intellectual self in action.[20]

Not one critical study has noticed that Heschel's conception of philosophy as radical self-understanding, as an act of thinking, is an extension of his method in *The Prophets*. The act of thinking is the proper subject of the inquiry and it views human consciousness in a phenomenological light.[21]

> The objection may be voiced that a psychological reaction is no evidence for an ontological fact, and we can never infer an object itself from a feeling a person has about it. The feeling of awe may often be the result of a misunderstanding of an ordinary fact; one may be overawed by an artificial spectacle or a display of evil power. That objection is, of course, valid. Yet what we infer from is not the actual feeling of awe but the intellectual certainty that in the face of nature's

grandeur and mystery we must respond with awe; what we infer from is not a psychological state but a fundamental norm of human consciousness, a categorical imperative. Indeed, the validity and requiredness of awe enjoy a degree of certainty that is not even surpassed by the axiomatic certainty of geometry.[22]

The "fundamental norm of consciousness" is the functioning of the objective fact of awe in correlation with the subjective act which perceives it. This is the noetic-noematic correlation forming the basis of Heschel's explanation of his experiential claim. It is the noetic-noematic correlation alone which allows the reader qua phenomenologist, to "watch the intellectual self in action."[23] Moreover, Heschel's use of phenomenology is in complete agreement with the defined theological study of religion. He retains the same parallel structure in his own philosophical works on Judaism that he used in *Die Prophetie* and *The Prophets*.

> Correspondingly, the study of religion has two major tasks to perform. One, to understand what it means to believe; to analyze *the act of believing*; to ask what it is that necessitates our believing in God. Two, to explain and to examine *the content of believing*; to analyze that which we believe in. The first is concerned with *the problem of faith*, with concrete situations; the second with *the problem of creed*, with conceptual relations....The religious situation precedes the religious conception, and it would be a false abstraction, for example, to deal with the idea of God regardless of the situation in which such an idea occurs.[24]

The novelty of Heschel's approach, which phenomenologically separates the creed of religion from the consciousness of religion, assures that the acts, events and insights of believing, not the content of believing, are the first proper themes of theological study. It is all too clear that Heschel's distinction of theology (creed) and depth-theology (phenomena) has been entirely overlooked. The methodological nature of depth-theology has not been recognized, yet Heschel's claim has been made straightforwardly.

> The theme of theology is the content of believing. The theme of the present study is the act of believing. Its purpose is to explore the depth of faith, the substratum out of which belief arises, and its method may be called *depth-theology*.[25]

From a philosophical point of view, radical self-understanding is the primary Heschelian category. From a theological point of view, an understanding of the origin of the act of believing, which is radically disconnected from the content of faith, is foremost.[26] Philosophically and theologically, Heschel considers the noetic act of thinking and believing in the same breath. Whichever comes first, and Heschel makes no decision, philosophy and theology come from the same source.[27] The noetic status of the original act of thought for radical self-understanding in philosophy and the act of believing in depth-theology, is similar. According to Heschel these two acts operate in the same manner. They each provide the antecedents of thought and faith respectively, that is to say, their phenomenological structures are similar. In this way, Heschel ensures that the method first used in *Die Prophetie* and in *The Prophets* is used in his own theological writings, *Man Is Not Alone* and *God in Search of Man*.

Again, one might be tempted to consider this case to be the exception and not the rule. One might claim that Heschel is a phenomenologist only when dealing with God's relationship to man as illustrated in his treatment of classical prophecy and the philosophy of religion. However, even stronger proof of this commitment to the phenomenological method is available in another of Heschel works that ignores theological claims. *Who is Man?* is a study of man and the nature of human being, not of prophecy nor of God. In Heschel's own words,

> The decisive form of human being is *human living*. Thus the proper theme for the study of man is the problem of living, of what to do with being. Living means putting being into shape, lending form to sheer being.[28]

Not surprisingly, *Who is Man?*, which offers Heschel's anthropological views, makes an outright reference to the phenomenological approach that gives form to being. Moreover it is the only work that identifies its philosophical source. The phenomenology of Brentano and Husserl, specifically the idea of intentionality, serves as the basis for Heschel's idea of self-consciousness.

> The self is inescapably beset by the question: What shall I do with my existence, with my being here and now? What does it mean to be alive? What does being alive imply for my will and intelligence? Its most characteristic condition is discontent with sheer being, generated by a challenge which is not to be derived from being around, being-here-too; it questions and transcends human being. Just as consciousness always posits an idea, as Brentano and Husserl have shown, self-consciousness posits a challenge. Consciousness of the self comes about in being challenged, in being called upon, in the choice between refusal and response.[29]

Throughout this entire volume Heschel is basing his treatment of man on an idea which he cryptically refers to only in passing. There are no statements about depth-theology to be found because it is not a theological tract which deals with the reality of God. Therefore, the noetic-noematic consciousness conjoined to prophetic religion is out of place. Rather, it is a profound philosophical essay on the nature of man and human existence. *Who is Man?* must be read from another phenomenological viewpoint, that of intentionality. The identifying of Brentano and Husserl[30] as positers of the concept that each act of consciousness posits an idea, is the basis of the book's philosophical strategy. The religious significance of self-consciousness positing a challenge must be viewed on the same noetic level as the idea of intentionality for consciousness. The idea of consciousness in *Who Is Man?* is purely deontological.[31] It is defined by the task that is given in consciousness.[32] These methodological concerns, the intentionality of consciousness and the challenge of self-consciousness, have equal standing in defining the problem of man's being and personality. Their similar value and their coinciding functionality point to the method of depth-theology, even though Heschel is bypassing their noetic-noematic correlation in *Who Is Man?*, because strictly speaking the book is not a theological exercise.[33] Husserl's phenomenological attitude is the basis of Heschel's view of both religious man's personality and the prophet's consciousness.

The reliance by Heschel on Husserl's idea of intentionality within the noetic-noematic correlation can be traced all the way back to the Introduction of *Die Prophetie*. The phenomenological approach of *Who Is Man?*, is clearly connected to Heschel's first study of prophecy. Upon completing his description of the structure of the prophet's consciousness in his early work, Heschel defines the starting point of the understanding of the prophetic act.

> The starting point is located neither in a genetic psychological, nor in an empirical psychological, nor in a symptomatic representative statement of the problem. Such a task, which would be grasped in its individuality, has its meaning as a psychological problem and finds only partial treatment. Here it is a total problem, of meaning and essence, not of action and details. Only then can knowledge and understanding of prophecy be attained, if the experience of the prophetic word is heard in relation to the personal totality and as a moment of a necessary genuine directedness of the 'I'.[34]

The directedness of the "I" is a general attitude and condition of knowledge and understanding of prophecy.[35] The "I" or understanding self must be directed or possess the intention of hearing the prophetic word in its totality. The overwhelming meaning of the event is only accessible if the "I" directs its attention essentially, that is, as a phenomenological possibility.

This theme is continued in the *The Prophets*. When Heschel introduces the idea of pathos, he gives it a phenomenological basis that echos his treatment of the prophetic act in *Die Prophetie*.

> It is not a passion, an unreasoned emotion, but an act formed with intention, rooted in decision and determination; not an attitude taken arbitrarily, but one charged with ethos; not a reflexive, but a transitive act. To repeat, its essential meaning is not to be seen in its psychological denotation, as standing as a state for the soul, but in its theological connotation, signifying God as involved in history, as intimately affected by events in history, as living care.[36]

This phenomenological statement is an explicit elaboration of his earlier statement in *Die Prophetie*. It demonstrates how phenomenology acts as the basic platform for Heschel's method and for the content of his major theological idea, revelation – the central concept that includes God's pathos and historical involvement.

The lack of recognition of Heschel as a religious thinker who employs a phenomenological method in all areas of religion has led to another oversight of immense proportions. After all, why does Heschel use a phenomenological method? Another philosophical program may have suited his purposes. What problem, internal to religion and Judaism, prompts this philosophical commitment?

Indeed, it is difficult to isolate that one problem or nexus of issues because of Heschel's unsystematic presentation of the claims of theology. Yet, in *God In Search Of Man*, Heschel spends the first one hundred and thirty-six pages describing the nature of insight in depth-theology. This insight, based on awe, radical amazement, sublimity and wonder, is not intended as an emotional appeal.[37] It is meant to support the claim which precedes it, that depth-theology is substantiated as an act of believing. The difficulty arises because the content of the act of believing cannot be conceptualized.

> True, the mystery of meaning is silent. There is no speech, there are no words, the voice is not heard. Yet beyond our reasoning and beyond our believing, there is a preconceptual faculty that senses the glory, the presence of the Divine. We do not perceive it. We have no knowledge; we only have an awareness. We witness it. And to witness is more than to give an account. We have no concept, nor can we develop a theory. All we have is an awareness of something that can be neither conceptualized nor symbolized.[38]

This remark is consistent with Heschel's attitude, originating in *Die Prophetie*,[39] that rejects genetic thought, i.e. the logical origin of conceptualization.[40] The problem of the noetic nature of depth-theology exists because of Heschel's suspected lapse into irrationalism or unrestrained subjectivism. But, these charges miss the point of Heschel's phenomenological method. If knowledge is not something gained through posthumous objects in a genetic fashion,[41] then it is gained through their presence. In *The Prophets* Heschel makes this point explicit.

> To comprehend what phenomena are, it is important to suspend judgement and think in detachment; to comprehend what phenomena mean, it is necessary to suspend indifference and be involved. To examine their essence requires a process of reflection. Such reflection, however, sets up a gulf between the phenomena and ourselves. Reducing them to dead objects of the mind, it deprives them of the power to affect us, to speak to us, to transcend our attitudes and conceptions.[42]

This is exactly what Heschel, in a cryptic manner, several years later, is referring to when speaking about the awareness of God.

> Thus, the certainty of the realness of God does not come about as a corollary of logical premises, as a leap from the realm of logic to the realm of ontology, from an assumption to a fact. It is, on the contrary, a transition from an immediate apprehension to a thought, from a preconceptual awareness to a definite assurance, from being overwhelmed by the presence of God to an awareness of His existence. What we attempt to do in the act of reflection is to raise that preconceptual awareness to the level of understanding.[43]

The transition from an immediate apprehension to a thought is supported in several other aspects of Heschel's thought and will be examined in their own context. Significantly, all of these references reject the presuppositions of genetic thinking in place of the acceptance of phenomenological intuition, which is based on the presence of objects.

The background of Heschel's phenomenological commitment now makes sense. Both depth-theology and conventional theology must come to terms with the problem of man's knowledge of God. From Heschel's perspective, God is never an object but always a subject.[44] Therefore, only awareness of His presence is possible and never knowledge of His essence.[45] Whatever knowledge or understanding the philosophical individual can grasp is a byproduct of the relationship that he experiences with God. Knowledge is gained only in relationship to God. The prophetic consciousness, which reflects a phenomenological structure, is the origin of this knowledge. The post-prophetic mind retains the guiding impulses of the prophetic phenomenological structure when it views the knowledge of God as subsequent to and not consequent to its premises.[46]

Abstract reasons could never have persuaded us, if God Himself had not entreated us. He has a stake in our attitude toward His word, and *His will that we believe* may work in ways not accessible to our own will to believe. And, indeed, there is a way of our receiving indirectly what the prophets received *directly*.[47]

This is an absolutely essential point in forming the philosophical part of Heschel's depth-theology. The origin of depth-theology is only accessible because the phenomenological method which employs a noetic-noematic correlation, allows subjects and objects to be viewed as presences and not as posthumous logical objects. In the analytical or genetic sense, depth-theology is not accessible as knowledge.[48] The postprophetic philosophical mind must operate within the parameters of this correlation too. As I demonstrated above, this means a total dependence on intentionality qua human consciousness. Theologically only one idea can originate and fulfill these criteria. Revelation is the primary idea that can operate in an intentional mode. All other theological concepts derive their significance from revelation and not vice versa. It is *the* concept, which requires a directedness of the individual toward God, because its prime assumption is that God directs His concern toward man.[49]

This phenomenological structure of faith and insight would be useless for Heschel's purposes if it could not explain the idea of revelation. According to Heschel, the experience of revelation illumines human existence because it alone can address man's total situation. Revelation, which contains the origin of man's experience of the supernatural, poses the foremost question for man.

Thus the issue which must be discussed first is not belief, ritual or the religious experience, but the source of these phenomena: the total situation of man; not how he experiences the supernatural, but why he experiences and accepts it.[50]

It is, therefore not surprising that the phenomenological structure of the first part of *God in Search of Man* is the groundwork for the second part – Revelation. The phenomenological structure of Part One, which interprets awe, wonder and radical amazement, is not merely the phenomenological basis from which revelation is possible. It is the phenomenological structure that is taken up in the concept of revelation.[51] Revelation becomes the phenomenological nexus in which knowledge and understanding become possible.[52] Yet, no critic has made the connection.

But if insights are not physical events, in what sense are they real? The underlying assumption of modern man's outlook is that objective reality is physical: all non-material phenomena can be reduced to material phenomena and explained in physical terms. Thus, only those types of human experiences which acquaint us with the quantitative aspects of material phenomena refer to the real world. None of the other types of experiences, such as prayer or the awareness of the presence of God, has any objective counterpart....This is the premise of faith: Spiritual events are real. Ultimately all creative events are caused by spiritual acts. The God who creates heaven and earth is the God who communicates His will to the mind of man.[53]

It should now be clear, that when Heschel rejects objective reality, he refers to natural events which are known by man because of the processes of which they consist.[54] When Heschel accepts spiritual events as real, he is referring to those events whose phenomenological structure begins with wonder, awe and radical amazement. This type of event is accessible through its noetic character. Only a phenomenological treatment of the idea of revelation allows Heschel to incorporate his method of depth-theology into the idea that must be accessible to both the antecedents and the content of faith.[55] If revelation consisted only of methodological integrity it would be an empty concept (this poses a problem of a different kind as will be discussed in Chapter Ten). It must possess some kind of content. One must carefully point out that "content" here does not have a natural or literal meaning but rather a phenomenological one. That is, like consciousness, which always posits an idea, revelation must always posit an intentional "content."[56]

The necessity of examining a spiritual phenomenon with a phenomenological structure leads directly into Heschel's prelude to revelation. "The voice of God is not always inaudible."[57] To be sure, it is not plainly audible either. The mysterious nature of revelation cannot be dealt with, either by empiricism, rationalism or irrationalism. When faced with the problem of intellectual content, only the phenomenologist can properly suspend his own prejudices and enter into the structure of the event, real or otherwise.[58] Revelation can only be phenomenologically explicated because it is an event and not a component of genetic knowledge. Genetic knowledge cannot be placed within the context of the event because it is posthumous. The separation of the context and content of revelation would irreparably damage its cognitive integrity.

What is the cognitive value of our insights? What is disclosed and what is retained out of such moments? When a person is hit by a bullet, he feels the pain, not the bullet. When a person is called to return, he feels his being called rather than the call. The guiding hand is hidden; what he may sense is his being *an object of concern*. There would be no call to man without a concern for man.[59]

The fact and value of God's concern for man, of revelation, is intellectually available only through a phenomenological evaluation. The plausibility and the possibility of revelation is only open to an investigation that, a priori, does not reject its cognitive aspect or the event itself because of its indescribability.[60]

The idea of revelation is comprehensible only as an event in the prophet's life.[61] The treatment of the problem of revelation in *Man Is Not Alone* and *God in Search of Man,* is the same treatment accorded prophecy in *The Prophets.* Heschel's methodology is the one feature of his depth-theology that unifies all the different aspects. The whole task of *God In Search Of Man* becomes an analysis of the act of prophetic inspiration *as the pious individual is capable of experiencing it.*[62] The impact of this analysis on religious life forms the last section of the book – appropriately titled "Response."

The uniqueness of revelation that precludes accessibility via rationalism or empiricism[63] demands phenomenological treatment. And without any treatment the presence of God remains an impenetrable mystery.[64] The first question that must be answered is not whether or not revelation took place. We must first understand what kind of fact revelation is,[65] and only the phenomenological method, which suspends its judgment from a natural viewpoint, enables Heschel to accomplish this.

It is my position that Heschel uses this phenomenological method outlined above to create his own ontology.[66] This will be treated in a separate chapter. However, the fact that many critics have overlooked this phenomenological attitude has led to claims against Heschel which he tries to avoid. For example, the special sense of intuition based on the awareness of God is not intended as a form of nature mysticism but is used by both Husserl and Heschel in an epistemological sense. The charge of nature mysticism against Heschel, a charge which claims revelation is a kind of emotional experience of nature without God, would preclude any intellectual content from his idea of revelation.[67] Furthermore, it would be impossible for Heschel to claim that his idea of revelation is connected to a standard rabbinic view. This second charge against Heschel would fragment his work into irreconcilable parts. Once again, the charge could be leveled against Heschel that his modernism is totally disconnected from the body of Jewish tradition.

Throughout his writings, Heschel constantly and consistently quotes rabbinic sources. Does he use them inspirationally or methodologically? It is my position that Heschel's use of rabbinic sources is fundamental to his philosophical writing and to his idea of revelation. The way in which he incorporates rabbinic texts into his philosophical writings must be systematically treated and must be done in conjunction with Heschel's major study of rabbinic theology, *Torah Min Hashamayim*.

Heschel claims, both in these volumes and in his philosophical works, that he is departing from the prevalent medieval Jewish philosophical methods of treating religion and revelation. In so doing, what kind of view of rabbinic theology is he using instead? Does his idea of revelation remain within recognizable rabbinic limits? These questions are seminal for his doctrine of revelation because they are influential in forming the content of that idea. While I do not intend to answer these questions here,[68] they are raised now, because *the methodological treatment that Heschel gives these rabbinic texts is as significant as the phenomenological treatment that he adopts as a philosophical program*. The challenge of treating rabbinic texts, with an attitude as critical and modern as the attitude he employs to describe faith is immense. Heschel's failure or success must be examined elsewhere. However the need to create a new framework for rabbinic theology is suggested by Heschel from the beginning of his phenomenological descriptions. His conception of rabbinic theology will be trivialized and rendered useless if seen in any other light.

---

[1]*The Prophets,* p. xvi.

[2]The personal self that Heschel establishes as the prophetic self is identical with the self that Husserl establishes. As Carr points out: "Of fundamental importance for Husserl is the concept of the person. His purpose is to distinguish the person from the psychophysical object of psychology and the epistemological subject of philosophy. The person is related to his world not causally but through motivation. 'The subject can be motivated only by what he "experiences," by what he is conscious of in his life, what is given to him subjectively as actual, as certain, as supposed, valuable, beautiful, good.' His world is an intersubjective one made up of 'things that are not mere physical bodies but value-objects, goods, etc.'" (Husserliana IV, p. 375). David Carr, *Phenomenology and the Problem of History,* (Evanston: Northwestern University Press, 1974), p. 197.

[3]*Die Prophetie,* p. 3.

[4]*Ibid.,* p. 5.

[5]*The Prophets,* pp. 430-431.

[6]*Ibid.,* p. 431.

[7]*Ibid.,* pp. 430-431.

[8]This same thought is expressed in *Man is Not Alone,* p. 20. "What the sense of the ineffable perceives is something objective which cannot be conceived by the mind nor captured by imagination or feeling, something real which, by its

very essence, is beyond the reach of thought and feeling. What we are primarily aware of is not our self, our inner mood, but a transubjective situation, in regard to which our ability fails. Subjective is the *manner*, not the *matter* of our perception. What we perceive is objective in the sense of being independent of and corresponding to our perception."

[9]*Man Is Not Alone,* p. 237, "What gives rise to faith is not a sentiment, a state of mind, an aspiration, but an everlasting fact in the universe, something which is prior to and independent of human knowledge and experience – *the holy dimension* of all existence. The objective side of religion, is the spiritual constitution of the universe, the divine values invested in every being and exposed to the mind and will of man; an ontological relation. This is why the objective or divine side of religion eludes psychological and sociological analysis."

[10]*Ibid.,* p. 5.

[11]*Ibid.*

[12]Nathan Rotenstreich, "On Prophetic Consciousness," *The Journal of Religion,* Vol. 54, No. 3, pp. 185-186.

[13]Heschel refers the reader of *God in Search of Man* (1955), p. 199, in the notes to Chapter Twenty, which is on revelation, to *Die Prophetie,* soon to be published in English, "for a phenomenological analysis of the prophetic event as reflected in the consciousness of the prophets." The fact that Heschel in effect makes no distinction of the method employed in either study strengthens the contention that he is not altering the method but only the emphasis when he limits it in the English edition, as I point out below.

[14]*Ibid.,* p. xii. Heschel's cryptic reference to the "impartiality" of the method he identifies as phenomenological is not explained in any text. Clarke assumes that this remark is rooted in Heschel's attempt to incorporate aspects of Dilthey's "understanding psychology" because of a rejection of Husserl (Clarke, p. 22). This may indeed be the case but a question still remains. What exactly is Heschel rejecting? He never rejects the presuppositionless character of the phenomenological method. Heschel never indicated what phenomenological impartiality was. It seems that Heschel may have erroneously concluded that the phenomenological method, since it strives to be presuppositionless, strives for absolute neutrality. This is never the case for Husserl and is clarified by Marvin Farber in an essay titled, "A Presuppositionless Philosophy," *Philosophical Essays in Memory of Edmund Husserl,* ed. M. Farber, (Cambridge: Harvard University Press, 1940), pp. 44-64.

[15]*The Prophets,* p. xix.

[16]*Ibid.,* p. 231.

[17]*The Prophets,* p. xvii.

[18]*Ibid.,* p. 360. The noetic character of the prophetic experience has cultural, linguistic and historical content which is inseparable from it.

[19]*Ibid.,* p. ix.

[20]*God in Search of Man,* p. 6.

[21]This is the radical "consciousnes of self" that Husserl speaks of in the First Cartesian Meditation.

[22]*Man Is not Alone,* p. 27.

[23]This intellectual self, as will be explained in Chapters Four and Five, is not placed primarily in the natural world. In considering the phenomena of awe, Heschel places this ego in a transcendental realm. This ego is a subject for pure consciousness not the natural attitude. This Heschelian position carried out throughout the entire first section of God in Search of Man, is stated by Husserl, "Thus the being of the pure ego and his *cogitationes*, as a being that is prior in itself, is antecedent to the natural being of the world – the world of which I always speak, the one of which I *can* speak. Natural being is a realm whose existential status is secondary; it continually presupposes the realm of transcendental being." Edmund Husserl, Cartesian Meditations, trans. D. Cairns, (Boston: Martinus Nijhoff, 1982), p. 21.

[24]*Ibid.*, p. 6.

[25]*Ibid.*, p. 7.

[26]Indeed, if one looks at the major internal Jewish criticisms of Heschel's thought by Petuchowski, Fox, Cohen and Berkovits, this is the most troubling issue. They criticize Heschel in the light of doctrinal issues when Heschel plainly argues that methodological issues must be allowed to set the tone for doctrinal ones.

[27]*God in Search of Man*, p. 19. For a "modernist," Heschel sounds very medieval.

[28]Abraham Heschel, *Who Is Man?*, (Stanford: Stanford University Press, 1965), p. 95.

[29]*Ibid.*, p. 105-106.

[30]The fact that Heschel lumps Brentano and Husserl together does not suggest that he did not differentiate their positions and impacts on the idea of intentionality. It does suggest that, like many others, Heschel assumed that there was a straight line of development from Brentano to Husserl. Another point of development, including Bolzano, is coherently argued by Dagfinn Follesdal, "Brentano and Husserl," *Husserl, Intentionality and Cognitive Science*, eds. Hubert L. Dreyfus and Harrison Hall, (Cambridge: The M.I.T Press, 1984), pp. 31-41.

[31]The significance of this fact is the main purpose of Chapter Eleven.

[32]"The first thought a child becomes aware of is his being called, his being asked to respond or to act in a certain way. It is in acts of responding to demands made upon him that the child begins to find himself as part of both society and nature. Without the awareness of a task to be done, of a task waiting for him, man regards himself as an outcast. The content of the task we must acquire, the search for a task is given with consciousness." *Who Is Man?*, p. 105.

[33]Rothschild, *Between God and Man*, p. 24.

[34]*Die Prophetie*, p. 4.

[35]*Ibid.*

[36]*The Prophets*, p. 231.

[37]Rothschild recognizes that the nature of insight is based on man's mode of responding to an objective aspect of reality, but he does not see the phenomenological significance of this structure, which is the task of this entire work. "There he finds six terms that describe grandeur and man's reaction to it

in three correlative pairs: the sublime and wonder, mystery and awe, the glory and faith. It must be borne in mind that in each of these three pairs of terms the first one refers to an objective aspect of reality and the second one to man's mode of responding to it." *Between God and Man*, p. 12.

[38]*God in Search of Man*, p. 108. See also p. 115 where Heschel emphasizes the immediacy of awareness that he is talking about.

[39]*Die Prophetie*, p. 4.

[40]Rothschild, *Between God and Man*, pp. 20-21. Rothschild also shows how this is tied into Heschel's idea of history.

[41]*Man Is not Alone*, p. 6 and p. 17.

[42]*The Prophets*, pp. xvi-xvii.

[43]*God in Search of Man*, p. 121.

[44]*Man Is Not Alone: A Philosophy of Religion:* (New York: Harper Torchbooks, 1966), pp. 125-129. *God in Search of Man*, pp. 159-160.

[45]*Man is Not Alone*, p. 68, p. 126 and p. 128. Here Heschel claims that understanding of God's essence based on intuition is possible. Man knows God not in His essence but only through what God asks man. This is clearly not similar to knowledge which proceeds from concepts. This interpretation is strengthened in a passage in *God in Search of Man*, p. 161. "We have no nouns by which to describe His essence; we have only adverbs by which to indicate the ways in which He acts toward us."

[46]*Ibid.*, p. 121. "In other words, our belief in His reality is not a leap over a missing link in a syllogism but rather *a regaining*, giving up a view rather than adding one, going behind self-consciousness and questioning the self and all its cognitive pretensions. It is an ontological pre-supposition."

[47]*God in Search of Man*, p. 251.

[48]Rothschild, *Between God and Man*, p. 22. Although Rothschild is not totally clear on this point, he seems to suggest that the dimension of depth does not enter the domain of knowledge from a scientific view.

[49]*The Prophets*, p. 231, *Man Is Not Alone*, pp. 143-150, *God in Search of Man*, pp. 136-143. These are some of the main references. This point is made repeatedly in the corpus of Heschel's work.

[50]*God in Search of Man*, p. 7, and *Man is Not Alone*, p. 55.

[51]The departure from the natural attitude to the phenomenological attitude, in the words of one Husserlian commentator, opens up the possibility of a universal structure that is continuous with the reality of the individual. As I will demonstrate, this is the exact claim that Heschel makes for revelation. "The shock that wrenches man out of the natural attitude into philosophical awareness is an intramundane event. *Wonder*, phenomenologically interpreted, is the recognition that the restricted field of my own experience is continuous with the whole of reality, that my own immediacy is, in its infrastructure, amenable to universal analysis, and that my own reality has a rational order, logos." Maurice Natanson, *Edmund Husserl: Philosopher of Infinite Tasks*, (Evanston: Northwestern University Press, 1973), p. 122.

[52]Since Heschel holds that reason and revelation are from the same source, then revelation must guarantee a form of knowledge and understanding which is not available through reason. Heschel makes this clear at the beginning of

the third section of *God in Search of Man*, p. 289. "Knowledge of God is knowledge of living with God." This forms the transition and the basis for his deontological explanation of the content of revelation.

[53]*God in Search of Man*, p. 142.

[54]*Ibid.*, pp. 209-212.

[55]Merkle's analysis of the antecedents of faith completely overlooks their phenomenological character. He never comes to terms with Heschel's use of "perception" in relation to the sublime (p. 58) and Heschel's rejection of natural processes. Merkle's attempt to explain away the difficulty by referring to Heschel's use of the sublime "as a nonsensuous perception" (p. 58) does not explain anything but only creates the impression of clarity when in fact it confuses the issue by creating an ambiguity. This lack of clarity ultimately cannot give an account of the more important problem of depth-theology's accessibility to the content of faith.

[56]*The Prophets*, p. 361. "The contributions of the ecstatic have to do with the sphere of subjective experience, not with that of objective insight and understanding. Prophecy, on the other hand, is meaningless without expression. Its very substance is a word to be conveyed, a message to be imparted to others. The habit of the mystic is to conceal; the mission of the prophet is to reveal." *Ibid.*, p. 144. "What is important in mystical acts is that something happens; what is important in prophetic acts is that something is said. Ecstasy is the experience of a pure situation, of an inner condition. It is an experience that has form but no content. Prophecy is the experience of a relationship, the receipt of a message. It has form as well as content."

[57]*Ibid.*, p. 145.

[58]*Ibid.*, p. xvi.

[59]*God in Search of Man*, p. 158.

[60]*Ibid.*, p. 172.

[61]*Ibid.*, p. 176.

[62]*Ibid.*, pp. 7-8. See *Man is Not Alone*, pp. 273-296.

[63]Rothschild, "Introduction," p. 13.

[64]*God in Search of Man*, p. 137.

[65]*Ibid.*, p. 78.

[66]Rothschild correctly points to the idea of concern as the root metaphor of Heschel's ontology. "...but the mode of *concern* or directed attention that is the ultimate datum of prophetic religiosity. He takes this fundamental fact of religious experience, analyzes its structure, and employs it as the *root metaphor* of his ontology. Thus the idea of concern becomes the basic philosophical category, a conceptual tool to render intelligible such different fields of inquiry as theology, ontology and ethics. *To be* means to be the object of divine concern. (*Between God and Man*, p. 23)" Rothschild does not make it clear that the method, based on phenomenological intentionality, is the basic conceptual tool. Without it, the intelligibility of concern could not be ascertained.

[67]*The Prophets*, p. 361 and p. 364.

[68]These issues are treated in Chapter Nine.

Chapter Three

The Interdependence of Philosophy and Theology

The analysis of Heschel's methodology leads to one important conclusion that affects every aspect of Heschel's thought. Depth-theology has the explicit intention of applying itself to the pretheological, presymboloic and preconceptual moments of faith.[1] Its subject matter is the antecedents of faith. The content of faith, on the other hand, is just the opposite – it is conceptual, symbolic and theological.[2]

Depth-theology cannot remain only in the pretheological realm. It would be an empty concept if it could not relate to the content of the theological act. Heschel is adamant about this continuity not only because of the impact of depth-theology on practical issues, but also because its theoretical necessity cannot be ignored.

> The moment of revelation is not to be separated from the content or substance of revelation. Loyalty to the norms and thoughts conveyed in the event is as essential as the reality of the event. Acceptance was not complete, the fulfillment has not occurred. The decisive moment is yet to come. The event must be fulfilled, not only believed in. What was expected at Sinai comes about in the moment of a good deed. A commandment is a foresight, a deed is a fulfillment. The deed completes the event. Revelation is but a beginning, our deeds must continue, our lives must complete it.[3]

To be sure, God's concern for man must be discernible in some way. The particulars behind this conception of God's concern are not salient at this point in the investigation.[4] However, the theoretical point is. If depth-theology is related to the content of theology, this relationship must be recognizable all the time. In theory, method and content must always retain the possibility of interacting on any level. They must always retain their interdependency. If method and content do not remain interdependent, Heschel's attempt at basing his own theology on the model of classical prophecy is inauthentic. The prophetic mind, which originated the love of God and one's neighbor, the observance of the sabbath and the laws of the Temple for example, cannot have its content separated from its structure and meaning.[5]

Similarly, according to Heschel, the philosophical mind, which is not approached through doctrine, has the same intention as the prophetic mind.

> There are two types of philosophy. Philosophy may be pursued as a process of thinking thought, of analyzing *the content of thinking,* such as principles, assumptions, doctrines. Or it may be pursued as thinking about thinking, as *radical self-understanding,* as a process of analyzing *the act of thinking,* as an act of introspection, of watching the intellectual self in action.[6]

This similarity, often overlooked, forms the basis of a crucial issue. The ideal content of Heschel's theology and philosophy of religion must be open to each other's criticism.[7] Method and content, either religious or philosophical, for all practical purposes, must be parallel. Heschel's theology and his philosophy must retain this aspect of interdependence or they both lose their meaning.[8]

This interdependence precludes the possibility that Heschel is only thinking religiously or theologically while consciously obscuring the differences of philosophy and theology. On the contrary, it is fundamental to Heschel's method that the differences between philosophy and religion are retained and used interdependently to explain the structure of depth-theology. Both the religious act of thought and the philosophical act of thought are generated in a radical way. They must share a common insight as well as an open intellectual structure that renders such insight understandable.

> Just as the mind is able to form conceptions supported by sense perception, it can derive insight from the dimension of the ineffable. Insights are the roots of art, philosophy and religion, and must be acknowledged as common and fundamental facts of mental life. The ways of creative thinking do not always coincide with those charted by traditional logicians; the realm where genius is at home, where insight is at work, logic can hardly find access to.[9]

Indeed, theology and philosophy have different contents, but their primary methodological concerns are identical and their contents must be equally available to intellectual analysis but not necessarily similar.[10] There cannot be two different kinds of truth,[11] one philosophical and one religious. More important, Heschel absolutely rejects the idea that theology can incorporate or employ any ambiguity.[12] All of these claims are based on the inclusive nature of the intellectual self as it applies to philosophy and religion.

The action in which the intellectual self is engaged takes place on two levels: on the level of insight and on the level of translating insights into concepts and symbols. Radical self-understanding must embrace not only the fruits of thinking, namely the concepts and symbols, but also the root of thinking, the depth of insight, the moments of immediacy in the communion of the self with reality.[13]

This attitude toward the intellectual self holds for philosophy and religion, and points to another important point of mutual concern. It is clear that for Heschel, religion is not within the limits of mere reason.[14] Yet, it cannot function without reason. In Heschel's eyes, reason and religion must cohere because they offer insights based on the same methodological concerns, even though they have different tasks.[15] This becomes clear when Heschel puts the sense of the ineffable, without which religion is meaningless, into its philosophical context. The cognitive aspect of the ineffable would clearly be meaningless without reason.

The sense of the ineffable is an intellectual endeavor out of the depth of reason; it is the source of cognitive insight. There is therefore, no rivalry between religion and reason as long as we are aware of their respective tasks and areas. The employment of reason is indispensable to the understanding and worship of God, and religion withers without it. The insights of faith are general, vague, and stand in need of conceptualization in order to be communicated to the mind, integrated and brought to consistency. Without reason faith becomes blind. Without reason we would not know how to apply the insights of faith to the concrete issues of living. The worship of reason is arrogance and betrays a lack of intelligence. The rejection of reason is cowardice and betrays a lack of faith.[16]

Just as religion is dependent on philosophy for explication through reason, philosophy is dependent on religion for the recognition of its limits.[17] The limitation of reason imposed by religion is not a strategy of obscuring truth. The limitation is a criticism of the powers of deduction, which cannot be extended as a means of evaluation for every aspect of reality. As Heschel says, "Evaluating faith in terms of reason is like trying to understand love as a syllogism and beauty as an algebraic equation."[18]

The interdependence of philosophy and religion is significant for Heschel not merely because it is an internal aspect of his theology.[19] It also forms the basis of depth-theology since this interdependence offers an intellectual self acceptable to both modes of thought. The insight of religion, which relegates reason to a certain status, must be examined because it is placed in a certain phenomenological context. It is clear that Heschel does not cherish reason's deductive power in relation to insight. It should be equally clear to those who realize this fact that

Heschel's method does emphasize the phenomenological structure of insight and the ineffable aspect of reality. As a result, Heschel consistently employs phenomenological ideas to explain his own reliance on insight, which do not destroy the integrity of reason.

> By the ineffable we do not mean the unknown as such; things unknown today may be known a thousand years from now. By the ineffable we mean that aspect of reality which by its very nature lies beyond our comprehension, and is acknowledged by the mind to be beyond the scope of the mind. Nor does the ineffable refer to a realm detached from the perceptible and the known. It refers to the correlation of the known and the unknown, of the knowable and the unknowable, upon which the mind comes in all its acts of thinking and feeling.[20]

This Heschelian emphasis on insight has eluded the critics, primarily because of its context. Heschel never explicitly describes an epistemological program. He chooses to make scattered phenomenological remarks or criticisms of Descartes,[21] Hegel,[22] Schleiermacher,[23] Kierkegaard,[24] Nietzsche,[25] Kant,[26] Spinoza,[27] Schelling,[28] Heidegger,[29] Otto,[30] and Tillich[31] without connecting those criticisms and presenting them in any organized fashion.[32] This leaves the reader with a serious problem, but it also strengthens the kerygmatic character of Heschel's work. Since Heschel never makes an absolute distinction between philosophy and religion, but depends on their interdependence, he sees no need to describe the kind of epistemological program that philosophers require.

Consequently, Heschel's philosophical remarks about insight are couched in religious terms. The reality of God and the nature of the ineffable provide the background from which the phenomenological nature of insight must be viewed. The understanding yielded by intuition is not a procedural abstraction but rather a sympathetic process.

> It is more appropriate to describe the ideas we acquire in our wrestling with the ineffable as understanding of God. For if He is neither an abstract principle or a thing, but a unique living being, our approach to Him cannot be through the procedures of knowledge but through a process of understanding. We know through induction or inference, we understand through intuition; we know a thing, we understand a personality; we know a fact, we understand a hint. Knowledge implies familiarity with, or even mastery of, something; understanding is an act of interpreting something which we only know by its expression and through inner agreement with it. There is no sympathetic knowledge but there is sympathetic understanding. Understanding, significantly, is a synonym for agreement. It is through agreement that we find a way of understanding.[33]

This type of intuition, according to Heschel, is not a form of knowledge but still has a recognizable process through which it is apprehended. By definition the process cannot presuppose blind agreement and therefore give up any claim to intelligibility. There are premises and conclusions which must be examined. A certain kind of inner logic must rule the expression if an inner agreement is to be reached. Heschel clarifies this movement from intuition to understanding in another book but within the same context.

> The ultimate question, moreover, is a question that arises on the level of the ineffable. It is phrased not in *concepts* but in *acts*, and no abstract formulation is capable of conveying it. It is, therefore, necessary to understand the inner logic of the situation, the spiritual climate in which it exists, in order to comprehend what the ultimate question implies. It is a situation in which we are challenged, aroused, stirred by the sublime, the marvel, the mystery and the Presence.[34]

The "act" to which Heschel is referring is the phenomenological experience and the "inner logic of the situation" is the noetic-noematic correlation which incorporates the idea of intentionality. This becomes even more clear when, two pages later, Heschel describes the moment lived on the level of the ineffable.

> Acts of love are only meaningful to a person who is in love, and not to him whose heart and mind are sour. The same applies to the categories of religion. For ultimate insight takes place on the presymbolic, preconceptual level of thinking. It is difficult, indeed, to transpose insights phrased in the presymbolic language of inner events into the symbolic language of concepts. In conceptual thinking, what is clear and evident at one moment remains clear and evident at all other moments. Ultimate insights, on the other hand, are events, rather than a permanent state of mind.[35]

The transition from intuition to concept must be made dynamically. It must be part of a process of thought that unfolds the power of the event. The state of mind that "conceives" an insight cannot give up the presence or the reality of the event.[36] Only a noetic-noematic correlation, based on the object as perceived and the subject as perceiving it, can retain the immediacy of the insight.

The description of Heschel's link between understanding and intuition offered here is supported by another Heschelian position. With the exception of Merkle, most critics have not noticed Heschel's use of understanding and knowing.[37] More often than not, Heschel makes a distinction between these two concepts. As we saw above, knowledge is inductive, indirect and procedural, which implies mastery over its object. Understanding is intuitive, immediate and sympathetic toward its object.[38] When discussing the ineffable Heschel often emphasizes its nondiscursive nature.

> Let us remember the fundamental fact of a universal nondiscursive perception of the ineffable which is a sense of transcendent meaning, of an awareness that something is meant by the universe which surpasses our power of comprehension.[39]

The idea of wonder imbedded here and spoken of elsewhere, is predicated on the opinion that transcendent meaning[40] is something "we apprehend but cannot comprehend."[41] These references clearly are based on the idea of understanding offered above. But, Heschel also indicates that wonder, meaning and knowledge may be used in a different manner. These concepts are not always used by Heschel to point out a distinction with understanding. They are used in combination to signify a positive content that cannot be reduced to sympathetic understanding.

> There is no insight into transcendent meaning without the premise of wonder and the premise of awe. We say 'premise' because wonder and awe are not emotions, but are cognitive acts involving value judgements.[42]

This type of usage is not only limited to the postprophetic mind, but is applied to the prophetic mind.

> But does the worth of wonder merely consist in its being a stimulant to the acquisition of knowledge? Is wonder the same as curiosity? To the prophets wonder is *a form of thinking*. It is not the beginning of knowledge but an act that goes beyond knowledge; it does not come to an end when knowledge is acquired; it is an attitude that never ceases. There is no answer in the world to man's radical amazement.[43]

This use of the term knowledge, which is positive and not employed in the same context of sympathetic understanding, is based on an idea of preconceptual thought. The section of *God in Search of Man* that includes this reference is decidedly philosophical. It is titled, "An Ontological Presupposition," and unambiguously and consistently refers to preconceptual knowledge.

> Indeed, knowledge does not come into being only as the fruit of thinking. Only an extreme rationalist or solipsist would claim that knowledge is produced exclusively through the combination of concepts. Any genuine encounter with reality is an encounter with the unknown, is an intuition in which an awareness of the object is won, a rudimentary, *preconceptual* knowledge. Indeed, no object is truly known, unless it was first experienced in its un-knowness.[44]

As if to warn the reader about mistakenly using knowledge and understanding synonymously, Heschel indicates that insight, the basis of both knowledge and understanding, is not a monolithic concept. Understanding and knowledge may have different insights.

> All insight stands between two realms, the realm of objective reality and the realm of conceptual and verbal cognition. Conceptual cognition must stand the test of a double reference, of the reference to our system of concepts and the reference to the insights from which it is derived.[45]

Insight, based on knowledge has its own purpose. It does not generate agreement as in the case of sympathetic understanding. It has exactly the opposite effect.

> The sense of the ineffable does not hush the quest of thought, but, on the contrary, disturbs the placid and unseals our suppressed impressionability. The approach to the ineffable leads through the depth of knowledge rather than through ignorant animal gazing. To the minds of those who do not make the universal mistake of assuming as known a world that is unknown, of placing the solution before the enigma, the abundance of the utterable can never displace the world of the ineffable.[46]

Clearly, Heschel does not consistently use knowledge and understanding synonymously, as Merkle attempts to demonstrate.[47] It is also impossible to infer that one use of wonder is temporary and the other is enduring. They are different in kind. The neglect of the texts that indicate this disparity only leads to a greater confusion of Heschel's intention. The task here is not to explain away a difficulty, as Merkle has done, but to penetrate the complexity of Heschel's philosophical position. While knowledge, which arises from preconceptual thinking, is not discursive and does not comprehend the transcendent, it is plainly objective.[48] It is still within the phenomenological realm of wonder, yet it never offers an act of apprehension equal to awareness.[49]

This collected background of knowledge indicates a phenomenological fact that has been completely overlooked. Heschel's use of knowledge corresponds to the noematic side of the noetic-noematic correlation that infuses Heschel's theological writing. Preconceptual knowledge is not only noetic as it refers to the objective realm and allows the mind to reflect on an event. It does not yield a sympathetic agreement because the objective structure is gained in reflection and not in direct participation. The objective structure cannot capture a sympathetic meaning because it is not *a situation lived in but reflected on.* "Acts of love are only meaningful to a person in love."[50] In

opposition to love, the primary meaning of knowledge is derived from
its premises, which must be questioned. Therefore, the apprehension
that can be attributed to knowledge must be available in concepts but its
origin must always lie beyond comprehension. Apprehension of the
structure of the experience is derived first from the event, and then, if
possible, comprehension is produced in concepts. It is an objective
structural knowledge that does not yield sympathetic understanding
because its structure is topical and does not penetrate the depth of
experience.

> In our religious situation we do not comprehend the transcendent; we
> are present at it, we witness it. Whatever we know is inadequate;
> whatever we say is an understatement. We have an awareness that is
> deeper than our concepts; we possess insights that are not accessible
> to the power of expression.[51]

This analysis demonstrates that there is no attempt by Heschel to
seek refuge in irrationalism or to obscure his dependence on intuition so
that it may hide his real intention.[52] The different uses of intuition
based on knowledge and understanding necessarily coexist within the
noetic-noematic correlation. Without these different usages, Heschel's
depth-theology could not bridge the gap to conventional theology.
Moreover, the subjective and objective aspects of religious consciousness
could not function together. They would be irreconcilable because of
their different requirements – subjective immediacy and objective
reflection. This phenomenological method consistently forms the basis
of Heschel's religious claims. It is to Heschel's discredit that he never
clarifies the use of the method or the philosophical meaning of
phenomenology but merely injects it into his religious thought creating
the impression that all questions of insight are self-evident, needing no
further explanation. This problem is the task of a later chapter. It is
now clear, however, that this method is the philosophical basis of
Heschel's claims and it utilizes an intelligible concept of insight, based
on a noetic-noematic correlation, that is not merely an appeal to
emotion or irrationalism.

---

[1] *God in Search of Man*, p. 108 and p. 115.
[2] *Ibid.*, pp. 6-7 and p. 115.
[3] *Ibid.*, p. 217.
[4] *Man is Not Alone*, pp. 135-150.
[5] *The Prophets*, p. ix.
[6] *God in Search of Man*, p. 6. This is specifically the point that Fackenheim
misses in all of Heschel's writing. The clearest example is the following; "We
have said that to the careful and well-intentioned reader it is clear that Heschel

engages in religious thinking, not in reflective thinking about religion. We must now add that to the not-quite-so-careful and well-intentioned reader this is not always clear. There are some passages in *God in Search of Man* which, at least at first sight, seem to argue, not on the basis of a commitment, but for a commitment, and whose argument would hence be circular unless taken as not based on a commitment. Possibly such passages have misled some of Heschel's critics into believing that Heschel offers detached thought about religion, rather than (or in addition to) committed religious thinking. If this were true, the critics would be quite right in considering the argument as inadequate. But it would appear that this is a misunderstanding. Heschel may not always be as careful in expression as one might wish him to be. But it does, on the whole, seem clear that his intention is to give us religious thinking and nothing else," (*Conservative Judaism*, Vol. 15, No. 1, p. 50). Fackenheim ignores Heschel's statements that argue against an absolutely "detached" or "impartial" thinking (*The Prophets*, p. xvi) and that argue for some form of detached thinking (*Ibid.*, pp. xvi-xvii). This point is the exact phenomenological fulcrum, that demonstrates Heschel's phenomenological reduction. This will be clarified in Chapters Four and Five. Here, Heschel clearly announces his intention to carry out reflective thinking about religion, in a phenomenological manner, as the act of thinking. This noetic reference is the basis of Heschel's philosophy of religion and not only his strategy for thinking religiously. It allows Heschel to carry out a criticism of the validity of religion from the point of view of philosophy (*God in Search of Man*, p.10).

[7] *Ibid.*, p. 17.

[8] *God in Search of Man*, pp. 9-14.

[9] *Man Is Not Alone*, p. 17. *Who is Man*, p. 78. "It is a cognitive insight, since the awareness it evokes adds to our deeper understanding of the world....There is no insight into transcendent meaning without the premise of wonder and the premise of awe. We say 'premise' because wonder and awe are not emotions, but are cognitive acts involving value judgements."

[10] *God in Search of Man*, p. 17.

[11] *Ibid.*, pp. 10-11.

[12] *Ibid.*, pp. 191-193. *Man Is Not Alone*, p. 173. "An essential disagreement between reason and revelation would presuppose the existence of two divine beings, each of whom would represent a different source of knowledge. Faith, therefore, can never compel the reason to accept that which is absurd."

[13] *God in Search of Man*, p. 6. *Man Is Not Alone*, p. 193, "If at the root of philosophy is not a self-contempt of the mind but the mind's concern for its ultimate surmise, then our aim is to examine in order to know."

[14] *God in Search of Man*, p. 20. This is clearly a rejection of Kant's well-known treatment of the problem. It is not, as is often assumed, based on Heschel's hasidic or mystical outlook. It is a seriously held philosophical opinion.

[15] *Ibid.*, p. 20. *Man Is Not Alone*, p. 173. "Neither reason nor faith is all-inclusive nor self-sufficient. The insights of faith are general, vague and stand in need of conceptualization in order to be communicated to the mind, integrated and brought to consistency. Reason is a necessary coefficient of faith lending form

to what often becomes violent, blind and exaggerated by imagination. *Faith without reason is mute; reason without faith is deaf."*

[16] *God in Search of Man,* p. 20.

[17] *Ibid.,* p. 18 and p. 189, "The goal is to train the reason for that which lies beyond reason."

[18] *Man is Not Alone,* p. 170.

[19] Merkle's excellent presentation of the interdependence of these areas does not analyze Heschel's reasoning behind this combination. Merkle's attempt to arrive at Heschel's depth-theology from his theology does not penetrate the former, because Merkle has not clarified the unity of Heschel's methodological statements. "The task at hand is to go beneath theological formulations and to reflect upon those 'acts which precede articulation and defy definition,' (*The Insecurity of Freedom* p. 123) says Heschel. The time has come to break through the bottom of theology into depth-theology" (*The Genesis of Faith,* p. 51). Nowhere in Heschel's writings is a reference of a transition from theology to depth-theology to be found. To penetrate depth-theology one must examine its raison d'etre and evaluate its philosophical concerns. Elaborating its content, no matter how well done, cannot yield its depth. The content analysis will expose only a lateral understanding of a concept that demands and presupposes a profound vertical knowledge.

[20] *God in Search of Man,* p. 104.

[21] *Who Is Man?,* p. 53, "It is not enough for me to be able to say 'I am'; I want to know *who I am,* and in relation to who I live." *Ibid.,* p. 111, "Do I exist as a human being? My answer is: I am commanded – therefore I am." *Man Is Not Alone,* p. 11, "Wonder rather than doubt is the root of knowledge. Doubt comes in the wake of knowledge as a state of vacillation between contrary or contradictory views; as a state in which a belief we had embraced begins to totter."

[22] *God in Search of Man,* p. 125, "To say that our search for God is a search for the idea of the absolute is to eliminate the problem which we are trying to explore. A first cause or an idea of the absolute – devoid of life, devoid of freedom – is an issue for science or metaphysics rather than a concern of the soul or the conscience." *Who Is Man?,* pp. 117-118, "The mind is in search of rational coherence, the soul in quest of celebration. Knowledge is celebration. Truth is more than equation of thing and thought. Truth transcends and unites both thing and thought. Truth is transcendence, its comprehension is loyalty." *Man Is Not Alone,* p. 48, "It is easy to raise verbally the question: Who is the subject, of which my self is the object? But to be keenly sensitive to its meaning is something which surpasses our power of comprehension. It is, in fact, impossible to comprehend logically its implications. For in asking the question, I am always aware of the fact that it is I who asks the question. But as soon as I know myself as an 'I', as a subject, I am not capable any more of grasping the content of the question, in which I am posited as an object. Thus on the level of self-consciousness there is no way to face the issue, to ask the absolute question."

[23] *Who Is Man?,* p. 109, "Religion has been defined as the feeling of absolute dependence. We come closer to an understanding of religion by defining one

of its roots as a sense of personal indebtedness. God is not only a power we depend on, He is a God who demands. Religion begins with the certainty that something is asked of us, that there are ends which are in need of us."

24 *Who Is Man?*, p. 48, "The acceptance of the sacred is an existential paradox: it is saying 'yes' to a no; it is the antithesis of the will to power; it may contradict interests and stand in the way of satisfying inner drives." *Ibid.*, p. 93, "God and the world are not opposite poles. There is darkness in the world, but there is also this call, 'Let there be light!' Nor are our body and soul at loggerheads. We are not told to decide between 'Either-Or,' either God or the world, either this world or the world to come. We are told to accept Either and Or, God and the world. It is upon us to strive for a share in the world to come, as well as to let God have a share in this world."

25 *Ibid.*, p. 48. *Ibid.*, p. 92, "Nietzsche's formula for the greatness of a human being is *amor fati*. Jewish tradition would suggest as the formula for the greatness of man his capacity for *kiddush hashem*, readiness to die for the sake of God, for the sake of the name."

26 There are too many anti-Kantian remarks interspersed throughout Heschel's writings to quote them all. These are representative of Heschel's position. *God in Search of Man*, p. 38, "According to Kant, *the beautiful* is what pleases apart from all interest and *the sublime* is what pleases through its opposition to the interest of sense....The sublime is not opposed to the beautiful, and must not, furthermore, be considered an esthetic category. The sublime may be sensed in things of beauty as well as in acts of goodness and in the search for truth." *Ibid.*, p. 97, "What then is reality? To the western man, it is *a thing in itself;* to the Biblical man, it is *a thing through God.*" *Ibid.*, p. 115, "The encounter with reality does not take place on the level of concepts through the channels of logical categories; concepts are second thoughts. All conceptualization is symbolization, an act of accommodation of reality to the human mind." *Ibid.*, p. 378, "Judaism would reject the Kantian axiom, 'I ought, therefore I can'; it would claim, instead, 'Thou art commanded, therefore thou canst." *Who Is Man?*, p. 109, "Thought is a response to being rather than an invention. The world does not lie prostrate, waiting to be given order and coherence by the generosity of the human mind. Things are evocative." *Man Is Not Alone*, pp. 84-85, "In other words our belief in the reality of God is not a case of first possessing an idea and then postulating the ontal counterpart to it; or, to use a Kantian phrase, of first having the idea of a hundred dollars and then claiming to possess them on the basis of the idea." *Ibid.*, p. 120, "The ultimate principle of ethics is not an imperative but an ontological fact. While it is true that what distinguishes a moral attitude is the consciousness of obligation to do it; yet an act is not good because we feel obliged to do it; it is rather that we feel obliged to do it because it is good. The essence of a moral value is neither in its being valid independent of our will nor in its claim that it ought to be done for its own sake." *Ibid.*, p. 194, "Man is not an all-inclusive end to himself. The second maxim of Kant, never to use human beings merely as means but to regard them also as ends, only suggests how a person ought to be treated by other people, not how he ought to treat himself. For if a person thinks that he is an end to himself, then he will use others as means."

[27] *God in Search of Man*, pp. 320-321, "It is important that we analyze a popular misunderstanding of Judaism which may be called 'religious behaviorism'. It signifies an attitude toward the law as well as a philosophy of Judaism as a whole. As an attitude toward the law, it stresses the external compliance with the law and disregards the importance of inner devotion. It maintains that according to Judaism, there is only one way in which the will of God need be fulfilled, namely, outward action; that inner devotion is not indigenous to Judaism; that Judaism is concerned with deeds not ideas; that all it asks for is obedience to the law....The theory of Judaism as a system of religious behaviorism goes back to Spinoza and Moses Mendelssohn."

[28] *God in Search of Man*, p. 92, "But what are the foundations of nature? To the Greeks who take the world for granted Nature, Order is the answer. To the Biblical mind in its radical amazement nature, order are not an answer but a problem: why is there order, being, at all?"

[29] *Who Is Man?*, p. 5, "Do we live what we are or do we live what we have or by what we have? Our difficulty is that we know so little about the humanity of man. We know what he makes, but we do not know what he is. In the characterization of man, for example, as a tool making or thinking animal reference is made to the functions, not to the being, of man. Is it not conceivable that our entire civilization is built upon a misinterpretation of man? Or that the tragedy of modern man is due to the fact that he is a being who forgot the question: Who is man?" *Ibid.*, pp. 94-95, "As sheer being man dissolves in anonymity. But man is not only being, he is also living, and if he were simply to 'surrender to being,' as Heidegger calls upon us to do, he would abdicate his power to decide and reduce his living to being." *Ibid.*, p. 97, "Heidegger's rhetorical question, 'Has the Dasein, as such, ever freely decided and will it ever be able to decide as to whether to come into existence or not?' has been answered long ago: 'It is against your will that you are born, it is against your will that you live, and it is against your will that you are bound to give account....' The transcendence of human being is disclosed here as life imposed upon, as imposition to give account, as imposition of freedom. The transcendence of being is commandment, being here and now is obedience."

[30] *Who Is Man?*, p. 110, "Unlike all other values, moral and religious ends evoke in us a sense of obligation. Thus religious living consists in serving ends that are in need of us. Man is a divine need, God is in need of man. Religion is not a feeling for the mystery of living, or a sense of awe, wonder or fear, which is the root of religion; but rather the question *what to do* with the feeling for the mystery of living, what to do with awe, wonder, or fear. Thinking about God begins when we do not know any more how to wonder, how to fear, how to be in awe. For wonder is not a state of aesthetic enjoyment. Endless wonder is endless tension, a situation at which we are shocked at the inadequacy of our awe, at the weakness of our shock, as well as the state of being asked the ultimate question."

[31] *God in Search of Man*, p. 127, " Yet there seems to be a third possibility: God is neither alive nor devoid of life but a *symbol*. If God is defined 'as a name for that which concerns man ultimately,' then He is but a symbol of man's concern, the objectification of a subjective state of mind. But as such God

would be little more than a projection of our imagination....Certainly God is more than 'a name for what concerns man ultimately.'" *Who Is Man?*, p. 56, "There is an appeal to which human being is exposed and is occasionally sensitive: an urging for significant being. Being as being is intransitive, going-on-ness, continuity: significant being is transitive, going beyond itself, centrifugal." *Ibid.*, p. 67, "The quest for the meaning of being is a quest for that which surpasses being, expressing insufficiency of sheer being. Meaning and being are, as said above, not coextensive. Meaning is a primary category not reducible to being as such. There may be meaning to that which is not yet, as there may be being destructive of meaning. Just as we are aware of being and coming into being, we are aware of meaning and of coming into meaning." *Ibid.*, p. 70, "Any ontology which disregards the wonder and mystery of being is guilty of suppressing the genuine amazement of the mind, and of taking being for granted. It is true that being's coming-into-being 'can neither be thought nor uttered.' Yet a fact does not cease to be fact because of its transcending the limits of thought and expression. Indeed the very theme of ontology, being *as* being, 'can neither be thought nor uttered.'"

[32] Heschel also criticizes the Pre-Socratics, Socrates, Plato and Aristotle but these arguments do not involve any aspects of modern phenomenology.

[33] *Man Is Not Alone*, p. 133.

[34] *God in Search of Man*, p. 130.

[35] *Ibid.*, pp. 131-132. It is interesting that Heschel quotes Maimonides, who supposedly reflects the creedal approach to theology, as a reference to this point (*God in Search of Man*, note 7, p. 135).

[36] "When detached from its original insights, the discursive mind becomes a miser, and when we discover that concepts bring no relief to our outraged conscience and thirst for integrity, we turn to the origin of thought, to the endless shore that lies across the logical. Just as the mind is able to from conceptions supported by sense perception, it can derive insights from the dimension of the ineffable. Insights are the roots of art, philosophy and religion, and must be acknowledged as common and fundamental facts of mental life." *Man Is Not Alone*, p. 17.

[37] Merkle, pp. 163-164.

[38] *Man Is Not Alone*, p. 133.

[39] *Ibid.*, p. 62.

[40] *Who Is Man?*, pp. 78-79.

[41] *Ibid.*, p. 20, and *God in Search of Man*, pp. 34 and 58.

[42] *Who Is Man?*, p. 78.

[43] *God in Search of Man*, p. 46.

[44] *Ibid.*, p. 115.

[45] *Ibid.*, p. 116.

[46] *Man Is Not Alone*, p. 15.

[47] Merkle, pp. 162-165. This misconception by Merkle forces him to misunderstand entirely the role of the ontological presupposition and the ineffable. "But Heschel usually suggests that it is apprehension of the divine, not the thought or the intellectual certainty of the divine, that leads us to the awareness of God's reality. Do we have the reverse with regard to the ineffable?

Perhaps such a reverse is suggested here, but some pages before the quotation under consideration, Heschel suggests that it is an experience that is the evidence of the reality of the ineffable. Recognizing this prompts another critical reflection. There is a sense in which, no matter how valuable the argument under consideration, it seems inconsistent with Heschel's basic approach. He says: 'What we *infer* from is...the intellectual certainty...that we must respond with awe.' Yet Heschel normally insists that we do not become aware of the ineffable – or certain of its realness – by way of inference but by way of immediate encounter and insight. Of course he never says that insight is infallible. Nonetheless it is not by way of inference that we become certain of the realness of the ineffable. Perhaps Heschel is using the method of inference here only because he is answering a possible objection. Thus he invokes an apologetic that is accidental to his own experience and understanding, but which can serve to vindicate rationally his experiential certainty. In this case he is not being inconsistent, but simply using a different terminology in his postexperiential dialogue with those who may raise objections." It is not surprising, given Merkle's failure to recognize the subtle distinction of types of insight and of the distinction of knowledge from understanding that Heschel sometimes uses, that he could call these inferences a different method only occasioned by an apologetic. Heschel's phenomenology clearly allows for a postexperiential reflection on the event of man's encounter with God. It demands this treatment as I have demonstrated. Without the ability to focus on the ontological presupposition, Heschel himself realizes there is no intellectual content to his claim. He says: "As a response, it is an act of raising from the depths of the mind an ontological presupposition which makes that response intellectually understandable" (God in Search of Man, p. 114).

[48] *God in Search of Man*, p. 116.

[49] *Ibid.* "Knowledge is not the same as awareness, and expression is not the same as experience. By proceeding from awareness to knowledge we gain in clarity and lose in immediacy. What we gain in distinctness by going from experience to expression we lose in genuineness."

[50] *Ibid.*, p. 131.

[51] *Ibid.*, p. 116.

[52] *Who Is Man?* p. 78. Heschel clearly differentiates finite from infinite meaning and applies the phenomenological categories to infinite meaning.

Chapter Four

Husserl's Phenomenological Program

Heschel's remarks about his own phenomenological method and its dependence on Husserl are neither exhaustive nor are they explanatory. Consequently, the philosophical significance of Heschel's method is left undeveloped. Even the most basic Husserlian ideas that Heschel explicitly uses, such as the noetic-noematic correlation and the intentionality of consciousness, are never fleshed out. Even more, the Husserlian ideas that Heschel implicitly uses are opaquely buried within his works.

The attempt to explain Heschel's philosophical significance and the philosophical nature of revelation, therefore must follow a basic elaboration of Husserl's program. It must explain the context of Husserl's phenomenological method and the natural standpoint from which it begins. This complex task is simplified somewhat by the fact that the noetic-noematic correlation appears in Husserl's work at a specific point in his career.[1] The *Logical Investigations* first published in 1900 is an intentional examination of the "rationalization of discourse as the form of scientific expression."[2] The first volume of *Logical Investigations*, while explaining the problems of logic, spends most of its energy attacking the contemporary views of logic. It does not contain a phenomenological program. The second volume of these investigations, which was reprinted in 1913, does not contain the noetic-noematic correlation[3] and makes no use of the basic tools of phenomenology, such as the phenomenological reduction, first introduced in *The Idea of Phenomenology*[4] in 1906 and employed throughout *The Ideas* published in 1913.

At the outset of this inquiry into Husserl's phenomenological method, it is clear that the period of his development that influenced Heschel includes the introduction of a new transcendentalism. It turns away from the objectivistic logic of the *Logical Investigations*, which sees phenomenology as a limited epistemological enterprise.[5] The new transcendentalism sees phenomenology as the universal foundation of philosophy[6] but refuses to go beyond the data available to consciousness. In Husserl's own words,

> We then understand ourselves, *not as a subjectivity which finds itself in a world ready-made...but a subjectivity bearing within itself, and achieving all the possible operations to which this world owes its becoming.* In other words, we understand ourselves...*as transcendental subjectivity,* where by 'transcendental', nothing more is to be understood than a regressive inquiry concerning the ultimate source of all cognitive formation.[7]

The transcendental nature of this later phenomenology is a result of the fact that "all that is required can be discovered by reflection on subjective acts with their inevitable objective correlates."[8] The transcendental is neither the object of the experince nor the subject having the experience.[9] It is, in the Kantian sense, the necessary conditions for experience. In conjunction with this new turn toward transcendental idealism there is a new understanding of immanence. The immanent here does not have a psychological sense. It is that which is in consciousness and can be reflected upon within the same stream of consciousness. The immanent means the "adequately self-given."[10] This is a transcendental immanence which is based solely on the given[11] and can be "accepted as the indubitable because it points to nothing outside itself, and what is intended here is adequately given in itself."[12] This description of immanence has a direct bearing on Heschel's formulation of the inquiry into prophetic consciousness. In *The Prophets,* Heschel makes the same claim about the immanence of consciousness vis-à-vis insight.

> Insight is a breakthrough, requiring much intellectual dismantling and dislocation. It begins with a mental interim, with the cultivation of a feeling for the unfamiliar, unparalleled, incredible. It is in being involved with a phenomenon, being intimately engaged to it, courting it, as it were, that after much perplexity and embarrassment we come upon insight – upon a way of seeing the phenomenon from within.[13]

This is the attempt by Heschel and Husserl to achieve a valid essential knowledge of being, that is "an analysis of the intentional structures of consciousness, wherein being appears."[14]

This attempt to achieve a valid essential knowledge of being based on the intentional structure of consciousness has another parallel in Heschel's thought. Heschel's dependence on the content of the noetic act, which originates in *Die Prophetie,*[15] is always presented as a correlation. The prophetic consciousness and the postprophetic consciousness are never conceived as things in themselves. They are consistently conceived as events in relation to a certain form and content.[16] For Husserl, the correlation which underlies the analysis of consciousness is not "conceived of as a one-dimensional sequence of events, consciousness must be defined as a noetico-noematic correlation, that is to say, a correlation between items pertaining to two heterogeneous planes: on the one hand that of temporal psychological events, and on the other hand, that of atemporal, irreal, that is to say, ideal entities that are the noemata, or meanings understood in the broader sense."[17]

Similarly, for Heschel, we find the exact correlation in use as the basis for prophetic consciousness and hence for postprophetic consciousness.[18]

> I have been led to distinguish in the consciousness of the prophet between what happened *to* him and what happened *in* him – between the transcendent and the spontaneous – as well as between content and form. The structure of prophetic consciousness as ascertained in the analysis was disclosed as consisting, on the transcendent level, of pathos (content of inspiration) and event (form), and on the personal level, of sympathy (content of inner experience) and the sense of being overpowered (form of inner experience).[19]

The transcendence and immanence of Husserl's noetic-noematic correlation, based on the heterogeneous temporal and atemporal planes of existence, provide Heschel a basis for the form and content of prophetic experience. This parrallelism, which is the basis of Husserl's noema and noesis[20] is evident throughout all of Heschel's work and is the basis of his ontology as will be demonstrated.[21] As such, form and content never become an aspect or quality of a subject-object dualism because they are intentional concepts, part of the noetic-noematic correlation, and cannot be represented as either thinking substance or as extended substance.[22] If this intentional structure is properly analyzed, then the object pole of the experience will be fully revealed[23] and the meaning of the experience can be understood. Within this context, Heschel's idea of form and content remain within the bounds of the phenomenological method first used by Husserl in the *Idea of Phenomenology* and then throughout his other works.[24]

The philosophical setting of Husserl, which clearly influenced Heschel's pretheological and preconceptual phenomenological method,[25] coincides with the period of Husserl's clarification of his own method. Husserl's need to elaborate the standpoint of his philosophical program rose to the surface principally in the *Idea of Phenomenology*, *Ideas*, *The Paris Lectures* and the *Cartesian Meditations*. We must turn to these works for an understanding of Husserl's position and of the basic concepts he employs to explicate it.

Only then, can we elaborate Heschel's method based on these fundamental Husserlian positions.

In a repetition of his rejection of empiricism, Husserl explains the origin of his method.

> As genuine standpoint-philosophers, and in obvious contradistinction to their principle of freedom from prejudice, the empiricists start from unclarified pre-conceived opinions whose truth has not been grounded. On the other hand, we take our start from what lies *prior to* all standpoints: from the total realm of whatever is itself given intuitionally prior to all theorizing, from everything that one can immediately see and seize upon – if only one does not let himself be blinded by prejudices and prevented from taking into consideration whole classes of genuine data.[26]

Husserl's desire to begin with an immediate seeing of what is prior to all standpoints is based on his desire to surpass what he calls the natural standpoint. Husserl conceives of the natural attitude as one which simply sees the spatio-temporal world as there before him. The definite objects of experience, through, sight, sound, touch, smell and taste are present as realities in our field of experience.[27] The spatial order of objects is copresent with a temporal horizon which extends into the past and the future.[28] We are part of the world and it is present to us. Therefore it is not merely a world of facts but also a world of values in which things are good, beautiful and ugly, and so forth, because they are objects for us, objects to be used.[29]

It is clear that the natural standpoint cannot be challenged by theoretical doubt or rejection of the data of the natural world. Knowledge is a fact of nature and must be considered a psychological fact in the most self-evident fashion. This is the underlying position of Husserl's preface to *The Idea of Phenomenology*[30] and it is the theme of the first lecture of that book. Husserl summarizes this view in *Ideas* some seven years later.

> I find the 'actuality', the word already says it, as a *factually existent actuality and also accept it as it presents itself to me as factually existing*. No doubt about or rejection of data belonging to the natural world alters in any respect the *general positing which characterizes the natural attitude*.[31]

The opposition to the natural attitude which Husserl began at the preface to the *The Idea of Phenomenology*, is developed more fully in *Ideas*. The basic problem with the natural attitude becomes the starting point for philosophical science or the phenomenological attitude.

What is taken for granted in natural thinking is the possibility of cognition. Constantly busy producing results, advancing from discovery to discovery in newer and newer branches of science, natural thinking finds no occasion to raise the question of the possibility of cognition as such. To be sure, as with everything else in the world, *cognition,* too, will appear as a problem in a *certain manner,* becoming an object of natural investigation. Cognition is a fact in nature. It is the experience of a cognizing organic being. It is a psychological fact. As any psychological fact, it can be described according to its kinds and internal connections, and its genetic relations can be investigated. On the other hand cognition is essentially *cognition of what objectively is;* and it is cognition through the *meaning* which is intrinsic to it; by virtue of this meaning it is *related* to what objectively is....However, the correlation between cognition as mental process, its referent (Bedeutung) and what objectively is, which has just been touched upon in order to contrast the psychology of cognition with pure logic and ontology, is the source of the deepest and most difficult problems. Taken collectively, they are the problem of the possibility of cognition.[32]

The transition from the natural attitude to the phenomenological attitude is a radical one.[33] Husserl brings it up in contrast to Cartesian doubt which wanted to bring "out a sphere of absolutely indubitable being."[34] The natural attitude was characterized primarily by its need to see the natural world always "on hand."[35] The phenomenological attitude is conceived by Husserl as a method of questioning this basic positing about the natural world. The transition from the natural attitude is a movement from "believingness of the natural attitude to the domain of transcendental subjectivity."[36] This shift in attention from the natural world does not lead to a new metaphysic. It is not a metaphysic in the Cartesian sense because Husserl places the emphasis on what lies in the essence of the act of cognition.[37]

In like manner, it is clear that the *attempt* to doubt anything intended to as something *on hand* necessarily *effects a certain annulment of positing* and precisely this interests us. The annulment in question is not a transmutation of positing into counter positing, of position into negation; it is also not a transmutation into uncertain presumption, deeming possible, undecidedness, into a doubt (in any sense whatever of the word): nor indeed is anything like that within the sphere of our free choice. *Rather it is something wholly peculiar. We do not give up the positing we effected, we do not in any respect alter our conviction* which remains in itself as it is as long as we do not introduce new judgement-motives: precisely this is what we do not do. Nevertheless the positing undergoes a modification: while it in itself remains what it is, we, *so to speak, 'put it out of action' we 'exclude it', we parenthesize it'.* It is still there, like the parenthesized in the parentheses, like the excluded outside the context of inclusion. We can also say: The positing is a mental process, but *we make 'no use' of it,* and this is not understood, naturally, as implying that we are would if we said of someone who was not conscious, that he made no use of a positing); rather in the case of this expression and all parallel expressions it is a matter of indicative designations of a definite, *specifically peculiar mode of consciousness* which is added to the original positing simpliciter (whether this is or is not an actional and even a predicative *positing* of existence) and, likewise in a specifically peculiar manner, changes its value. *This changing of value is a matter in which we are perfectly free, and it stands over against all cogitative position-takings* coordinate with the positing and incompatible with the positing in the unity of the 'simultaneous', as well as over against all position-takings in the proper sense of the term.[38]

At this point Husserl's method comes into being. The parenthesizing that Husserl refers to here is the epoche.[39] It is a refraining from judging the existence of objects in the natural world. The epoche allows one to bracket existence so that no judgment is made for or against it.

We shall direct our attention to the fact that the phenomenological epoche lays open (to me, the meditating philosopher) an infinite realm of being of a new kind, as the sphere of a new kind of experience: transcendental experience.[40]

The purpose of the epoche is to admit to knowledge whatever is necessary and to exclude whatever is contingent. The epoche does not construct anything. It is never a positive factor with regard to what is there.[41] The epoche has positive counterparts in the reductions which are carried out on the residue after the epoche has been accomplished.[42] This new attitude is also extended to the sciences which use the natural world as their basis.[43] The validity of these sciences is also excluded[44] and all judgments about spatiotemporal factual being are suspended.[45]

Husserl's desire to uncover the essence of the stream of consciousness requires another reduction.[46] Pure phenomena as such do not yield universality. We cannot ascertain phenomenologically, the idealization of objectivity without performing the eidetic reduction.[47] This procedure, which can yield the universal necessary structure of these phenomena must exclude whatever is transcendent and not absolutely self-given to pure intuition.[48] The eidetic reduction alone fulfills this purpose. It is based on Husserl's attempt to understand the givenness of objects and their properties not as instances but as essences.[49] The following serves as an example of the eidetic reduction.

What you see when you see Oscar's color, is an instance of the essence yellow. Now, in order to get acquainted, not with an instance, but with the essence, you must perform a shift in mental attitude, you must perform what Husserl calls an 'eidetic reduction'. You must pay attention, not to the perceived instance, but to the essence of which it is an instance. After this shift has taken place, you will 'see' the essence yellow just as directly as you earlier saw (the aspects of!) the instance yellow. But this is not all. With this mental set, through eidetic reflection, you also 'perceive' connections among essences. You discern, for example, that yellow is lighter than midnight blue, or that the essence triangle necessitates having inner angles adding up to two right angles, or that the essence mental act requires that all acts have objects.[50]

This objectivity, based on the apriority of absolute self-given data, is the objectivity of essences.[51] It is the phenomenality of objects with everything that is not purely phenomenal removed from the objects.[52]

It is this reduction which brings the basic issues of phenomenology into view. The subject matter of phenomenology are the essences and not the facts of experience. These essences are "seen" in intuition as pure eidetic objects.

> The essence (Eidos) is a new sort of object. Just as the datum of individual or experiencing intuition is an individual object, so the datum of eidetic intuition is a pure essence.[53]

Underlying this usage of essences within intuition is the essential universality of experience which is to be analyzed in intuition without the correspondence to an object.[54]

> Intuition of essences – taken as it has been up to now – as a consciousness analogous to experience, to seizing upon a factual existence, as a consciousness in which an essence is seized upon as an object just as something individual is seized upon in experience, is not the only consciousness which involves essences while excluding every positing of factual existence. Essences can be an intuitive consciousness of essences, in a certain manner they can also be seized upon, without becoming 'objects about which'.[55]

Since these essences are posited without the real conditions of the world, their causal nature is of no importance.[56] Their apriority does not consist of a cause and effect which proceeds in strict logical fashion.[57] To be sure, there are laws and principles of logic which must have an a priori nature.[58] But, phenomenology analyzes the ultimate meaning of these logical requirements "if the logical concepts as unities of meaning are taken in the way they manifest themselves in original intuition, and such an intuition is, in turn, possible only by means of an ideating abstraction on the basis of concrete experiences."[59]

Upon the completion of the epoche and the eidetic reduction, the phenomenological reduction is employed.[60] The phenomenological method demands a universal insight into the "essence of any consciousness whatever."[61] This insight in the stream of consciousness points to mental processes "purely with respect to their essence, or of *pure essences* and of that which is 'a priori' *included* in the essences *with unconditional necessity.*"[62]

> It then becomes evident that every mental process belonging to the stream which can be reached by our reflective regard has an *essence of its own* which can be seized upon intuitively, a 'content' which allows of being considered *by itself in its ownness*. Our concern is to seize upon and to universally characterize this own content of the cogitation in its *pure* ownness by excluding everything which does not lie in the cogitatio with respect to what the cogitatio is in itself.[63]

It should be noted, that these reductions are not successive operations carried out to validate knowledge. They are "interdependent factors in an overall process known as 'intentional constitution', which at one and the same time renders knowledge completely immanent and hence capable of complete verification, and completely necessary for subjectivity as such, which gives it its universal objective validity."[64]

Unlike the epoche which has a negative result, the phenomenological reduction has a definite positve result even though it is often approached somewhat negatively.[65]

> Instead, then, of living naively in experience and theoretically exploring what is experienced, transcendent Nature, we effect the 'phenomenological reduction'. In other words, instead of naively *effecting* the acts pertaining to our Nature – constituting consciousness with their positings of something transcendent, and letting ourselves be induced, by motives implicit in them, to effect ever new positings of something transcendent – instead of that, we put all these positings 'out of action', we do not 'participate in them'; we direct our seizing and theoretically inquiring regard to *pure consciousness in its own absolute being*. That, then is what is left as the sought-for *'phenomenological residuum'*, though we have 'excluded' the whole world with all physical things, living beings, and humans ourselves included. Strictly speaking, we have not lost anything but have rather gained the whole of absolute being which, rightly understood, contains within itself, 'constitutes' within itself, all worldly transcendencies.[66]

These reductions, employed correctly, indicate something left over from the natural attitude. In fact it is this realm which Husserl wanted all along to uncover. The residue of the phenomenological reduction is that realm of consciousness which was unknown previous to its discovery by Husserl. This residue forms the basis for the analysis of pure consciousness and allows the intuitive life to be the origin of being.[67] As such the world and all other subjects do not simply exist. They are phenomena of being instead of things that really are.[68]

Moreover, these phenomena attain any meaning they may have in and through the pure ego.

> The ego seems to be there continually, indeed, necessarily, and this continualness is obviously not that of a stupidly persistent mental process, a 'fixed idea'. Instead, the Ego; belongs to each coming and going mental process; its 'regard' is directed 'through' each actional cogito to the objective something....In contradistinction the pure Ego would, however, seem to be something essentially *necessary*; and, as something absolutely identical throughout every actual or possible change in mental processes, it *cannot in any sense be a really inherent part or moment* of the mental processes themselves.[69]

It is the nature of the residue that is of supreme significance because it indicates the nature of the self that conceives it. This residue of the phenomenological reduction, the "pure" subject, is in no way objectified.[70] The empirical self which observed the world before the reduction was accomplished has given way to the "phenomenological observer concerned with the 'world' as the intentional correlate of transcendental subjectivity."[71] The character of the transcendental ego appears incompatible with the natural attitude.

> All the attributes we could apply to it would be inadequate because they have been borrowed from the 'world', whereas the ego is 'extraworldly'. Moreover the very step by which we must manage to grasp this ultimate reality in its purity is in some sense ineffable.[72]

The only data that can be accepted as absolute data are those which are genuinely immanent[73] and not reproductions of an existing object.[74] Pure phenomena become the only realities which cognition is concerned with.[75] Henceforth, the basic problem of phenomenological epistemology is not the fact that an inner mental process must reach a thing "out there." The new emphasis on the immanent and transcendental shapes the epistemological focus of phenomenology. The problem is functional.[76] It is a problem of "determining how the pure phenomena of cognition can reach something which as such is not immanent in them, that is to say, of how the absolute self-giveness of cognition itself can reach something which is not self-given in the same way."[77] Husserl's solution to this problem is based on his idea of constitution. Since Husserl does not rely on a causal relation between the object and consciousness,[78] he must examine the "object" as it is constituted in consciousness. The transcendental function of subjectivity accomplished through the reduction is precisely this "constitution."[79] This subjectivity is based on a knowledge "transcendentally related to the objects which are its intentions"[80] because for Husserl there is no other objectivity than that which is intentional.[81]

It is at this point that the stream of consciousness is constituted. The residue of the eidetic and phenomenological reductions brings the nature of consciousness into view. It has been Husserl's goal to show that consciousness has an entirely unique being of its own[82] because it remains unaffected by the phenomenological reduction.[83] It is here that Husserl's doctrine of intentionality comes to the fore.

> All mental processes having these essential properties in common are also called 'intentive mental processes' (acts in the broadest sense of *Logische Untersuchungen*); in so far as they are conscious of something they are said to be 'intentively referred' to this something.[84]

It is the nature of consciousness to be consciousness of something even though not every moment of the concrete unity of the mental process has the character of intentionality.[85] The schema of the structure of consciousness – the ego-cogito-cogitatum – contains any kind of intentional experience.[86] Through the cogito and its intentionality we can arrive at the unity of the world. Just as there is no abstract experience,[87] there is no "abstract crossing from the object to the subject but the concrete, lived realization that the entire sense of the world is to be the *cogitatum* of a subject that transcends it."[88] The object of thinking is revealed as an object-for-a-subject and conversely the subject is seen as the subject-for-this-object.[89] Consciousness is that act which makes us see, "the whole world and all that exists generally is for me only what 'holds' for me, that is, it exists for me only as *cogitatum* of my changing and, while changing, interconnected *cogitationes.*"[90] The ego-cogito-cogitatum interrelationship allows consciousness to be directed toward something other than itself. The intentional character of consciousness precludes the idea that consciousness ever has a problem dealing with transcendence because the ego is outside the world but is always directed toward it.[91] It is the role of the cogitatum to inform us that experiences vary because experience is only understood through the object intended in it.[92] As a result, the act of meaning and the object meant form the constitutive nature of consciousness. The becoming of the world has its origin in transcendental subjectivity and the constitutions of phenomena have their origin in consciousness.[93]

It is Husserl's attempt to understand the universal self-givenness of pure phenomena that leads him to consider the content of our cogitations. That which is intuited by the pure Ego must be lifted into universal consciousness.[94] Each cogito must retain a certain Ego-relatedness.[95] This prompts Husserl to introduce a distinction that is found in every cogitation. The discussion of cogitationes is based on the distinction of the givenness of the appearing and the givenness of that which appears.

> Accordingly, there are always distinguished – in spite of the necessary relatedness to one another – *the mental process itself* and the *pure Ego* pertaining to the mental living. And, again: [there are always distinguished] the *purely subjective moments of the mode of consciousness* and, so to speak, the rest of the *content of the mental process turned away from the Ego*. As a consequence, there is a certain, extraordinarily important two-sidedness in the essence of the sphere of mental processes, of which we can also say that in mental processes there is to be distinguished a *subjectively oriented* side and an *objectively oriented* side.[96]

Absolute phenomenological data have not one but two aspects. They are the noesis and the noema.[97] The noesis is the giveness of the appearing and the noema is the giveness of that which appears. The noetic aspect is the subject-in-relation-to-the-object and the noema is the object-in-relation-to-the-subject[98] or the content of the mental act. These are not two distinct components of the act of consciousness, but two different ways of analyzing the act of consciousness.[99]

> Rather the terms signify that the one act is structured in two ways, the one real and the other intentional, and can, therefore, be analyzed in two distinct ways. We might say that the noesis is the intentional act *looked at* as a real subjective operation, while the noema is the same act *looked at* as intentionally structured. It is the function of the act as noetic to 'give' a sense; it is the function of the same act as noematic to 'contain' an objective sense.[100]

The noetic-noematic correlation supplies the basic structure of consciousness.[101] Without it, consciousness cannot be consciousness of something nor can its necessity surpass the psychological realm.[102]

> Owing to its noetic moments, every intentive mental process is precisely noetic; it is of its essence to include in itself something such as a 'sense' and possibly a manifold sense on the basis of this sense-bestowal....Such noetic moments are, e.g., directions of the regard of the pure Ego to the objects 'meant' by it owing to sense-bestowal, to [the object] which is 'inherent in the sense' for the Ego....Corresponding in every case to the multiplicity of Data pertaining to the really inherent noetic content, there is a multiplicity of Data, demonstrable in actual pure intuition, in a correlative 'noematic content' or, in short, in the 'noema'.[103]

The relationship of the noesis and the noema defines the structure of consciousness. It is a strictly correlative relationship. Since the knowing act and the object known cannot be reduced along the lines of a Cartesian dualism it is never a question of an object "out there" being known "in here." The "object" is known through an act of meaning which is related to the meant object.[104] According to Husserl, things are not in consciousness like matches in a box. Things are presented in consciousness intentionally and

> the noetic-noematic correlation is what has to be meant by the term intentionality. In this light, the formula 'consciousness of something' is to be understood: a conscious act is an act of awareness, presenting the subject who experiences it with a sense, an ideal atemporal unity, identical, i.e. identifiable.[105]

The noetic-noematic correlation is based on the most basic idea of Husserl's phenomenology. It is the peculiar characteristic of consciousness to be consciousness of something.[106] Intentionality is the general theme of phenomenology because it is the universal character that "characterizes *consciousness* in the pregnant sense and which, at the same time, justifies designating the whole stream of mental processes as the stream of consciousness and as the unity of *one* consciousness."[107] Intentionality is not a property of consciousness, but the very mode of its existence.[108] Intentionality is what makes up the very subjectivity of subjects.[109] From the objective pole of cognition Husserl consistently claims that things are constituted by their being present to a knowing subject. This element of constitution is the basic correlation of the noesis and the noema.[110] Constitution is the process of building a meaning, the self-generating dynamic of consciousness or the building up of reality.[111] According to Husserl the only reality which can have significance is a constituted reality.[112]

> We see at once that what has been said here by way of example for the constitution of the material *physical thing* – and, more particularly, what was said with respect to the constitution in the system of multiplicities of experience *prior* to all thinking – must be extended to all *regions of objects* with respect to problems and with respect to methods.[113]

This is "another way of saying that a judgment will be true when the 'state of affairs' constituted in it has been phenomenologically guaranteed. All of which brings us back to the a priori laws of phenomenological constitution; that is truly objective which has been constituted in accord with the *necessary* laws of subjectivity."[114] Based on this model, the world is a constituted sense or a unity of sense.[115]

> Unities of sense presuppose (as I again emphasize: not because we can deduce it from some metaphysical postulates or other, but because we can show it by an intuitive, completely indubitable procedure) a *sense bestowing* consciousness which, for its part, exists absolutely and not by virtue of another sense-bestowal.[116]

This idea[117] or sense of constitution is not a certain manner of being but the foundation of an ontology by transcendental phenomenology.[118] Hence, the otherworldy nature of the "I" in relation to the world as a whole, including the transcendent and the immanent, forms constitution as a relation which is neither receptive nor productive.[119] This is the explicit point Heschel makes at the conclusion of *The Prophets*. There is no reciprocal succession of events in prophetic consciousness.[120] There is only a parallelism of form and content. In Husserl's eyes the relation is not causal, nor is it in a 'metaphysical space'[121] because it is contained in intuition.[122] Consequently when Heschel adopts the phenomenological method, he adopts the function of intuition that is essential to it. This creative intuition really creates its object in consciousness because consciousness must always anticipate something.

It is evident that constitution makes the structures of intentionality progressively clearer. Yet, the transcendental nature of constitution forbids it description and prima facie constitution seems to fall prey to either of two possibilities:

> Either to say nothing of constitution, since it transcends the world, which is the domain of all language, so that phenomenology ends in a kind of mysticism; or else to speak of it, and so fall back into the world, lowering transcendental idealism to the level of psychological idealism, which, precisely, it claims to oppose.[123]

Both of these ends transform the doctrine into something it is clearly not meant to be and disregard its intuitional nature. The constituting life of the ego cannot be adequately described in active or in passive terms.[124] The understanding gained through the syntheses of cogitata related to the same intentional object are "seen" and not constructed.[125]

This use of intuition is not defined as a concept by its sensual counterparts[126] but by the fact that intuition realizes a meaning.[127] As such, judgment is not the essential component of knowledge.[128] The analysis of judgments, if they can be realized by intuition, give us access to knowledge.[129] There is no attempt, in Husserl's theory of knowledge, to prove the adequacy of thought to things, which allows truth to be deduced from the judgment. Truth is the function of a judgment which is correlated to its intuition because judgments presuppose truth[130] and intuition is the very course of thought toward truth,[131] a rational penetration into the data of experience.[132]

This explication of Husserl's phenomenological method is incomplete without consideration of the idea of reflection employed throughout its development. Reflection, or philosophical intuition, must be directed "toward the pure, primary, and eminently concrete consciousness discovered by phenomenological reduction."[133] It reveals the intentive nature of consciousness and is basically an "apprehension of the entire noetic-noematic complex."[134] Reflection turns the intentional correlate of an act into an object.[135] As an act of reflection, with the phenomenological reduction we turn our attention away from the object considered and away from our psychological experience of being directed toward that object and "turn our attention to the act, more specifically to its intentional content, thus making our representation of the conditions of satisfaction of the intentional state our object."[136]

> In great measure what one has held to be act-analysis, noetic analysis, is gained entirely from the the direction of regard to the 'meant as meant,' and thus it was noematic structures which one described in that analysis.[137]

In so doing, phenomenology assumes a content, a prereflective object in consciousness because the object of the intention must exist prior to the act of reflection on it.[138] The objectivity of so-called naive consciousness is based on an ontological presupposition which, even though bracketed, is the transcendental guide of all phenomenological investigations.

> In the particularization of that type, and of its description, the intentional object (on the side belonging to the cogitatum) plays, for easily understood reasons, the role of 'transcendental clue' to the typical infinite multiplicities of possible *cogitationes* that, in a possible synthesis, bear the intentional object within them (in the manner peculiar to consciousness) as the same meant object. Necessarily the point of departure is the object given 'straightforwardly' at the particular time. From it reflection goes back to the mode of consciousness at the time and to the potential modes of consciousness included horizonally in that mode, then to those in which the object might be otherwise intended as the same, within the unity (ultimately) of a possible conscious life, all the possibilities of which are included in the 'ego'.[139]

It is the nature of Husserl's phenomenological method, through its reductions which lead back to this data,[140] to rediscover and analyze this pure data as a correlate of an immanent intentional function[141] and to lay open an "infinite realm of being of a new kind."[142]

---

[1] Paul Ricoeur, *Husserl: An Analysis of his Phenomenology*, trans. E. Ballard and L. Embree, (Evanston: Northwestern University Press, 1967), p. 27. According to Lauer, this correlation is the most important contribution of *Ideas*, "Perhaps the most important contribution of the *Ideas* of 1913 was to develop this correlative structure of the intentional act. As he so often did when

he wished to emphasize the novelty of a notion, Husserl sought Greek terms to designate the two structures. The subjective (real) structure became the 'noetic' structure, or simply noesis; and the objective became the 'noematic' structure, or simply noema." Quentin Lauer, *The Triumph of Subjectivity*, (New York: Fordham University Press, 1978), p. 93.

2 Quentin Lauer, *Phenomenology and the Crisis of Philosophy*, (New York: Harper and Row, 1965), p. 51.

3 "By the time he published *Ideas*, thirteen years after the *Logical Investigations*, he had moved to a stronger view of what the intentional content is and how it works. He argued that an act of consciousness or noesis does not, on its own, do the work of representing an object and its relation to the subject; rather, the act has intentionality only by virtue of an 'abstract form' or noema correlated with the act." H. Dreyfus, "Introduction," *Husserl, Intentionality, and Cognitive Science*, ed. H. Dreyfus and H. Hall, (Cambridge: M.I.T. Press, 1984), p. 7.

4 Edmund Husserl, *The Idea of Phenomenology*, trans. W. Alston and G. Nakhnikian, (The Hague: Martinus Nijhoff, 1970), p. xiii.

5 J. Kockelmans, *A First Introduction to Husserl's Phenomenology*, (Pittsburgh: Duquesne University Press, 1967), p. 17. Lauer concisely formulates Husserl's program at its early stage of development. "But at this early stage Husserl is concerned only with making it clear that there is such an objective term, or intention and that logic, whose function is to lay down rules of thought, is to be a study of traditional logical concepts precisely from the point of view of the mind's operational function in which they originate." *The Triumph of Subjectivity*, p. 30.

6 Herbert Spiegelberg, *The Phenomenological Movement. A Historical Introduction*, (The Hague: Martinus Nijhoff, 1960), Vol. 1, p. 74. Kockelmans, p.xxi, also p. 19.

7 Edmund Husserl, *Experience and Judgment*, ed. L. Landgrebe, trans. J. Churchill and K. Ameriks, (Evanston: Northwestern University Press, 1973), p. 49. Spiegelberg, p. 113, also points to the nature of the transcendental as the attempt to "reach back" into the structure of pure consciousness. He bases this expanded meaning on Husserl's last publication, *The Crisis of European Sciences and Transcendental Phenomenology*, trans. D. Carr, (Evanston: Northwestern University Press, 1970), section 26, p. 97 and 98. "It is the motif of inquiring back into the ultimate source of all the formations of knowledge, the motif of the knower reflecting upon himself and his knowing life in which all the scientific structures that are valid for him occur purposefully, are stored as acquisitions, and have become and continue to become freely available."

8 Lauer, *Phenomenology and the Crisis of Philosophy*, p. 23. Lauer, *The Triumph of Subjectivity*, p. 37 and 38.

9 D. Stewart and A. Mickunas, *Exploring Phenomenology*, (Chicago: American Library Association, 1974), p. 38.

10 Kockelmans, p. 31.

11 *The Idea of Phenomenology*, p. 27-29.

12 Kockelmans, p. 31.

13 *The Prophets*, p. xvi.

14 Lauer, *Triumph of Subjectivity*, p. 52. This is the exact starting point of Heschel's inquiry in *Die Prophetie* and *The Prophets*. He is solely concerned with the intentional structure of prophetic consciousness as it contains the appearance of God.

15 See p. 5.

16 *Die Prophetie*, pp. 4-5. *The Prophets*, p. xix.

17 A. Gurwitsch, "Husserl's Theory of the Intentionality of Consciousness in Historical Perspective", ed. E. Lee and M. Mandelbaum, *Phenomenology and Existentialism*, (Baltimore: The Johns Hopkins Press, 1967), p. 49.

18 One commentator refers to the paradox of the reduction which "lies in the peculiar traffic between two worlds: the world in its historical becoming and the becoming of the world in transcendental consciousness." M. Natanson, *Edmund Husserl: Philosopher of Infinite Tasks*, (Evanston: Northwestern University Press, 1973), p. 77. As will be demonstrated about Heschel's idea of revelation for the postprophetic mind, its polarity also lies in its "peculiar traffic" between these two worlds.

19 Heschel, *The Prophets*, p. xix.

20 *Ideas*, p. 311, "Thus the noema too is related to an object and possesses a 'content' by 'means' of which it relates to the object; in which case the object is the same as that of the noesis; as then the 'parallelism' again completely confirms itself."

21 Heschel clearly refers to it as a parallelism and not a succession of acts in *The Prophets* Vol. II, p. 268, "Man's awareness of God is to be understood as God's awareness of man, man's knowledge of God is transcended in God's knowledge of man, the subject – man – becomes object, and the object – God – becomes subject. Not a reciprocal succession of acts, not a distinguishable alteration of sound and echo, but rather in every event of the religious consciousness it is a question of a dual mutual operation, a twofold mutual initiative. Every apprehension of God is an act of being apprehended by God, every vision of God is a divine vision of man."

22 This is the basis of Husserl's rejection of Descartes position. See Stewart, p. 4 and pp. 8-10, and the introduction to *The Idea of Phenomenology* by G. Nakhnikian, pp. xv-xvii. Nakhnikian correctly identifies the idea of immanency that Husserl rejects in Descartes' thinking and the idea that Husserl uses in its place. "The crucial sense of immanence, on the other hand, is the sense in which it is the intentionally in existent essences that are immanent. They are the referents of intentional acts. Their immanence consists in their self-givenness (Selbstgegebenheit to pure intuition. At the same time, they are transcendent in that their nature and reality are independent of their being actually in commerce with mind via some mode of mental activity or other, for example, being imagined, desired, believed, and so on."

23 Lauer, *The Triumph of Subjectivity*, pp. 41-42. "It must be possible to find within consciousness a criterion for determining whether consciousness intends being correctly. If we want to determine what something really is, I must turn to the experience in which the something is present to my consciousness; therein I will find an intentional structure, and that intentional structure properly analyzed will reveal to me all that can be revealed with

regard to the object toward which my experience is oriented. The structure of intentionality is the fundamental structure of any phenomenon."

24 D. Stewart and A. Mickunas, *Exploring Phenomenology*, (Chicago: American Library Association, 1974), p. 4 and 5.

25 *God in Search of Man*, p. 108 and p. 121. See above p. 33 (27 and 31)

26 Edmund Husserl, *Ideas Pertaining to a Pure Phenomenology and to a Phenomenological Philosophy*, trans. F. Kersten, (Boston: Martinus Nijhoff, 1983), p. 38.

27 *Ideas*, p. 51.

28 *Ibid.*, p. 52.

29 *Ibid.*, p. 53.

30 *The Idea of Phenomenology*, p. 1, "*Natural thinking* in science and everyday life is untroubled by the difficulties concerning the possibility of cognition. *Philosophical thinking* is circumscribed by one's position toward the problems concerning the possibility of cognition."

31 *Ideas*, p. 57.

32 *The Idea of Phenomenology*, p. 15.

33 *Ideas*, p. 57.

34 *Ibid.*

35 *Ibid.*

36 M. Natanson, *Edmund Husserl: Philosopher of Infinite Tasks*, p. 65.

37 *Ibid.*

38 *Ideas*, pp. 58-59.

39 *Ibid.*

40 *Cartesian Meditations*, p. 27.

41 Lauer, *The Triumph of Subjectivity*, p. 50.

42 *Ibid.*, p. 50.

43 *Ideas*, p. 61.

44 *Ibid.*, p. 62.

45 *Ibid.*, p. 61.

46 Lauer sees six levels of reductions and explains them coherently as "six stages in seeing the implications of the original radical epoche." *The Triumph of Subjectivity*, p. 51.

47 *Ibid.*, p. 53.

48 *Ibid.*, p. 32.

49 R. Grossmann, *Phenomenology and Existentialism: An Introduction*, (Boston: Rutledge & Kegan Paul, 1984), p. 138.

50 *Ibid.*, p. 138 and 139.

51 Lauer, *The Triumph of Subjectivity*, p. 32.

52 *Ibid.*, p. 48.

53 *Ideas*, p. 9.

54 Lauer, *The Triumph of Subjectivity*, p. 78.

55 *Ideas*, p. 12.

56 Lauer, *The Triumph of Subjectivity*, p. 146.

57 D. Stewart and A. Mickunas, p. 8. Essences have an intentional character and intentionality "was not a causal relationship to objects but an activity of consciousness which is identical with the meant object."

[58] The role that these a priori laws play in consciousness is clearly stated by Lauer in *The Triumph of Subjectivity*, p. 76. "Since all operations of consciousness are subject to determinable a priori laws – and it is the function of phenomenology to determine them – the constituitive operations wherein objects are rendered really present are also subject to such laws; and the determination of these laws is a logic – not merely a formal logic – concerned with the laws governing correct thinking, but above all a transcendental logic concerned with the laws governing the way consciousness gives content to its thought."

[59] *Ibid.*, p. 79.

[60] *Ideas*, p. 65 and 66.

[61] *Ibid.*, p. 65.

[62] *Ibid.*, p. 73.

[63] *Ibid.*, p. 69.

[64] Lauer, *The Triumph of Subjectivity*, p. 62.

[65] *Ibid.*, p. 53.

[66] *Ideas*, p. 113.

[67] E. Levinas, *The Theory of Intuition in Husserl's Phenomenology*, trans. A. Orianne, (Evanston: Northwestern University Press, 1973), p. 93.

[68] Kockelmans, p. 160.

[69] *Ideas*, p. 132.

[70] Lauer, *The Triumph of Subjectivity*, p. 53.

[71] Natanson, p. 74.

[72] G. Berger, *The Cogito in Husserl's Philosophy*, trans. K. McLaughlin, (Evanston: Northwestern University Press, 1972), p. 49. Berger also cites a letter of Fink's concerning the relation of the ineffable to language, "that it cannot be presented by means of simple sentences of the natural attitude. It can be spoken of only by transforming the natural function of language (E. Fink, letter of May 11, 1936)." The transforming of natural language is the exact strategy Heschel employed throughout his thinking and explained in *God in Search of Man*, pp. 176-183. This will be taken up in due course.

[73] Kockelmans, p. 31.

[74] Lauer, *The Triumph of Subjectivity*, p. 55.

[75] *Ibid.*

[76] *Ideas*, p. 207.

[77] Lauer, *The Trimph of Subjectivity*, p. 55.

[78] *Ibid.*, p. 55.

[79] *Ibid.*

[80] *Ibid.*

[81] *Ideas* p. 199. Lauer, *The Triumph of Subjectivity*, p. 55.

[82] *Ideas*, p. 63 and 64.

[83] Kockelmans, p. 142.

[84] *Ideas*, p. 73.

[85] *Ibid.*, p. 75.

[86] Lauer, *The Triumph of Subjectivity*, p. 91.

[87] *Ibid.*, p. 91.

[88] Berger, p. 43.

89 *Phenomenology: The Philosophy of Edmund Husserl and its Interpretation,* ed. J. Kockelmans, (Garden City: Anchor Books, 1967), p. 68. In *The Triumph of Subjectivity,* pp. 65-66, Lauer, puts this Husserlian position into an historical perspective which Husserl himself ignored.

90 *Cartesian Meditations,* p. 140.

91 Berger, p. 110.

92 Lauer, *The Triumph of Subjectivity,* p. 91.

93 Natanson, p. 96.

94 *Ideas,* p. 172, Kockelmans, p. 33.

95 *Ideas,* p. 191.

96 *Ibid.,* p. 191.

97 *Ibid.,* p. 213 and 214.

98 *Ibid.,* p. 253 and *Cartesian Meditations,* p. 36. Richard Schmitt, "Husserl's Transcendental-Phenomenological Reduction," In *Phenomenology: The Philosophy of Edmund Husserl and its Interpretation,* ed. J. Kockelmans, (Garden City: Doubleday, 1967), p. 67.

99 Lauer, *The Triumph of Subjectivity,* p. 93.

100 *Ibid.,* p. 93.

101 *Ideas,* p. 221 and 222. *Formal and Transcendental Logic,* pp. 184-188.

102 Lauer, *The Triumph of Subjectivity,* p. 141. As Lauer points out, this is precisely the task of *Formal and Transcendental Logic.* "It is, accordingly an *intentional explication of the proper sense of formal logic...*the explication turns back to the intentionality of the *scientists,* from whom the Objective stock of concrete scientific theory originated – since, indeed, the logician directs his attention to the sciences that are given him beforehand. The intentionality that comes to life in any actual following and understanding is asked what it is properly aiming at. Reflective sense-explication, as critical clarification, must yield the answer." E. Husserl, *Formal and Transcendental Logic,* trans. D. Cairns, (Martinus Nijhoff: The Hague, 1969), p. 10 and 11. The necessary correlation of noema and noesis is also discussed in this work, p. 261 and 262.

103 *Ideas,* pp 213-214.

104 *Ibid.,* p. 311 and 312.

105 A. Gurwitsch, "Intentionality, Constitution and Intentional Analysis." In *Phenomenology,* ed. Kockelmans, p. 135.

106 *Ideas,* p. 200.

107 *Ibid.,* p. 199.

108 E. Levinas, *The Theory of Intuition in Husserl's Phenomenology,* (Evanston: Northwestern University Press, 1973), p. 40 and 41, "Intentionality in Husserl cannot be taken as a property of consciousness, i.e., as a character which is unrelated to the mode of existing of consciousness, as simply a modality of the contents of consciousness. It is precisely the very mode of existence of consciousness that the notion of intentionality tries to characterize."

109 Levinas, p. 41.

110 Ricoeur, p. 27.

111 Natanson, p. 94.

112 Lauer, *The Triumph of Subjectivity,* p. 101.

113 *Ideas,* p. 364.

[114] Lauer, *The Triumph of Subjectivity*, p. 101.
[115] *Cartesian Meditations*, p. 107.
[116] *Ideas*, p. 129.
[117] *Cartesian Meditations*, p. 51 and 52.
[118] *Ideas*, p. 282, Berger, p. 76.
[119] Berger, p. 78.
[120] *The Prophets*, p. 488.
[121] Berger, p. 79.
[122] *Ibid.*, p. 85.
[123] *Ibid.*, p. 91.
[124] *Ibid.*, p. 93.
[125] *Ibid.*
[126] *Ideas*, p. 36.
[127] Levinas, p. 78.
[128] *Ibid.*, p. 83.
[129] *Ibid.*
[130] *Ibid.*, p. 89.
[131] *Ibid.*, p. 92.
[132] Lauer, *The Triumph of Subjectivity*, p. 62.
[133] Levinas, p. 154.
[134] Zaner, p. 134.
[135] H. Dreyfus, "Husserl's Perceptual Noema." In *Husserl, Intentionality and Cognitive Science*, ed. H. Dreyfus and H. Hall, (Cambridge: M.I.T. Press, 1984), p. 100
[136] H. Dreyfus, "Introduction," *Husserl, Intentionality and Cognitive Science*, p. 6.
[137] *Ideas*, p. 308.
[138] Lauer, *The Triumph of Subjectivity*, p. 88.
[139] *Cartesian Meditations*, p. 50.
[140] The etymological sense of reduction "means a return or a leading back." Natanson, p. 94.
[141] Lauer, *The Triumph of Subjectivity*, p. 90.
[142] *Cartesian Meditations*, p. 27.

Chapter Five

Heschel's Phenomenology

Heschel's reliance on Husserl's phenomenological method can be demonstrated on many levels. Even though Heschel never thoroughly adopted nor systematically used Husserl's method, it forms the basic philosophical building blocks of his theology. The philosophical significance of Heschel's theology has been neglected because of the oversight of its phenomenological principles and structure.

The attempt to understand Heschel's depth-theology without its phenomenological roots has led to many misunderstandings. Aside from the phenomenological content of Heschel's thought, which does not directly concern us here, his remarks about awe, wonder, radical amazement and the sublime have been taken completely out of context. Most important, Heschel's critics have not recognized the fact that Heschel is explicating these antecedents of faith from within the epoche and the phenomenological reduction. The presuppositionless aspect of Husserl's phenomenology is the ground from which Heschel's reduction grows.

> Part company with preconceived notions, suppress your leaning to reiterate and to know in advance of your seeing, try to see the world for the first time with eyes not dimmed by memory or volition, and you will detect that you and the things that surround you – trees, birds, chairs – are like parallel lines that run close and never meet. Your pretense of being acquainted with the world is quickly abandoned.[1]

This attempt by Heschel to liberate the mind of presuppositions is based on another idea. Husserl's rejection of the natural attitude sets the tone for Heschel's concept of nature.

> But what are the foundations of nature? To the Greeks who take the world for granted, Nature, Order is the answer. To the Biblical mind in its radical amazement, nature, order are not an answer but a problem: why is there order, being at all?...The world is not an ontological necessity.[2]

The existence or nonexistence of nature is not essential to the consciousness which Heschel's theology is trying to elucidate. The natural attitude is itself problematic because it is the source of all contingency.[3] The natural world is never completely negated by Heschel as it wasn't by Husserl. To be sure, the natural world must be the source of the data required for further reductions. But, the existence of the natural world is inconsequential for religious consciousness which is authenticated in intuition.

> Awe, then, is more than a feeling. It is an answer of the heart and mind to the presence of mystery in all things, *an intuition for a meaning that is beyond the mystery*, an awareness of the *transcendent worth of the universe*.[4]

The awareness of God, which is the content of Heschel's phenomenological reduction, is located in consciousness through the same method Husserl employs. Just as the reductions were thoroughly reflective for Husserl, they are for Heschel. The reduction is a return to or a leading back to the essential cognitive content that is presented in consciousness.

> In other words, our belief in His reality is not a leap in a missing link in a syllogism but rather *a regaining*, giving up a view rather than adding one, going behind self-consciousness and questioning the self and all its cognitive pretensions. *It is an ontological presupposition*.[5]

This use of the reduction and its attendant reflection is not employed by Heschel only on a temporary basis. When Heschel describes his ontological presupposition,[6] he makes it clear that the preconceptual thinking based on the reduction is the basis of every encounter with reality.

> The encounter with reality does not take place on the level of concepts through the channels of logical categories; concepts are second thoughts. All conceptualization is symbolization, an act of accommodation of reality to the human mind. The living encounter with reality takes place on a level that precedes conceptualization, on a level that is responsive, immediate, preconceptual and pre-symbolic. Theory, speculation, generalization, and hypothesis are efforts to clarify and to validate the insights which preconceptual experience provides.[7]

Heschel's use of the reduction must be seen through his description of reflection as a theological tool and is consistent with his abstention from asking and answering disconnected epistemological questions.

We do not have to discover the world of faith; we only have to recover it. It is not a *terra incognita,* an unknown land; it is a forgotten land, and our relation to God is a palimpsest rather than a *tabula rasa.*[8]

This implied reduction is present in Heschel's anthropology as well.

Man is not a tabula rasa. Unlike other objects, the desire to know himself is part of his being. To know himself he must first question himself, and that means questioning his self-knowing, disturbing what might be a narcissistic relationship of the self to its conceits, ingrown thinking. To raise such questions is more than to seek an approach to an answer; it is a breakthrough.[9]

The act of reflection, which characterizes man's search for self-understanding according to Heschel, is the consistent theme of *Who Is Man?* and consistently uses an implied reduction.

His search, his being puzzled at himself is above all an act of disassociation and disengagement from sheer being, animal or otherwise. The search for self-understanding is a search for authenticity of essence, a search for genuineness not to be found in anonymity, commonness, and unremitting connaturality.[10]

For Heschel, as for Husserl, the reductions are a means of opening the reflective mind to essential knowledge. This search for authenticity of essence by Heschel, which originates in its disassociation from being, is the phenomenological reduction in explicit use. It has its origins in the introduction to *The Prophets.*

To comprehend what phenomena are, it is important to suspend judgement and think in detachment; to comprehend what phenomena mean, it is necessary to suspend indifference and be involved. To examine their essence requires a process of reflection. Such reflection, however, sets up a gulf between the phenomena and ourselves. Reducing them to dead objects of the mind, it deprives them of the power to affect us, to speak to us, to transcend our attitudes and conceptions.[11]

The phenomenological reduction is the only available philosophical tool for Heschel's theological analysis because it alone can penetrate the immanence of consciousness, as I have explained at the outset of Chapter Four.

The ultimate question, moreover, is a question that arises on the level of the ineffable. It is phrased not in *concepts* but in *acts,* and no abstract formulation is capable of conveying it. It is, therefore, necessary to understand the inner logic of the situation, the spiritual climate in which it exists, in order to comprehend what the ultimate question implies.[12]

Reflection is not an abstraction. The mental act, together with its context, must be grasped at once to understand the prophetic consciousness or any consciousness for that matter.[13] According to Heschel, any other philosophical strategy insists on a type of reflection which cannot give the onlooker the proper exegesis to understand "the prophet in terms and categories of prophecy."[14] The encounter with the ineffable only takes place when the existence of the world is subject to the phenomenological reduction.

> Part company with preconceived notions, suppress your leaning to reiterate and to know in advance of your seeing, try to see the world for the first time with eyes not dimmed by memory or volition, and you will detect that you and the things that surround you – trees, birds, chairs – are like parallel lines that run close and never meet. Your pretense of being acquainted with the world is abandoned quickly.[15]

The reduction and the residue of consciousness that remains after Heschel employs it, point to the intentional nature of consciousness and its functional nonsubstantial character.

> In the awareness of my personhood I do not come upon sheer consciousness or a block of reality called the self, but upon the power to create events. Being human is not a thing, a substance; it is a moment that happens; not a process but a sequence of acts or events. The self that I am, the self that I come upon, has the ability to combine a variety of functions and intentions in order to bring about a result, the meaning or value of which transcends my own existence.[16]

The residue of consciousness left over after the application of the reduction indicates a directedness of the "I" that we saw in the German edition of *The Prophets*[17] and which is infused in Heschel's other works.[18] For Heschel, it is the nature of consciousness to be intentional so that the states of existence and meaning must be directed at each other.

> Imbedded in the mind is a certainty that the state of existence and the state of meaning stand in a relation to each other, that life is assessable in terms of meaning. The will to meaning and the certainty of the legitimacy of our striving to ascertain it are as intrinsically human as the will to live and the certainty of being alive.[19]

This will to meaning that is imbedded in the mind is not blind nor is it a mere passion.[20] Neither is this will to meaning an isolated aspect of the human mind. It corresponds to divine pathos, "an object of human experience."[21] Just as the will to meaning displays an intentional character, so does the divine pathos to which it corresponds.[22]

It is not a passion, an unreasoned emotion, but an act formed with intention, rooted in decision and determination; not an attitude taken arbitrarily, but one charged with ethos; not a reflexive, but a transitive act.[23]

The directedness of the "I" forms the basis of Heschel's phenomenological dialectic. But, intentionality is not only a cognitive concept according to Heschel.

We cannot, on the other hand, analyze man as a being only here and now. Not only here, because his situation is intentional with the situation of other men scattered far and wide all over the world. Not only now, because his total existence is, in a sense, a summation of past generations, a distillation of experiences and thoughts of his ancestors.[24]

Intentionality must function in a living reality and as such does not originate only in the mind. Heschel's use of intentionality is inconceivable without an evolved relationship.

What do we mean by direction? A personal event is an act of communication in which an intention is conveyed to another person. It means addressing a person. An act of communication has a direction. The turning is the genesis of the event, the direction its realization. It is a moment in which an act within a person becomes an act for the sake of another person. A relationship is established, the event has reached its end; it has assumed form; it is a maximum of eventuation.[25]

This use of intentionality and consciousness for Heschel, is certainly not limited to intrapersonal human relationships. On the contrary, the intentionality of consciousness arises within a relationship with God and bestows meaning on all other relationships.

Prophetic consciousness, it must be stressed again, does not spring from the depths of the human spirit; it is based upon anticipation or inclusion of man in God.[26]

While God is seen by Heschel as an intentional agent, this act of anticipation or of intentionality retains its Husserlian roots because it emphasizes the parallel nature of the noema and noesis of consciousness as a form.[27] The subject and object poles of consciousness must be mutually correlated and not seen as successive in nature. If they are not correlated in this manner, then consciousness lapses into a mere psychological representation of fact, the significance of which can never be known. For Heschel, the consciousness of prophetic religion is always presented in a polarity of the "I" and the "object" of experience.

> A specific aspect of prophetic religion or of the religious phenomenon in general, as opposed to the purely psychological, lies in the fact of the mutual inherence of the "I" and the object of religious experience, for an intention of man toward God produces a counteracting intention of God toward man. Here all mutual relations end, not in an original decision, but in a relationship which represents a counteraction.[28]

The intentionality included in Heschel's idea of consciousness exhibits the noetic-noematic correlation throughout his work, which he had claimed as the basis of prophetic consciousness in the German edition of *The Prophets*.[29] This act of consciousness consists not only of a direction of the I toward an object of religious experience, but also of a subjective and objective structure.

> It is important to distinguish between the objective and the subjective aspect of the prophetic consciousness of God. By the objective aspect we mean that which is given to the prophet as a reality transcending his consciousness. By the subjective we mean the personal attitude or the response of the prophet to that reality.[30]

Each component of its respective structure takes on its quality. For instance, since consciousness is consciousness of something, the "something" which is purely intentional demands that the objective components cannot be real. The components of the objective structure are "unreal" or "ideal."[31] Similarly the noetic aspect of prophetic consciousness must be recognizable in its ideal components. Heschel clearly points out these ideal components in prophetic consciousness.

> The noetic character of prophecy is reflected in most of its aspects. Its message had to be relevant to the contemporary situation and capable of changing the minds of those who held the power to change the situation. The Inspirer in whose name they spoke was not a God of mystery, but a God Who has a design for history, Whose will and law are known to His people. The prophet is not a person who has had an experience, but one who has a task, and the marks of whose existence are the consistency and wholeheartedness in the dedication to it. The noetic character of the prophetic experience is, furthermore, reflected in the noetic character of the prophetic utterance. Unlike the stammering of the ecstatic or the language of negation of the mystic, the prophet's word is like fire, like a hammer which breaks the rock in pieces.[32]

These subjective and objective structures demonstrate that Heschel is in complete agreement with Husserl's description of consciousness because he consistently analyzes the event of prophecy[33] and the situation of theological thinking,[34] totally rejecting the substance of prophecy as absolute content and the concept of theology as a pure act of reason, i.e. without correlative elements.

The use of the noetic-noematic correlation by Heschel is not blind. That is, Heschel is fully aware of the consequences of the correlation. This is born out by a statement made in connection to his phenomenological treatment of pathos in *Who is Man?*

> Indebtedness is the pathos of being human, self-awareness of the self as committed; it is given with the awareness of existence. Man cannot think of himself as human without being conscious of his indebtedness. Thus it is not a mere feeling, but a constitutive feature of being human. To eradicate it would be to destroy what is human in man.[35]

The constitution of the noetic-noematic correlation, central to Husserl's conception of consciousness, is employed by Heschel as the general feature of his treatment of pathos. It is also seen by Heschel as an existential feature of human consciousness, without which man's humanity could not function.

The phenomenological constitution of human being and consciousness is also employed by Heschel in relation to intuition in general. Heschel's doctrines of transcendence and meaning, which are intertwined in his concept of intuition, demonstrate the constitutive aspect of intuition which is the focal point of his phenomenological method.

> The secret of being human is care for meaning. Man is not his own meaning, and if the essence of being human is concern for transcendent meaning, then man's secret lies in openness to transcendence. Existence is interspersed with suggestions of transcendence, and openness to transcendence is a constitutive element of being human. Such is the structure of our situation that human being without an intuition of meaning cannot long remain a fact; it soon stares us in the face as a nightmare. Indeed, the concern for meaning of human being is what constitutes the truth of being human. Its ontological relevance is rooted in the very being of man, since human being devoid of the possibility of being human is an absurdity.[36]

This description of intuition, constituted by transcendence and meaning, has profound philosophical import. The verification of judgments is based on constitutive intuition because Heschel's use of a constitutive intuition places it in the same relation to judgment as Husserl's concept does (see above, Chapter Four p. 57). Transcendent meaning attains truth when the state of affairs constituted in it has been phenomenologically guaranteed. Transcendent meaning becomes objective when it has been constituted in accord with the necessary laws of subjectivity.[37] This function of intuition is summarized concisely in one of Heschel's early works.

> It is not in a roundabout way, by analogy or inference, that we become aware of the ineffable; we do not think about it *in absentia*. It is rather sensed as something immediately given by way of an insight that is unending and underivable, logically and psychologically prior to judgement, to the assimilation of subject matter to mental categories; a universal insight into an objective aspect of reality, of which all men at all times are capable; not the froth of ignorance but the climax of thought, indigenous to the climate that prevails at the summit of intellectual endeavor, where such works as the quartets of Beethoven come into being. It is a cognitive insight, since the awareness it evokes is a definite addition to the mind.[38]

The transcendent role of intuition in Heschel's idea of depth-theology has a definite and consistent role to play throughout his phenomenology. As we have seen, it is the nature of insight in Heschel's theology to be ontologically presupposed.[39] Heschel gives this ontological presupposition two functions in relation to the reality of God.

> Certainty of the realness of God comes about, *as a response* of the whole person to the mystery and transcendence of living. As a response, it is an act of raising from the depths of the mind an *ontological presupposition* which makes that response intellectually understandable.[40]

Clearly the second response, is elaborated from his phenomenological method. The experience of the reality of God within consciousness is preconceptual and prereflective. As such, it can be recaptured in the mind with the use of the phenomenological method. The anticipation of the mind, or its intentionality, is directed toward God, and His reality can be summoned from the depths of the mind, within the noetic-noematic correlation. The attempt to include the temporality of intentionality and the non-temporality of the object intended, i.e. the reality of God, in one act of consciousness, would be inconceivable without the noetic-noematic correlation. The act of "seeing" is, with its object, the phenomenological view of reality available through radical amazement.

> Radical amazement has a wider scope than any other act of man. While any act of perception or cognition has as its object a selected segment of reality, radical amazement refers to all of reality; not only to what we see, but also to the very act of seeing as well as to our own selves, to the selves that see and are amazed at their ability to see.[41]

As we noted previously, since consciousness cannot be "conceived of as a one-dimensional sequence of events, consciousness must be defined as a noetic-noematic correlation, that is to say, a correlation between items pertaining to two heterogeneous planes: on the one hand that of temporal psychological events, and on the other hand, that of atemporal, irreal, that is to say, ideal entities that are the noemata, or meanings understood in the broader sense."[42]

This progression of phenomenological ideas within Heschel's use of intuition, has a definite effect on Heschel's theology. Heschel's theological belief about the reality of God is based on a content which is phenomenologically presented and can never be demonstrated deductively. This content, the reality of God, is phenomenologically available, but must exist prior to the act of reflection on it.[43] It is not another name for the ineffable nor does it indicate the defeat of reason.[44] Phenomenological reflection does not produce objects, rather it progressively clarifies the structure of intentionality and the content that it is directed at. Our analysis of Husserl's reliance on the objectivity of the naive consciousness produced the same result (see above, Chapter Four, pp. 17-18). The objectivity of so-called naive consciousness is based on an ontological presupposition which, even though bracketed, served as the transcendental guide of all phenomenological investigations[45] (see above Chapter Four, p. 19). This transcendental structure functions in the same manner in Heschel's depth-theology.

The ontological presupposition, which functions as a transcendental clue within Heschel's phenomenology, also leads to another important conclusion that has escaped the critics. The values and objects which Heschel talks about, such as man, justice, mercy, love, and concern must be placed within this context. Friedman has claimed that Heschel is inconsistent in presenting these values because he talks about them as objective entities, things in themselves, while sometimes claiming that our conceptions of them can change.[46]

These values and objects, which constitute the relationship of man and God, and are not seen as attributes of God, reside in the phenomenological consciousness. They are clearly not things in themselves, which are absolutely rejected by the phenomenological method (see above, Chapter Four, p. 9). They are universal essences.[47] As Heschel makes clear, the humanity of human being is disclosed in essential modes.

> Man is not only a special kind of being. His being human depends upon certain relations without which he ceases to be human. The decision to give priority to the question what is human about a human being is based upon the assumption that the category of human is not simply derived from the category of being. The attribute 'human' in the term 'human being' is not an accidental quality, added to the essence of his being. It is the essence. Human being demands being human. An analysis of the human situation discloses a number of

essential modes of being human, a few of which I should like to refer
to in the next chapter.[48]

These phenomenological objects are not assertions about matters of
fact,[49] neither mental nor psychological.[50] Their essences are known as
a result of the eidetic reduction and they come to consciousness in the
noetic-noematic correlation. As such the are "meant objects" which
correspond to the meaning of the subjective act.[51] Their non-temporal
being does not render them objects of imagination, so Heschel speaks of
them as one would speak of objects of sensory perception. Heschel's use
of objective talk in relation to values within the phenomenological
method, necessitates the use of intentionality which presupposes
changes in attitude and perspective without negating their negative
aspects. In other words, they are correlated on an atemporal and
temporal plane of consciousness. The overlooking of this seminal point
neglects the entire thrust of Heschel's phenomenological method,
which constitutes consciousness with objects of meaning.

---

[1] *Man Is Not Alone*, p. 5.

[2] *God in Search of Man*, pp. 92 and 93.

[3] "What do we mean by 'the world'? If we mean an ultimate, closed, fixed and
self-sufficient system of phenomena behaving in accord with the laws known to
us, then such a concept would exclude the possibility of admitting any super-
mundane intervention or penetration by a voice not accounted for by these
laws. Indeed, if the world as described by natural science is regarded as the
ultimate, then there is no sense in searching for the Divine which is by
definition the ultimate. How could there be one ultimate within the other?"
God in Search of Man, p. 210. It is clear that the expansion of experience
intended here by Heschel, while based on the same rejection of the natural
attitude as Husserl, is motivated by another reason, the revelation of God to
man. Clearly this motivation stands at the center of Heschel's adoption of
phenomenological principles.

[4] *Ibid.*, p. 106.

[5] *Ibid.*, p. 121, also p. 141

[6] *Ibid.*, pp. 114ff.

[7] *Ibid.*, p. 115

[8] *Ibid.*, p. 141.

[9] *Who Is Man?*, p. 5.

[10] *Ibid.*, p. 22. This same point, from a different perspective, is made on pp. 32
and 42.

[11] *The Prophets*, pp. xvi-xvii.

[12] *God in Search of Man*, p. 130.

[13] This is the nature of the mental act as described by Husserl in *Ideas*, pp. 78
and 79.

[14] *The Prophets*, p. xviii.

[15] *Man Is Not Alone*, p. 5.

[16] *Who Is Man?*, p. 42.

[17] See Chapter Two, p. 20.

[18] *Who Is Man?*, pp. 42 and 99.

[19] *Man Is Not Alone*, p. 193.

[20] *The Prophets*, pp. 278, 298, 314 and 318.

[21] *Ibid.*, Vol. II, p. 11.

[22] *Ibid.*, Vol. II, p. 267.

[23] *Ibid.*, Vol. II, p. 11.

[24] *Who Is Man?*, p. 99.

[25] *The Prophets*, p. 437.

[26] *The Prophets*, p. 486.

[27] See Chapter Four, p. 19.

[28] *The Prophets*, p. 487.

[29] *Die Prophetie*, pp. 3-5.

[30] *The Prophets*, p. 307.

[31] Lauer, *The Triumph of Subjectivity*, p. 93.

[32] *The Prophets*, p. 360.

[33] *Ibid.*, Vol. II, p. 11.

[34] *God in Search of Man*, p. 5.

[35] *Who Is Man?*, p. 108.

[36] *Ibid.*, p. 66.

[37] Lauer, *The Triumph of Subjectivity*, p. 101.

[38] *Man Is Not Alone*, p. 19.

[39] *God in Search of Man*, p. 114ff.

[40] *Ibid.*, p. 114.

[41] *God in Search of Man*, p. 46.

[42] A. Gurwitsch, "Husserl's Theory of the Intentionality of Consciousness in Historical Perspective", ed. E. Lee and M. Mandelbaum, *Phenomenology and Existentialism*, (Baltimore: The Johns Hopkins Press, 1967), p. 49.

[43] Lauer, *The Triumph of Subjectivity*, p. 88.

[44] "On the other hand, the fact of our being able to sense it and to be aware of its existence at all is a sure indication that the ineffable stands in some relationship to the mind of man. We should, therefore, not label it as *irrational*, to be disregarded as the residue of knowledge, as dreary remains of speculation unworthy of our attention. The ineffable is conceivable in spite of its being unknowable." *Man Is Not Alone*, p. 32. Merkle's rejection of Friedman's and Cohen's criticisms of the ontological presupposition (*The Genesis of Faith*, pp. 247-248), while correct, does not recognize Heschel's adherence to phenomenological principles which guarantee validity within their own limits.

[45] *Cartesian Meditations*, p. 50.

[46] M. Friedman, "Divine Need and Human Wonder, The Philosophy of Abraham Heschel" [Hebrew], *Hagut Ivrit Ba-Amerika: Studies on Jewish Themes by Contemporary American Scholars*, eds. M. Zohori, A. Tartakover

and H. Ormian, (Tel Aviv: Brit Ivrit Olamit, Yavneh Publishing House, 1973), p. 409.

[47] *Who Is Man?*, pp. 13, 22 and 31.

[48] *Ibid.*, p. 29.

[49] *Ideas*, p. 12.

[50] Kockelmans, p. 111.

[51]"What the sense of the ineffable perceives is something objective which cannot be conceived by the mind nor captured by imagination or feeling, something real which, by its very essence, is beyond the reach of thought and feeling. What we are primarily aware of is not our self, our inner mood, but a transubjective situation, in regard to which our ability fails. Subjective is the manner, not the matter of our perception. What we perceive is objective in the sense of being independent of and corresponding to our perception. Our radical amazement responds to the mystery, but does not produce it. You and I have not invented the grandeur of the sky nor endowed man with the mystery of birth and death. We do not create the ineffable, we encounter it." *Man Is Not Alone*, p. 20.

Chapter Six

Heschel's Idea of Revelation

As we have seen, Heschel's idea of the prophetic consciousness is based on Husserl's noetic-noematic correlation. His philosophical explication of prophecy and the theology he elaborates from that exposition are inseparable. Heschel's phenomenological understanding of classical prophecy is the structure upon which his own modern theology is erected. It should come as no surprise that the idea that sets the tone for postprophetic consciousness, revelation, is infused with the same phenomenological significance that informs classical prophecy. Heschel makes this clear in the conclusion to *The Prophets.*

> Revelation means, not that God makes Himself known, but that He makes His will known; not God's disclosure of His Being, His self-manifestation, but a disclosure of the divine will and pathos, of the ways in which he relates Himself to man. Man knows the word of revelation, but not the self-revelation of God. He experiences no vision of God's essence, only a vision of appearance.[1]

The meaning of revelation or the vision of appearance of God for post-prophetic man in Heschel's theology, is phenomenologically available through the noetic-noematic correlation and the corresponding phenomenological principles outlined in Chapter Five. Consciousness, and hence revelation is not a "mere unidimensional sphere composed of acts, as real psychical events, which coexist with and succeed one another."[2] Consciousness and revelation are two dimensional acts,[3] in which the noetic and noematic planes must correspond. As a result, the phenomenological description of revelation does not and cannot possess an absolute beginning and a process whose course is rationally evident.[4] That is to say, there is no text, temporal succession, deduction of cause and effect or psychic act to which one may point and say, that is revelation.[5] Consequently, the attempt to fix the content of revelation within boundaries that are constant and necessarily specified is impossible.[6] The idea of revelation, according to Heschel, must be continuously rethought. That does not, however, deny the possibility of establishing necessary principles that engender the content of revelation. The phenomenological treatment that Heschel extends to revelation is precisely that claim. It must be remembered that revelation and its phenomenological content are not real, i.e. they cannot be defined by natural means through cause and effect. Judaism, in the form of the Bible, confronts man with the result of revelation.[7] Revelation and its phenomenological content are "irreal" or "ideal." For Heschel this guarantees that the content is a result of a transcendental origin which cannot operate without rules. From Heschel's theological viewpoint, any other claim would sever its ties to Biblical prophecy and the authenticity of ensuing Jewish traditions. Revelation is always more than man experiences but never less than man can indicate in an ideal way.[8]

This radical result of Heschel's phenomenological thesis and its ontological presupposition, in relation to the idea of revelation, has been neglected and misunderstood. The neglect and misunderstanding have been so thorough that Heschel's critics have not properly evaluated his ontology, the content of revelation, the nature of pathos and the rabbinic origins of his idea of revelation. It is certainly accurate to claim that Heschel himself has not helped to clarify these positions because he has not collected and explained his methodology and its content in any one place. But, as I have demonstrated, theoretically and practically, there is no aspect of his writing that is devoid of his method and its content. All of Heschel's work is an attempt to explain the significance of the correlation of man and God. Even *Who Is Man?*, an essay on human existence, and not on theology, uses categories of revelation to describe the transcendence of man.[9] None of Heschel's work is situated outside the ideal of revelation. The phenomenological significance of revelation touches each and every aspect of his thought because the interrelation of God and man is the nexus of Heschel's theology.[10] The purpose of this chapter is to present a clarification of the internal issues of revelation based on Heschel's own phenomenological exposition of the problem of revelation.

Heschel's principal treatment of revelation forms the second of three main sections of *God in Search of Man*. It is clear from this location, that the act of revelation, i.e. its phenomenological structure and not a rhetorical theological presentation and defense of it, is Heschel's main concern.[11]

> In entering this discourse, we do not conjure up the shadow of an obscure phenomenon, but attempt to debate the question whether to believe that there is a voice in the world that pleads with us in the name of God.[12]

This is even more evident if one pays the slightest amount of attention to the limits which Heschel sets to evaluate revelation. Revelation cannot be examined by looking at its substance.[13] Only its ideal structure and the consequences of that structure have any authenticity for Heschel.

> Thus it is not the claim alone, or even primarily, that draws us to the Bible. It is *what* the prophets say that is a challenge to our life, to our thinking, and that drives us in our efforts to understand the meaning of that claim. It is, therefore, necessary to distinguish between three aspects of the problem of revelation: *the idea, the claim* and *the result*.[14]

As an idea, the significance of revelation is seen by Heschel apart from its historical foundation. The accumulative historical experience of the prophets or of the Jewish people is not what Heschel has in mind in his consideration of revelation.

> It is not historical curiosity that excites our interest in the problem of revelation. As an event of the past which subsequently affected the course of civilization, revelation would not engage the modern mind any more than the Battle of Marathon or the Congress of Vienna. If it concerns us, it is not because of the impact it had upon past generations but as something which may or may not be of perpetual, unabating relevance.[15]

According to Heschel, the problem of revelation for modern man, is rooted in modern man's absurd notion of self-sufficiency[16] and unworthiness.[17] It is compounded by modern man's consideration that God is too distant from man and the meaninglessness of claiming that divine human interaction can take place.[18] These objections can be found throughout the history of philosophy from Spinoza to the Deists and to all manner of modern thinkers. Heschel clearly places these objections to revelation into an historical-philosophical context. But, his answer is not given within the same historical-philosophical context and perhaps has lead critics to conclude that Heschel's answer is not intended as a philosophical solution. Heschel does not reject these arguments in a systematic fashion. The problem of revelation according to Heschel is its ideal validity. In the midst of the objections he interjects a remark that seems to have little more than rhetorical significance.

> Let us pause for a moment to consider the constant interaction that exists between the somatic and the psychic. A touch of the finger tips is translated into a concept, while an intention of the mind is communicated to the body. How this interaction takes place remains indescribable. Are we, then, because of the indescribability of revelation, justified in rejecting a priori as untrue the assertion of the

prophets that, at certain hours in Israel's history, the divine came in touch with a few chosen souls? That the creative source of our own selves came in touch with man? If there are moments in which genius speaks for all men, why should we deny that there are moments in which a voice speaks for God? That the source of goodness communicates its way to the human mind?[19]

Heschel's language is carefully chosen here and is the key to the concept he is employing. The reality of intentionality is the seminal issue. The description of intentionality cannot be conveyed in physical terms. Intentionality is not consistent with the natural attitude. There is no way to explain "how it takes place," yet, it is real.[20] Similarly, in the case of revelation, intentionality is indescribable in natural terms. There is no way to explain the "how" of revelation. But, there is certainly a way to explain the "what" of revelation. The "what" of revelation is the intentional structure that becomes clear as a result of the phenomenological reduction. Heschel's analogy leads him to conclude that the major problem of revelation, the indescribability of its idea of intentionality, should not lead us to reject a priori the reality of revelation. The intentional structure of revelation is guaranteed by his method and its application to prophetic consciousness through the noetic-noematic correlation, just as Husserl guaranteed the validity of intentional structures[21] (see above Chapter Four, p. 4).

Heschel's theological rhetoric, "the most serious problem is the absence of the problem,"[22] misleads the reader who has not captured the phenomenological heart of the issue. Heschel's statements about the reality of revelation in the Bible can only make sense within the phenomenological method he employs.[23] The idea of revelation is not a rhetorical device. It is a complex intentional structure that is clarified through the use of depth-theology and not an element of fantasy or the imagination.[24] The reality of God, His presence to the mind is never an object but only an intentional object. This is seminal to the problem of the idea of revelation.

> The idea of revelation remains an absurdity as long as we are unable to comprehend the impact with which the realness of God is pursuing man, every man. However, collecting the memories of the sparks of illuminations we have perceived, the installments of insight that have been bestowed upon us throughout the years, we will find it impossible to remain certain of the impossibility of revelation.[25]

The fact that the Bible contains the idea of revelation, which is accessible through the phenomenological method, is the basis for Heschel's second contention about revelation. While Heschel presented the idea of revelation phenomenologically he requires a concrete locus for the act of revelation, since prophetic acts no longer take place.

> A clarification of this question will depend on our dealing with another question, namely, why do we turn to the Bible in our search for the voice of God in the world? It is because the Bible does more than posit the idea or possibility of revelation. In the Bible we are confronted with a claim, with prophets who claim to convey the will of God; a fact that dominated the history of Israel. Thus, in approaching the Bible, it is not a principle, a general idea, or a metaphysical possibility which we discuss, but specific prophetic acts which, according to the Bible, happened in the life of the people of Israel between the time of Moses and the time of Malachi.[26]

The claim of revelation does not ignore the phenomenological context that its idea necessitated. If anything, the claim of revelation strengthens the phenomenological presentation because Heschel is evaluating "specific prophetic acts" and not the substance of prophecy.[27] The meaning of the prophetic act is the crucial point. Although Heschel does not consistently distinguish between the noetic and the noematic aspects of meaning, he clearly uses this distinction. The similarity to the meant object of the noetic-noematic correlation is the first concern of Heschel's analysis of the claim of revelation. In using language that is essential to the description of the nature of revelation, Heschel speaks of the meant object.

> The word 'revelation' is like an exclamation; it is an indicative rather than a descriptive term. Like all terms that express the ultimate, it points to its meaning rather than fully rendering it.[28]

This phenomenological remark is indicative of another important phenomenological issue that lies beneath the surface of Heschel's procedure in dealing with revelation.

> It is our task to deal with two questions: what is the meaning of prophetic inspiration and what is the truth about prophetic inspiration? The first question inquires: what kind of act is described by prophetic inspiration? The second question inquires: is it true? Did it really happen?[29]

The order of Heschel's questions is also not to be taken as insignificant.[30] The analysis of Husserl's idea of constitution yielded important conclusions about the function of truth and judgments. According to Husserl, the analysis of judgments, if they can be realized by intuition, give us access to knowledge.[31] There is no attempt, in Husserl's theory of knowledge, to prove the adequacy of thought to things, which allows truth to be deduced from the judgment. Truth is the function of a judgment which is correlated to its intuition because judgments presuppose truth[32] and intuition is the very course of thought toward truth,[33] a rational penetration into the data of experience.[34] This is "another way of saying that a judgment will be true when the 'state of affairs' constituted in it has been phenomenologically guaranteed. All of which brings us back to the a priori laws of phenomenological constitution; that is truly objective which has been constituted in accord with the *necessary* laws of subjectivity."[35] Heschel's desire to explicate the "state of affairs," in this case the prophetic act, and then decide its truth based on a judgment correlated to its intuition, is in agreement with Husserl's idea of constitution and the necessary laws of subjectivity. This motivation clearly underlies Heschel's procedure as it was quoted above.

Yet, Heschel points out, the postprophetic mind needs a location to grasp the meaning of revelation.[36] The noetic-noematic structure cannot be the only way to grasp the meaning of revelation. Language is itself part of the constitution of consciousness. The ideal meaning of revelation would be empty if the words used to convey it were not understood in their proper context. Therefore, imbedded within the meaning of the claim of revelation is a thorough explanation of Heschel's use of language.[37] The five points which he enumerates become the basis of Heschel's idea of the content of revelation and are best examined when that issue is fully treated.

These procedural issues of judgment and meaning lead to Heschel's third consideration vis-à-vis revelation. The idea and the claim of revelation lead directly to the result of revelation or the words.[38] The first two concepts closely follow Heschel's announced phenomenological program and are the direct focus of that method. The result of revelation must coincide with these goals or Heschel's theology will be inconsistent.

The result of revelation, from a phenomenological perspective, must first be apprehended through its structure. From a theological viewpoint this is not acceptable because revelation is located in the Bible, through the words which are communicated from God to man.[39] Revelation cannot be guided by an abstraction.[40] But, the post-prophetic mind can gain an awareness of it, through phenomenological intuition.

> Souls are introduced to a range of mountains through the courtesy of a definition. Our goal, then, must not be to find a definition, but to learn how to sense, how to intuit the will of God in words. The essence of intuition is not in grasping what is describable but in sensing what is ineffable. The goal is to train the reason for the appreciation of that which lies beyond reason. It is only through the sense of the ineffable that we may intuit the mystery of revelation.[41]

The idea of consciousness that Heschel employs and his idea of revelation are not unidimensional events, but two dimensional acts (see above p. 1). It is significant for Heschel's theological purposes that, within phenomenological intuition, revelation has divine and human aspects.[42] Heschel's use of these aspects is the preeminent structural bond in the idea of revelation.

> This is at the core of all Biblical thoughts: God is not a being detached from man to be sought after, but a power that seeks, pursues and calls upon man. The way to God is a way of God. Israel's religion originated in the initiative of God rather than in the efforts of man. It was not an invention of man but a creation of God; not a product of civilization, but a realm of its own. Man would not have known Him if He had not approached man. God's relation to man precedes man's relation to Him.[43]

Revelation can only take place when God initiates it and man is receptive to God's initiative no matter how overwhelming the event. Individually, the divine and human aspects of revelation are necessary but not sufficient for its understanding. The correlation of man and God in revelation is explicitly intentional. The divine and human aspects of the event also have two phases, which are called turning and direction.[44] These two phases represent the genesis and the termination of the event from the respective points of view. This becomes clear in Heschel's contrast of the mystic and prophetic outlooks.

> The mystic experience is man's turning toward God; the prophetic act is God's turning toward man. The former is first of all an event in the life of man, contingent on the aspiration and initiative of man; the latter is first of all an event into the life of God, contingent on the pathos and initiative of God. From the mystic experience we may gain an insight of man into the life of God; from the prophetic act we learn of an insight of God into the life of man.[45]

The "turning" of God to man is not an empty gesture on the part of God. It is the bestowal of a content and the delivery of a message. This theological aspect of correlation of man and God indicates how the form of the relation is complemented by a content.

> What is important in mystical acts is that *something happens;* what is important in prophetic acts is that *something is said.* Ecstasy is the experience of a pure situation, of an inner condition. It is an experience that has form but no content. Prophecy is the experience of a relationship, the receipt of a message. It has form as well as content.[46]

The human phase of revelation is, as Heschel has maintained from the outset in *The Prophets,*[47] one of form and content. The prophet is sympathetic to God's intention.[48] The prophet's inner experience is a response to the call of God.

> Sympathy is a prophetic sense. Compatible with God, the prophet is sensitive to the divine aspect of events. To be sure, such sensitivity is not regarded by him as an innate faculty. Sympathy is a response, not a manifestation of pure spontaneity. The prophet has to be called in order to respond, he has to receive in order to reciprocate.[49]

This is only a partial explanation of the human phase of revelation. If revelation truly has a human aspect it must originate in the purely spontaneous will of the prophet. If the prophet is not to be a mere vessel for divine words, then his consciousness must retain its own integrity.[50] As opposed to inspiration of the ecstatic or poetic type, for the prophet, inspiration is an act

> in which the prophetic person stands over against the divine person. It is characterized by a subject-subject structure: the self-conscious active 'I' of the prophet encounters the active, living Inspirer. The prophet, unlike the ecstatic, is both a recipient and a participant. His response to what is disclosed to him turns revelation into dialogue. The prophets asserted that many of their experiences were not moments of passive receptivity, mere listening to a voice or mere beholding a Presence, but dialogues with God. By response, pleading, and counterspeech, the prophet reacts to the word he perceives. The prophet's share in the dialogue can often give the decisive turn to the encounter, evoking a new attitude in the divine Person and bringing about a new decision. In a sense, prophecy consists of a revelation of God and a co-revelation of man.[51]

According to Heschel, the human phase of revelation clearly demonstrates an antinomy. In the moment of encounter with God, a dialectical tension arises in the prophet's consciousness that leads to the human aspect of revelation.

> He is both active and passive, free and forced. He is free to respond to the content of the moment; he is forced to experience the moment, to accept the burden of his mission. Thus the effect of the impact of inspiration is to evoke in him both a sense of freedom and a feeling of coercion, an act of spontaneity and an awareness of enforced receptivity. This note of dialectic tension is of essential significance in the structure of the prophetic personality.[52]

The phenomenological significance of Heschel's idea of revelation resides in the prophet's self-consciousness as it is related to God's pathos. In the prophetic consciousness, revelation is "an experience of an act of God."[53] In the postprophetic consciousness of depth-theology, revelation may be partially understood through its structural presentation. This subject-subject structure is thoroughly intentional.

Consequently, the meaning of revelation for the postprophetic mind is captured in prophetic consciousness as a noetic-noematic correlation. The object pole of the correlation must have a content to assure that it is something self-given in intuition. Borrowing the language of perception which is tied to Husserl, Heschel makes this structure evident.

> Therefore, to characterize revelation as a prophetic insight or experience is to reduce a reality to a perception. Seen from man's aspect, to receive a revelation is to witness how God is turning toward man. It is not an act of gazing at the divine reality, a static and eternal mystery. The prophet is in the midst of a divine event, of an event in the life of God, for in addressing the prophet, God comes out of His imperceptibility to become audible to man. The full intensity of the event is not in the fact that 'man hears' but in the 'fact' that 'God speaks' to man. The mystic experience is an ecstasy of man; revelation is an ecstasy of God.[54]

The phenomenological structure of prophetic religion is mainly characterized by the correlation of the prophetic "I" and the object of the experience. God is clearly not the object of experience. God's pathos is the object of prophetic experience that is incorporated into the intentionality of prophetic experience as a phenomenological fact.[55] The prophet does not mystically create this object but he is challenged by it.[56] The content of the prophet's inner experience, his sympathy, has no cosmological significance.[57] Sympathy is an anthropological and religious category that points to the structure of the prophet's personality and his consciousness of revelation.[58] The "turning" of the prophet and postprophetic man toward God, allows the phenomenological object "to be seen." Conversely, when God turns toward man, man becomes the object of God's pathos because God's intention is directed at him.

> A specific aspect of prophetic religion or of the religious phenomena in general, as opposed to the purely psychological, lies in the fact of a mutual inherence of the 'I' and the object of religious experience, for an intention of man toward God produces a counteracting intention of God toward man. Here all mutual relation end, not in the original decision, but in a relationship which represents a counteraction. In turning toward God, man experiences God's turning toward him. Man's awareness of God is to be understood as God's awareness of man, man's knowledge of God is transcended in God's knowledge of man, the subject – man – becomes object, and the object – God – becomes subject.[59]

---

[1] *The Prophets*, p. 485.

[2] A. Gurwitsch, "Intentionality, Constitution and Intentional Analysis," p. 135.

3 Heschel constantly refers to his idea of revelation as a co-revelation. "In a sense prophecy consists of a revelation of God and a co-revelation of man. The share of the prophet manifested itself not only in what he was able to give but also in what he was unable to receive. Revelation does not happen when God is alone. The two classical terms for the moment at Sinai are *mattan torah* and *kabbalat torah*, 'the giving of the Torah' and 'the acceptance of the Torah.' It is both an event in the life of God and an event in the life of man." *God in Search of Man*, p. 260.

4 This is made clear by Heschel's remarks about the difference of process and event in connection to the remoteness of revelation from modern man. "Prophetic inspiration must be understood as *an event*, not as *a process*. What is the difference between process and event? A process happens regularly, following a relatively permanent pattern; an event is extraordinary, irregular. A process may be continuous, steady, uniform; events happen suddenly, intermittently, occasionally. Processes are typical; events are unique. A process follows a law, events create a precedent." *God in Search of Man*, p. 209. The non-absolute nature of the content of revelation is also asserted in another context. In reference to the nature of pathos and its functional character, Heschel makes the following remark: "The basic features emerging from the above analysis indicate that the divine pathos is not conceived of as an essential attribute of God, as something objective, as a finality with which man is confronted, but as an expression of God's will; it is a functional rather than a substantial reality; not an attribute, not an unchangeable quality, not an absolute content of divine Being, but rather a situation or the personal implication in His acts." *The Prophets*, p. 231.

5 *God in Search of Man*, pp. 184-185.

6 "The experience of having been spoken to by Him, who is more than heaven and earth, has a grandeur in comparison to which all words lose their weight. An examination of the psychic and historic circumstances would be of little relevance. Whatever answer may be found to the question – How did prophecy happen? Was it an inner or an external experience? What was its historic background? – will revolve around the adventitious, just as a discussion of colons and semicolons will hardly bring out the content of a sentence. The words and their meaning have to be grasped first." *God in Search of Man*, p. 178.

7 "The idea of revelation we discussed in the previous chapter. It is the claim to which we wil turn now before we discuss the words or the result." *God in Search of Man*, p. 177. "We must not try to read chapters in the Bible dealing with the event at Sinai as if they were texts in systematic theology. Its intention is to celebrate the mystery, to introduce us to it rather than to penetrate or to explain it. As a report about revelation the Bible itself is a midrash." *God in Search of Man*, p. 185.

8 "If revelation were *only* a psycho-physical act, then it would be little more than a human experience, an event in the life of man. Yet just as a work of sculpture is more than the stone in which it is carved, so is revelation *more* than a human experience. True, a revelation that did not become known by experience would be like a figure carved in the air. Still its being a human experience is but a part

of what really happened in revelation, and we must, therefore, not equate the event of revelation with man's experience of revelation." *God in Search of Man*, p. 184.

[9] *Who Is Man?*, pp. 74ff. The meaning of man is man's being an object of divine concern.

[10] Rothschild, *Between God and Man: An Interpretation of Judaism*, p. 11.

[11] A. Cohen, *The Natural and the Supernatural Jew*, pp. 234ff. Cohen's specific charge against Heschel is centered in the following (pp. 244-245), "The prophet exemplifies what Heschel has described as 'situational thinking' by contrast with the philosopher's 'conceptual thinking.' This distinction, as many of Heschel's favorite distinctions, ought not to be scrutinized too rigorously. Heschel's distinctions are too fragile. They possess rhetorical power, but they are not intellectually resilient. Clearly the prophet is different from the philosopher. Something happens to the prophet which cannot happen to the sound philosopher – namely, his reason is overwhelmed by an experience, whose nature and source his awe of the numinous restrains him from investigating. This is all well and good; but to say that the difference between 'situational thinking' and 'conceptual thinking' is that the former 'involves an inner experience', while the latter is 'an act of reasoning' is simply not true." It is plainly evident that Cohen has overlooked the phenomenological character of Heschel's thought which explicates the 'inner experience' of the prophets (see above Chapter Four, p. 52 and Chapter Five pp. 75-76) and is not a rhetorical device that cannot be scrutinized. A little further on Cohen states, "Man is not God's object." According to Heschel, the opposite is the case. This position is the basis of Heschel's phenomenology. Heschel claims that man's awareness of God is limited to man's being known as God's object. As I have shown, Heschel's meaning is phenomenological and therefore he is talking of a phenomenological object. Cohen's misunderstanding of these points leads him to misunderstand the real intention of Heschel's rhetoric. As I have demonstrated previously (see above Chapter Three pp. 38-39) Heschel is not against the use of reason. He rejects the act of reason when it is outside the phenomenological consciousness and when it is not allied with the insights of religion. Heschel never supports an antirational or irrational claim. Heschel does accept claims which include nonrational elements. The important citation brought by Cohen is certainly rooted in these Heschelian rejections which are phrased rhetorically and does not reflect a Heschelian desire to negate reason.

[12] *God in Search of Man*, p. 168.

[13] "In order to comprehend the form or the essential structure of that encounter, it will be necessary to subtract from it its accidental aspects, or whatever does not belong indispensably to it. In other words, we must disregard all features not essential to revelation as such. We are therefore excluding from our present consideration not only the substantial elements (e.g., the pathos motive), but also all contingent formal elements, such as the outward form of the experience (whether it was an act of hearing or seeing)." *The Prophets*, p. 430.

[14] *God in Search of Man*, p. 177.

[15] *Ibid.*, p. 168.

[16] *Ibid.*, p. 169.

[17] *Ibid.*, p. 170.

[18] *Ibid.*, p. 172.

[19] *Ibid.*, pp. 172-173.

[20] "To convey what the prophets experienced, the Bible could use either terms of description or terms of indication. Any description of the act of revelation in empirical categories would have produced a caricature. This is why all the Bible does is to state that revelation happened; how it happened is something they could only convey in words that are evocative and suggestive." *Ibid.*, p. 185.

[21] Merkle's analysis of revelation as event (*The Genesis of Faith*, pp. 114-115) recognizes the aspect of will, freedom and decision as primary, but he completely misses the intentional structure of revelation as event. Merkle's notion that Heschel accepts process as an historical concept and not as a natural one is correct: "According to Heschel, in the biblical tradition, revelation is 'not thought of as proceeding out of God like rays out of the sun'; rather it is 'an act proceeding from His will and brought about by a decision to disclose what otherwise would remain concealed. In this sense, it was an act within the life of God.' (*The Prophets*, p. 436.) This I contend, is what Heschel is really driving at when he claims that revelation is an event rather than a process. Again, it is will and decision that make it an event, not the fact that it happens suddenly, intermittently, and occasionally. Even a process-event may be informed by will and decision." (*The Genesis of Faith*, p. 115.) But, Merkle's emphasis on this point has lead him to neglect the intentionality of God and man in the event, that is responsible for its meaning and points to its phenomenological exposition. This is evident when Merkle resorts to meaning as an explanation for the welding of the "various revelatory events into one" (p. 251, #37), without taking into account its phenomenological context.

[22] *God in Search of Man*, p. 168.

[23] Heschel's theological rhetoric is never completely separated from his phenomenological principles. His prose, which is intended to be inspiring and convincing, always maintains some association to the phenomenological problem at hand. The following rhetoric about revelation and the Bible incorporates the "directedness of the "I." "The Bible is an answer to the supreme question: what does God demand of us? Yet the question has gone out of the world. God is portrayed as a mass of vagueness behind a veil of enigmas, and His voice has become alien to our minds, to our hearts, to our souls. We have learned to listen to every 'I' except the 'I' of God. The man of our time may proudly declare: nothing animal is alien to me but everything divine is. This is the status of the Bible in modern life: it is a sublime answer, but we do not know the question any more. Unless we recover the question, there is no hope of understanding the Bible." *God in Search of Man*, pp. 168-169.

[24] *Man Is Not Alone*, p. 237.

[25] *God in Search of Man*, pp. 174-175.

[26] *Ibid.*, p. 176. This passage indicates that Heschel supports the standard rabbinic view that prophecy ceased with Malachi (Sotah 48b).

[27] This explanation is based on *God in Search of Man*, pp. 177-178 and p. 184, "If revelation was a moment in which God succeeded in reaching man, then to try to describe it exclusively in terms of optics or acoustics, or to inquire was it a vision or a sound? was it forte or piano? would be even more ludicrous than to ask about the velocity of "the wind that sighs before the dawn." Of course, the prophets claim to have seen, to have heard. But that kind of seeing and hearing cannot be subjected to psychological or physiological analysis. An analysis of the poet's ability to hear the wind sigh would have no relevance to our understanding of the poem. Did the prophet claim to have encountered God in the way in which he met one of his contemporaries or in the way in which Aristotle met Alexander the Great?" This is amplified by Clarke p. 118, "In describing the prophetic act Heschel excludes from consideration both the substantial elements, such as the pathos motive, and the contingent formal elements, such as the outward form of the experience – whether it is an act of hearing or seeing."

[28] *God in Search of Man*, p. 185.

[29] *Ibid.*, p. 177.

[30] Heschel himself calls our attention to the order in which the questions must be answered and intimates the underlying phenomenological purpose. "Our inquiry must begin with the first question, for it is obviously necessary to know what prophetic inspiration is before attempting to prove or disprove its having taken place. What kind of fact is described by the term prophecy? What does it signify?" *God in Search of Man*, pp. 177-178.

[31] Levinas, p. 83.

[32] *Ibid.*, p. 89.

[33] *Ibid.*, p. 92.

[34] Lauer, *The Triumph of Subjectivity*, p. 62.

[35] *Ibid.*, p. 101.

[36] *God in Search of Man*, pp. 176-177.

[37] *Ibid.*, pp. 176-183.

[38] *Ibid.*, p. 177.

[39] "The dogmatic theologian who tries to understand the act of revelation in terms of his own generalizations takes himself too seriously and is guilty of oversimplification. Revelation is a mystery for which reason has no concepts. To ignore its mysterious nature is an oversight of fatal consequence. Out of the darkness came the voice to Moses; and out of the darkness comes the Word to us. The issue is baffling." *Ibid.*, p. 189.

[40] *Ibid.*, p. 197.

[41] *Ibid.*, p. 189.

[42] *Ibid.*, p. 194.

[43] *Ibid.*, p. 198.

[44] *The Prophets*, p. 435, pp. 361, 364, 365 and 440.

[45] *God in Search of Man*, p. 198.

[46] *The Prophets*, p. 364.

[47] "...on the personal level, of sympathy (content of inner experience) and the sense of being overpowered (form of inner experience)." *Ibid.*, p. xix.

[48] *Ibid.*, pp. 308-309.

[49] *Ibid.*, p. 311.

[50] "There is no indication in the prophets' reports of their experiences of that emptying of consciousness which is the typical preparation for ecstasy, of a loss of self-consciousness or of a suspension of mental power during the reception of revelation. Unlike mystical insight, which takes place in 'the abyss of the mind', in 'the ground of consciousness', prophetic illumination seems to take place in the full light of the mind, in the very center of consciousness." *Ibid.*, p. 359.

[51] *Ibid.*, p. 366.

[52] *Ibid.*, p. 445.

[53] *God in Search of Man*, p. 198.

[54] *Ibid.*, pp. 198-199.

[55] "Sympathy, the fundamental feature of the prophet's inner life, assumed various forms. Common to them all as an essential element is the focusing of the attention on God, the awareness of divine emotion, intense concern for the divine pathos, sympathetic solidarity with God. However, following Max Scheler's classification, we may distinguish two types of sympathy: (1) community of feeling, or sympathy *with* God; (2) fellow feeling, or sympathy *for* God. The first type of relationship obtains when two friends are standing at the coffin of a beloved friend. They feel in common the 'same' sorrow, the 'same' anguish. It is not that A feels this sorrow and B feels it also. What obtains here is a *feeling in common.* A's sorrow is in no way an 'external' matter for B here, as it is, e.g. for their friend C, who joins them and commiserates 'with them' or 'upon their sorrow'. The feeling of A and the feeling of B are independent of each other; the sorrow of one is neither caused nor reinforced by the sorrow of the other. 'On the contrary, they feel it together, in the sense that they feel and experience in common, not only the self-same value situation, but also the same keenness of emotion in regard to it.' The sorrow and the grief are here one and identical. Since the prophets are, so to speak, confronted with the same object or reality as God, namely the spiritual and moral plight of the people, of Israel, and the standard and motivation of the divine pathos worked in them in similar fashion, the prophets may react in the same mode as God, in sorrow or indignation, in love or anger. The second type of relationship is fellow feeling, or sympathy for God. It involves the prophets' intentional reference of the feeling of joy or sorrow to God's experience. Here God's pathos is first presented as A's in an act of understanding and it is to this pathos that the prophet's primary commiseration is directed. In other words, the prophet's sympathy and God's pathos are phenomenologically two different facts, not *one* fact as in the first case." *The Prophets*, pp. 313-314.

[56] *Ibid.*, p. 316.

[57] *Ibid.*, p. 315.

[58] *Ibid.*, p. 315.

[59] *Ibid.*, pp. 487-488.

Chapter Seven

The Nature of Pathos

In the previous chapter the object of revelation was demonstrated in its phenomenological context. According to Heschel, God in His essence is clearly not the object of prophetic experience or revelation.[1] The object of revelation is God's pathos.[2]

> Pathos means: God is never neutral, never beyond good and evil. He is always partial to justice. It is not a name for a human experience, but the name for an object of human experience. It is something the prophets meet with, something eventful, current, present in history as well as in nature.[3]

Heschel clearly distinguishes the phenomenological object of his inquiry from the essence of God, lest one wrongly conclude that Heschel is obscuring that object in spite of its essential mystery or confusing it with the object of classical theology.

> The prophet reflects, not on heavenly or hallowed mysteries, but on the perplexities and ambiguities of history. He never discloses the life of the beyond, but always speaks of an appearance, God as turned toward man. The anthropotropic moment is the object of his experience; God in His eternal self-existence, never.[4]

Pathos is the object of prophetic experience that is incorporated into the intentionality of prophetic experience as a phenomenological fact.[5] The prophet does not merely feel this reality or mystically create this object. The prophet is challenged by it.[6] As such, pathos is matched in prophetic consciousness by sympathy.[7]

This intentional structure of prophetic consciousness, represented in postprophetic consciousness by the noetic-noematic correlation, makes God's pathos a concept easily misunderstood. The prophetic act of consciousness is a constituted reality based on the noetic-noematic correlation, and its object, pathos, is a nonsubstantial reality. This phenomenological context of pathos has been ignored. The constitutive and nonsubstantial reality of pathos has not been given any consideration. Consequently, Heschel's theology has had serious charges leveled against it.[8] In Berkovits' critique, the phenomenological function of pathos is completely overlooked and Berkovits accuses Heschel of ignoring the anthropomorphic and anthropopathic consequences of his theology.[9] Katz, in an important critique of Berkovits' assertions, conclusively demonstrates Berkovits' textual, methodological and analytical errors.[10] They need not be replayed here. Unfortunately, Katz suggests there are serious problems with Heschel's philosophical presentation[11] without constructing Heschel's position, a fault Katz himself attributes to Berkovits.

The main issue of Heschel's idea of divine pathos must be its phenomenological context because pathos is the essential phenomenological object, that becomes the central theological concept. Pathos is the phenomenological content of the temporal and atemporal noetic-noematic correlation.

> In sum, the divine pathos is the unity of the eternal and the temporal, of meaning and mystery, of the metaphysical and the historical. It is the real basis of the relation between God and man, of the correlation of Creator and creation, of the dialogue of the Holy One of Israel and His people.[12]

The attempt to understand pathos without its phenomenological context is either self-contradictory[13] or ignorant of Heschel's theological purpose. Pathos, is the transcendental content of inspiration in Heschel's theology.[14]

> The idea of the divine pathos is not a personification of God but an exemplification of divine reality, an illustration or illumination of His concern. It does not represent a substance, but an act or a relationship.[15]

Pathos is not a self-evident concept. It is not merely given. It is accessible through the ontological presupposition which supplies the transcendental clue to the reality of God (see Chapter Five, p. 73). Furthermore, this Heschelian position is elaborated in an historical-philosophical context but its connection to his ontological presupposition ought to have been partially clear to Heschel's critics because the name of the section in which this link is found is, 'The Ontological Presupposition'. Pathos, which requires a change in the appearance of God to the prophet, must correspond to an ontology that reflects the changeability and dynamics of being.

> The Eleatic premise that true being is unchangeable and that change implies corruption is valid only in regard to being as reflected in the mind. Being in reality, being as we encounter it, implies movement. If we think of being as something beyond and detached from beings, we may well arrive at an eleatic notion. An ontology, however, concerned

with being as involved in all beings or as the source of all beings, will find it impossible to separate being from action or movement, and thus postulate a dynamic concept of divine Being.[16]

The identification of being and action or movement is based on a further assumption. The ontological presupposition revolves around the mystery of being and not about being itself.[17] According to Heschel, being is not a self-sufficient ontological category. This is a form of biblical thinking that Heschel identifies with his own ontology. It is free of an ontocentric predicament because it can conceive the end of being or not-being[18] and need not beg the question of being. Consequently, the ontology of the Bible, is focused on how God acts and not on how He is. This is the basis of pathos and its historical existence. Heschel's use of pathos in depth-theology is based on the ontological biblical presentation of pathos.

> Biblical ontology does not separate being from doing. What *is*, acts. The God of Israel is a God who acts, a God of mighty deeds. The Bible does not say how He is, but how He acts. It speaks of His acts of pathos and of His acts in history; it is not as 'true being' that God is conceived, but as the *semper agens*. Here the basic category is action rather than immobility. Movement, creation of nature, acts within history rather than absolute transcendence and detachment from the events of history, are the attributes of the Supreme Being.[19]

While this biblical ontology of being and non-being is at the root of Heschel's idea of pathos, depth-theology's treatment of pathos is the seminal issue. Pathos cannot be treated as an object of speculation.[20] But, it does have objective status of a phenomenological kind. This objective status is based on "the a priori laws of phenomenological constitution; that is truly objective which has been constituted in accord with the *necessary* laws of subjectivity."[21]

Heschel's description of pathos within the ontological presupposition would be useless if his use of intuition was not consistent with these assumptions. Heschel is aware of this problem and takes the appropriate measures to explain it and guard intuition from becoming an irrational activity (see Chapter Five, pp. 78-79). Placing pathos outside of these assumptions, as Berkovits does, will inevitably lead to a misunderstanding of Heschel's use of pathos.[22] But, this is not the most difficult aspect of the problem that Heschel addresses with the use of pathos.

The manner in which pathos exists in prophetic intuition is the problematic issue. Pathos is either a substantial or a functional reality. If pathos is a substantial reality in prophetic intuition, the charges of anthropomorphism and anthropopathism leveled against Heschel are justified. If pathos is a functional reality, i.e. it connotes the way in which intuition functions or how it responds to God's actions, but not what intuition is, then these charges are unjustified. If pathos is a substantial reality, it will have a substantial effect on God's essence. That is to say, if pathos is an attribute of God, it will cause a change in the divine essence because changes in God's attributes (in this case His feelings or thoughts), will then have a direct relation to His essence.[23] Secondly, if God is subject to change initiated by man, then God is passible and not perfect within the limits of classical Aristotelian metaphysics. This will lead Heschel's theology down the path of anthropopathism. Heschel outrightly rejects an anthropopathic theology and absolutely distinguishes depth-theology from it.[24]

The other alternative is to maintain the functional intelligibility of pathos. As such, pathos is the mental and moral intentionality of God.[25] There is no substantial link between God's essence and His relatedness (existence) if pathos is only functionally available to man. Pathos causes no change in the divine essence because all mental and moral actions are by definition and by nature intentional and God, in His essence, exhibits all mental and moral intentions.[26] This tie between intentionality and God in Heschel's theology has been completely overlooked and has forced a mistreatment of Heschel's idea of divine pathos.[27] In this instance, pathos is reduced to emotional affectedness, when it is clearly used by Heschel as moral intentionality including reason and emotion.

> In ascribing a transitive concern to God, we employ neither an anthropomorphic nor an anthropopathic concept but an idea that we should like to characterize as an *anthropopneumatism (anthropo + pneuma)*. We ascribe to Him not a psychic but a spiritual characteristic, not an emotional but a moral attitude.[28]

God's has an intellectual content because of its intentionality. Pathos is not an appeal to mere emotion. But there are appeals to emotion made by Heschel. In the light of Heschel's criticism of a religion of reason,[29] these appeals to emotion are based on his desire to use a full fledged concept of reason. If pathos is "not a passion, an unreasoned emotion,"[30] then it surely is a reasoned emotion. Heschel's rhetorical appeal to a kind of personal thinking is not a blind alley. It is meant to support and demonstrate the eminent rationality of pathos as the essential object of religious consciousness.

> We have been trained to draw a sharp distinction between reason and emotion. The first is pure spontaneity, the drawing of inferences, the ordering of concepts according to the canons of logic. Emotion, on the other hand, is pure receptivity, an impression involving neither

cognition nor representation of the object. Such a contrast, however, is hardly tenable when applied to religious existence. Is religious thinking ever to be completely separated from the stream of emotion that surges beneath it? Religious reason is more than just thinking, and religious emotion is more than just feeling. In religious existence, spontaneity and receptivity involve each other. Is there no reason in the emotional life? True, if emotion is unreasonable, it tends to distort a person's thinking. But emotion can be reasonable just as reason can be emotional, and there is no need to suppress the emotional roots of one's life in order to save the integrity of one's principles. Receptivity and spontaneity involve each other; the separation of the two is harmful to both.[31]

The intentionality of pathos is the form of relation that God and man share. The intentionality of God is the basis of Heschel's idea of God's oneness.[32] In God's essence, intentionality would be absolutely self-constituting. But, in God's relatedness, intentionality is constituted with man. Consequently, this second alternative, the functional intelligibility of pathos, is the strategy chosen by Heschel.[33] God in relation to man, but not in His essence, is affected by human actions and the course of history. This is the anthropological meaning of pathos according to Heschel. Human consciousness is capable of understanding divine pathos, even though there is a reliance on bodily description. The prophet is expressing the intentionality of man through the ascription of divine characteristics to man and not vice versa.[34]

The idea of divine pathos has also anthropological significance. It is man's being relevant to God. To the biblical mind the denial of man's relevance to God is as inconceivable as the denial of God's relevance to man. This principle leads to the basic affirmation of God's participation in human history, to the certainty that the events in the world concern Him and arouse His reaction. It finds its deepest expression in the fact that God can actually suffer. At the heart of the prophetic affirmation is the certainty that God is concerned about the world. Beyond these implications for the meaning of history and human deeds, the idea of pathos reflects a high estimation of human nature. The consciousness of the high dignity and sanctity of man, his soul and body alike, accounts for the extreme development of anthropomorphic views in Jewish and Christian tradition, as the rejection of such consciousness played a part in the radical opposition to anthropomorphism. The *analogia entis* as applied to man having been created in the likeness of God and as expressed in the commandment, 'You shall be holy, for I the Lord your God am holy' (Lev 19:2), points to what may be called a *theomorphic anthropology*. Soul, thought, feeling, even passion, are often regarded as states imbued by God. It is perhaps more proper to describe a prophetic passion as theomorphic than to regard the divine pathos as anthropomorphic.[35]

Heschel retains this distinction of theomorphic anthropology in thought and in reality because this affection of God is never substantial.[36] Pathos is the prophetic statement of God's aliveness,[37] and it only receives functional treatment in Heschel's theology. Its structure connotes the way in which God turns and directs His attention to man.[38] This treatment, like the noetic-noematic correlation from which it derives, is based on Husserl's idea of functional consciousness.[39] As such, Heschel's use of pathos never departs from the phenomenological roots of consciousness.

> The basic features emerging from the above analysis indicate that the divine pathos is not conceived of as an essential attribute of God, as something objective, as a finality with which man is confronted, but as an expression of God's will; it is a functional rather than a substantial reality; not an attribute, not an unchangeable quality, not an absolute content of divine Being, but rather a situation or the personal implication in His acts.[40]

---

[1] "The Prophets never identify God's pathos with His essence, because for them the pathos is not something absolute, but a form of relation." *The Prophets,* p. 231. No doubt this is similar to Heschel's position in *Man Is Not Alone,* pp. 99-100. "We cannot express God, yet God expresses His will to us. It is through His word that we know that God is not beyond good and evil. Our emotion would leave us in a state of bewilderment, if not for the guidance we received."

[2] "The idea of pathos is an answer to the question of content only, not to that of form, and it by no means implies the event of revelation. Pathos is the object of communication, but it does not necessarily of itself engender the latter. The need to reveal itself is not intrinsic to it." *The Prophets,* p. 438.

[3] *Ibid.,* p. 231.

[4] *Ibid.,* p. 485.

[5] See Chapter Six, pp. 13-14.

[6] *The Prophets,* pp. 316 and 443.

[7] "To us, wisdom is the ability to look at all things from the point of view of God, sympathy with the divine pathos, the identification of the will with the will of God." *God in Search of Man, p.* 75.

[8] Berkovits, pp. 192-224.

[9] Berkovits' major objection is centered on his rejection of the separation of God from His pathos (p. 204). "The life-giving significance of God's relatedness to the world is not in the act of relatedness but in the fact that it is God who relates Himself. It is the very essence of God, God as he exists in his absoluteness and perfection, that determines the value of His care for man. It is not possible to separate the essence of God from His pathos. The prophet does not have sympathy with pathos; experiencing God's pathos, he sympathizes with God, the Absolute and Perfect, the Supreme Being, the creator of heaven and earth. The theological dilemma is therefore inescapable.

It cannot be overcome by abstaining from any claim to comprehend God's essence. Of course, one may well take the position that it is all a mystery, but one should not speak of a *theology* of pathos."

Whether or not Berkovits can claim to comprehend God's essence (Heschel plainly refuses this task, *The Prophets*, p. 484), Berkovits has seriously misrepresented Heschel's position. According to Heschel, pathos is a phenomenological object and God is never an object of any kind. Without the existential distinction of God's essence and His relation to man, God must remain absolutely separate from man and totally irrelevant to him, which flies in the face of Heschel's overall strategy (*The Prophets*, p. 259). The forms of God's relation to man are ideal, "The Prophets never identify God's pathos with His essence, because for them the pathos is not something absolute, but a form of relation" (*The Prophets*, p. 231), and Berkovits' attempt to render them literally (pp. 194 and 205), smacks of insincerity.

[10]Steven T. Katz, "Eliezer Berkovits and Modern Jewish Philosophy," *Tradition*, Vol. 17, No. 1, (Fall 1977), pp. 92-138, and especially pp. 124-132.

[11] Berkovits, p. 131.

[12] *The Prophets*, p. 231.

[13]Katz says the following of Berkovits' self-contradictory attempt (p. 129), "Berkovits summarizes Heschel's view in the following manner: 'The reality of God is experienced by the prophet as God's care and concern for His creation.' [Man stands under God's 'concern' is the basic message of all prophecy.] Berkovits then acknowledges his agreement with this view by adding: 'These are, of course, familiar thoughts, well understood by all who have some knowledge of Biblical theology or religious philosophy.' But what does Berkovits mean when he agree's to speak of 'God's care and concern?' Can he make out a philosophical case in which these terms retain their intelligibility while avoiding the anthropopathetic errors he attributes to Heschel? Berkovits does not seem aware that the position he advances is logically self-contradictory, for he does not attempt any resolution of the self-referential inconsistency."

[14] *The Prophets*, p. xix.

[15] *Ibid.*, p. 273.

[16] *Ibid.*, p. 262.

[17] *Ibid.*, p. 263.

[18] *Ibid.*, p. 263.

[19] *Ibid.*, p. 264.

[20] "It is of extreme importance that theology should endeavor to operate with categories indigenous to the insights of depth-theology instead of borrowing its categories from speculative philosophy or science. What is regarded as the ultimate in philosophy must not be regarded as the ultimate in theology. What man thinks or what man says is the ultimate theme of philosophical analysis. To theology, the ultimate theme is that which man is unable to objectify, which he refuses to conceptualize." *Ibid.*, p. 265.

[21] Lauer, *The Triumph of Subjectivity*, p. 101.

[22] "The characteristic of the prophets is not foreknowledge of the future, but insight into the present pathos of God." *The Prophets*, p. 231.

[23] Heschel is explicitly aware of this danger, a point Berkovits (p. 202) completely overlooks. "In the language of Maimonides, 'belief in unity cannot mean essentially anything but the belief in one single idea.' An attribute is either identical with the essence of that to which it is attributed, or different from it. If it is identical, then its attribution is either a tautology (e.g. man is a reasoning animal). Such attributes are impossible with reference to God. God cannot be described by His definition because He cannot be defined. On the other hand, if the attribute is different from the thing to which it is attributed, and thus an idea added to that thing, then it denotes an accident of that essence. Yet such an attribute would imply a plurality (of essence and accidents) in the divine Being. These difficulties arise from the attempt to reduce the biblical insight to an exact rational category. To be sure, the rational component is central to the biblical understanding of unity. However, the biblical intention is not to stress an abstraction, an idea in general, but the fullness of the divine Being; the certainty that the Creator *is* the Redeemer, that the Lord of nature is the Lord of history. *God's* being One means more than just being one. It means, we may say, that He is One, not many; unique and only (one-ly), the center and the circle, all-embracing and involved." *The Prophets*, p. 267.

[24] *The Prophets*, pp. 268-278, *God in Search of Man*, pp. 187-188. *Man Is Not Alone*, pp. 135 and 144.

[25] "Pathos is not conceived as an essential attribute of God, as something objective, as a finality with which man is confronted, but as an expression of God's will." *The Prophets*, p. 231.

[26]This is undoubtedly, the basis of Heschel's idea of God's perfection. Since God's essence is never grasped (*God in Search of Man*, p. 160), the direction of the mind is altered and focused on His intention. Heschel makes this clear in the following. "How do we know that our interpretation of what is given to us in moments of religious insight is correct? How do we know that it is a living God, the creator of heaven and earth, whose concern reached the soul? What is the standard by which to test the veracity of religious insights? Such a standard would have to be an idea, not an event. It would have to be an ultimate idea, worthy of serving as an identification of the divine and at the same time the supreme idea in human thinking, a universal idea. Such an idea is *oneness or love*, which is an expression of oneness. All knowledge and understanding in science, art, ethics, as well as in religion, rest upon its validity. Oneness is the norm, the standard and the goal. If in the afterglow of a religious insight we can see a way to gather up our scattered lives, to unite what lies in strife – we know it is a guidepost on His way."

Katz, even though he does not supply the idea (p. 126), points to the fact that Berkovits misses Heschel's idea of perfection and its context by trying to inject a medieval notion. "There is a curious blindness to Berkovits' appeal to the medievals. He notes that Maimonides rejected the attributes of emotional predicates to God on the philosophical grounds of God's mutability. To make such attributions would challenge God's immutability and hence His perfection according to Maimonides' inherited Aristotelian notion of perfection. What Berkovits fails to appreciate is that the notion of perfection here involved is perhaps inappropriate and needs to be rethought. Heschel makes this precise point and Berkovits refers to it (p. 202), but Berkovits misses the force of this remark thinking it is only a historical point about the origin of the Eleatic idea of perfection." Katz, p. 126.

Merkle (p. 133), without taking note of the phenomenological background, notes the changeless essence of God and the changing intention of God. "Pathos may not be 'an essential attribute of God,' but Heschel would have to admit that passibility is. For pathos is only possible in a being that is in essence passible. But this does not mean that the divine essence is changeable. The fact that God's modes of reacting to the world are changeable does not mean that God changes in essence. To be in essence passible is to be by nature a being who may change modes of action and reaction; to have a passible essence is to have a changing nature – for example, now human, now divine, or now living now inanimate. God's nature may be immutable while the modes of God's being-in-relation may change. Specifically, while God *is* the transcendent, transitive concern for being, the expressions of that concern are historical and subject to change."

[27] The analogy between divine pathos and prophetic sympathy is based on intentionality. This is the meaning of Heschel's ontological statement about the Bible. "The Bible speaks of man as having been created in the likeness of God, establishing the principle of an analogy of being. In his very being, man has something in common with God. Beyond the analogy of being, the Bible teaches the principle of an analogy in acts. Man may act in the likeness of God. It is this likeness of acts – 'to walk in His ways' – that is the link by which man may come close to God. To live in such likeness is the essence of imitation of the Divine." *God in Search of Man*, p. 289.

[28] *Man Is Not Alone*, p. 144.

[29] *God in Search of Man*, pp. 18-19.

[30] *The Prophets*, p. 231.

[31] *Ibid.*, p. 256.

[32] See *Man is Not Alone*, pp. 111-123. The perfection and oneness of God does not originate in a speculative position. It may seem that Heschel is ignoring the classical attempt to defend these positions because he does not see them as primary in importance. Heschel's strategy is to present the oneness and perfection of God as it arose in the biblical and rabbinic contexts, apart from initial metaphysical concerns. The phenomenology of God's oneness and perfection is intuited through the history of God's interaction with Israel. God's oneness and perfection can only be intuited as an ideal form of relation (see above note 6). Heschel never implies that this contradicts the classical position, but only that it is a superior explanation of God and man because it does not leave man in existential isolation.

[33] "Indeed, prophecy would be impossible were the divine pathos in its particular structure a necessary attribute of God. If the structure of the pathos were immutable and remained unchanged even after the people had 'turned', prophecy would lose its function, which is precisely to influence man as to bring about a change in the divine pathos of rejection and affliction." *The Prophets*, p. 231.

[34] "The greatest challenge to the biblical language was how to reconcile in words the awareness of God's transcendence with His overwhelming livingness and concern. Had the biblical man recoiled from using anthropomorphic words, he never would have uttered; 'The Lord is my shepherd, I shall not want.' On the other hand, to assume that the psalmist, in using the word 'shepherd' had the image of a shepherd in his mind is to misunderstand the meaning of that passage." *The Prophets*, p. 276.

[35] *The Prophets*, pp. 259-260.

[36] "The idea of the divine pathos is not a personification of God but an exemplification of divine reality, an illustration or illumination of His concern. It does not represent a substance, but an act or a relationship." *The Prophets*, p. 273.

[37] "All expressions of pathos are attempts to set forth God's aliveness. One must not forget that all our utterances about Him are woefully inadequate. But when taken to be allusions rather than descriptions, understatements rather than adequate accounts, they are aids in evoking our sense of His realness." *The Prophets*, p. 277.

[38] "In the light of these structural categories, religious events must be divided into two types. They are experienced either as a turning of a transcendent Being toward man, or as a turning of man toward a transcendent Being. The first may be called *anthropotropic*, the second *theotropic*...Prophetic inspiration as a pure act may be defined as anthropotropism, as a turning of God toward man, a turning in the direction of man." *The Prophets*, p. 440.

[39] "Nonetheless, the greatest problems of all are the functional problems, or those of the 'constitution of consciousness-objectivities.' [These problems] concern the way in which noeses, e.g., with respect to Nature, by animating stuff and combining it into manifold-unitary continua and syntheses bring about consciousness of something such that the Objective unity of the objectivity allows being harmoniously 'made known', 'legitimated' and 'rationally' determined. In this sense '*function*' (in an entirely different sense in contrast to the mathematical one) is something wholly unique, grounded in the pure *essence* of noesis. Consciousness is precisely consciousness 'of' something; it is of its essence to bear in itself 'sense', so to speak, the quintessence of 'soul', 'spirit', 'reason'. Consciousness is not a name for 'psychical complexes', for 'contents' fused together, for 'bundles' or streams of 'sensations' which, without sense in themselves, also cannot lend any 'sense' to whatever mixture; it is rather through and through 'consciousness', the source of all reason and unreason, all legitimacy and illegitimacy, all reality and fiction, all value and disvalue, all deed and misdeed....The point of view of function is the central one for phenomenology....In place of analysis and comparison, description and classification restricted to single particular mental processes, consideration arises of single particularities from the 'teleological' point of view of their function, of making possible a 'synthetical unity'." *Ideas*, pp. 207-208.

This function, in terms of the noesis and the noema, must be understood as components of a single act of consciousness as Lauer points out. "Rather the terms signify that the one act is structured in two ways, the one real and the other intentional, and can, therefore, be analyzed in two distinct ways. We might say that the noesis is the intentional act *looked at* as a real subjective operation, while the noema is the same act *looked at* as intentionally structured. It is the function of the act as noetic to 'give' a sense; it is the function of the same act as noematic to 'contain' an objective sense." *The Triumph of Subjectivity*, p. 93.

[40] *The Prophets*, p. 231.

Chapter Eight

The Content of Revelation

The noetic-noematic act of consciousness which provides the basic structure of Heschel's idea of revelation, includes a specific concept of content. This content has two aspects: a noetic and a noematic aspect. According to Husserl, the meaning of the intentive mental process and the meaning as meant each possess a content.

> As soon as we go into it more precisely we are immediately cognitively aware that indeed the distinction between 'content' and 'object' is to be made not only for the 'consciousness', for the intentive mental process, but also for the *noema taken in itself*. Thus the noema too is related to an object and possesses a 'content' by 'means' of which it relates to the object; in which case the object is the same as that of the noesis; as then the 'parallelism' again completely confirms itself.[1]

The intentional object of consciousness, *the something* which is constituted in consciousness, has a specific content, the meaning as meant. In the case of prophetic consciousness, as in any act of consciousness, each act has its "What."[2] This allows the phenomenologist to

> acquire by explication and conceptual comprehension a closed set of formal or material, materially determined or 'undetermined' ('emptily' meant) 'predicates' and these in their modified signification determine that 'content' of the object-core of the noema which is spoken of.[3]

This noematic content is available in a separate and central noematic moment, not only as a predicate.[4] Heschel's use of the noetic-noematic correlation as the foundation of prophetic consciousness and its noematic content for the intentional object, entails a content for revelation that many of Heschel's critics have not fully understood. The functional nature of pathos, the object of communication between God and man, implies a content in revelation, but does so in a way that many have found confusing. This confusion is most unfortunate because Heschel is clear and thorough about the content of revelation.

The first content of revelation considered by Heschel is explicitly treated. The noetic content of the prophetic act is evident in the personalities and words of the prophets themselves. In principle, disagreement over the existence of this content is futile. Its purpose may be argued, but its validity is certain.[5]

> The noetic character of prophecy is reflected in most of its aspects. Its message had to be relevant to the contemporary situation and capable of changing the minds of those who held the power to change the situation. The Inspirer in whose name they spoke was not a God of mystery, but a God who has a design for history, Whose will and law are known to His people. The prophet is not a person who has had an experience, but one who has a task, and the marks of whose existence are the consistency and wholeheartedness in the dedication to it. The noetic character of the prophetic experience is, furthermore, reflected in the noetic character of prophetic utterance. Unlike the stammering of the ecstatic or the language of negation of the mystic, the prophet's word is like fire, like a hammer which breaks the rock in pieces.[6]

Without ignoring the most fundamental texts and purposes of Heschel, it is impossible to contend that the noetic content of revelation is absent. In fact this is the main purpose of the first eleven chapters of *The Prophets*, which include expositions on some of the prophet's lives.

The major point of confusion concerns the noematic content of revelation. Is the content of revelation, according to Heschel, only subjective and not objective? Is there an objective content of revelation that is tied to the moment of revelation? If attention is given only to the noetic content of prophecy there would seem to be no content in the pure event. But, Heschel is adamant about this content and its link to the moment of revelation.

> And yet mere attachment to events does not fully express the essence of Jewish living. Event is a formal category, describing the fact of pure happening. However, to speak of a pure event, of an event in and by itself, is to speak of an artificial abstraction that exists nowhere except in the minds of some theologians. The moment of revelation must not be separated from the content or substance of revelation. Loyalty to the norms and thoughts conveyed in the event is as essential as the reality of the event. Acceptance was not complete, the fulfillment has not occurred. The decisive moment is yet to come. The event must be fulfilled, not only believed in. What was expected at Sinai comes about in the moment of a good deed. A commandment is a foresight, a deed is a fulfillment. The deed completes the event. Revelation is but a beginning, our deeds must continue, our lives must complete it.[7]

Since this objective content is not an abstraction, another question must be put to Heschel. His contention that revelation has transcendental meaning must be grounded in the event as a formal category. What is the content of revelation qua meaning and truth? Does an objective content of revelation exist and if it does, does revelation have any content that can be identified with judgments of truth? These questions all focus on the same aspect of the problem and originate from the same problem. If there is no objective content of revelation, then there is no way to authenticate any particular content of revelation.[8] We would then be led to the conclusion that Heschel's subjectivity, even though it isn't irrational, makes no ultimate or ontological claims. This is clearly not the case. Heschel makes many statements, from an internal theological point of view, that support the position of an objective content of revelation. Many of these statements are centered around halachah as an objective aspect of religious life. Yet, citing these statements concerning the fixed nature of halachah does not prove that Heschel held there was an ideal objective content of revelation. The statements about halachah only support a procedural strategy about halachah and do not lend themselves to an extrapolation of philosophical ideas. At best these statements lead to a metahalachic stance. As has been suggested from the beginning, Heschel's methodological statements must first be examined.

There are no methodological statements which would suggest that Heschel rejects an objective content of revelation. Indeed, every methodological statement indicates that Heschel thought there was an objective content of revelation.[9] The doubt or confusion about Heschel's position exists because the objective status of this content is impossible to define or describe. The use of the phenomenological method, which alone is responsible for the accessibility of revelation and its content, precludes any natural description of revelation and its content.[10] Any reference to intellectual substance or natural morality cannot exist within the limits of the phenomenological reduction. Our examination must turn to his understanding of language.

Heschel's explanation of the status of the content of revelation is buried within his examination of prophetic language. Heschel, in *God in Search of Man*, where he considers "The Prophetic Understatement," explains the phrase, "God spoke."[11] He identifies three possible positions which explain the phrase and the content of revelation. The words of the prophets can be understood either, literally, symbolically or responsively.[12] These positions, although placed in connection to Heschel's theory of language, must be seen in the context of another of Heschel's assumptions about revelation. Heschel never equates the event of revelation with man's experience of it.

> If revelation were *only* a psycho-physical act, then it would be little more than a human experience, an event in the life of man. Yet just as a work of sculpture is more than the stone in which it is carved, so is

revelation *more* than a human experience. True, a revelation that did not become known by experience would be like a figure carved in the air. Still its being a human experience is but a part of what really happened in revelation, and we must, therefore, not equate the event of revelation with man's experience of revelation.[13]

This idea is significant as it partially underlies Heschel's rejection of literal-mindedness. The ineffable aspect of revelation demands that language can never portray revelation accurately.[14] There has never been a complete match or identification of the content of revelation and the language that conveys it.[15] Furthermore, there can never be a complete match or identification of the content of revelation and the language used to explain it. These results are an outcome of an idea that has already been considered. Heschel's distinction of the idea, the claim and the result of revelation was predicated on the exact same point. The result of the idea of revelation is not identical with the event.

It is, therefore, necessary to distinguish between three aspects of the problem of revelation: *the idea, the claim* and *the result*. The idea of revelation we discussed in the previous chapter. It is the claim to which we will turn now before we discuss the words or the result.[16]

The words, i.e. the written text of the Bible, are the result of the event of revelation and not coterminous nor coextensive with it.[17] The prophet is responsible for the phrasing used to convey the message and its noetic content.[18] This is Heschel's point in the rejection of a literal content for revelation.

The surest way of misunderstanding revelation is to take it literally, to imagine that God spoke to the prophet on a long-distance telephone.[19]

Not only is there a theological point to Heschel's discussion here, there is a phenomenological one as well. The object of revelation, pathos, must be identified with the content of revelation according to Heschel. But, Heschel insists that the words are themselves not the terminus ad quem of revelation. In phenomenological terms, things do not exist in consciousness like matches in a box. Objects are constituted in consciousness by a creative act of intuition. Revelation is not an interference with nature.[20] Pathos, and its content, are therefore not available except through the creative intuition of the prophet. They can only be recaptured through the noetic-noematic correlation and its attendant act of intuition. There is no direct reference between object and content, such that the words used to convey revelation can also be identified as the content.[21] Nonetheless, there is an objective meaning as meant in consciousness. This is certainly the meaning and context of the following paragraph and its rejection of a literal content. Here, the theological and phenomenological aspects of Heschel's thought come together.

> The meaning of revelation is given to those who are mystery-minded, not to those who are literal-minded, and decisive is not the chronological fact but the theological fact; decisive is that which happened between God and the prophet rather than that which happened between the prophet and the parchment. We accept the authority of the Pentateuch not because it is Mosaic, but because Moses was a prophet.[22]

This rejection of the literal content of revelation is but one aspect of Heschel's treatment of the problem. With equal disdain and vigor Heschel also denies that revelation has a symbolic content.

> 'God spoke.' Is it to be taken symbolically: He did not speak, yet it was as if He did? The truth is what is literally true to us is a metaphor compared with what is metaphysically real to God. A thousand years to us are a day to Him. And when applied to Him our mightiest words are feeble understatements. And yet, that 'God spoke' is not a symbol. A symbol does not raise a world out of nothing. Nor does a symbol call a Bible into being. The speech of God is not less but more than literally real.[23]

This repudiation of the symbolic content of revelation is not an isolated remark by Heschel. It fits Heschel's encompassing phenomenological strategy which seeks to understand what takes place in the prophet and postprophetic man when he is touched by God's pathos.[24] Heschel is examining the immediacy of God's reality and not its logical representation.[25] Heschel is not at all interested in discovering a supermundane reality through an intellectual strategy.

> Symbolism is so alluring because it promises to rehabilitate beliefs and rituals that have become meaningless to the mind. Yet, what it accomplishes is to reduce belief to make-believe, observance to ceremony, prophecy to literature, theology to esthetics....The quest for symbols is a *trap* for those who seek the truth. Symbols may either distort what is literally true or profane what is ineffably real. They may, if employed in the inner chamber of the mind, distort our longing for God into mere esthetics....Symbolism undermines the certainty of history, implying that even God did not succeed in conveying His will to us, and that we did not succeed in understanding His will. Man speaks in symbols; God speaks in events and commands. Realizing all this, one begins to wonder whether symbolism is an authentic category of prophetic religion. Or whether it is not a device of higher apologetics, a method of rationalization?[26]

What does all this do for Heschel? The rejection of these positions would seem to leave Heschel without a defensible strategy vis-à-vis the consciousness or content of revelation. Literalism and symbolism seem to include the most viable explanations of the content of revelation. Heschel does not want to deny that the event literally took place and he does not want to symbolize revelation reducing its meaning to a fiction.[27]

The explanation of this dilemma is found in Heschel's description of religious language. Heschel's paradigm of prophecy in contrast to mysticism clearly signifies a content in the prophetic act.[28] According to Heschel, "In all forms of prophetic experience the content, the word, proceeds from a personal Inspirer rather than from a mysterious unknown."[29] If this is so, then Heschel's theory of religious language must negate the literal and symbolic content of revelation and propose a third alternative.

Heschel's use of language is summarized systematically in one location in his work. Not coincidentally it is found in the section of revelation in *God in Search of Man*, immediately following Heschel's guidelines for the treatment of the idea of revelation. Heschel outlines five points which define his theory of religious language. These five points are,

> (1) things and words have many meanings. (2) the prophet's statements are understatements. (3) the language of the prophet is the language of grandeur and mystery. (4) there is a distinction between descriptive and indicative words. (5) the statements of the prophets must be taken responsively.[30]

It is clear that Heschel considers these five points exhaustive and comprehensive. Concerning the content of revelation, the fourth and fifth points directly bear on the issue.

The distinction of descriptive and indicative language is present at the outset of any phenomenological examination. The fluidity of words and reality that is sought with indicative usage incorporates the intuition of the participant in the event. Within the limits of the phenomenological reduction, the objects of nature and science are not regarded for their existence or nonexistence. Pathos, the essential phenomenological object, is understood because it arouses the sympathy of the prophet. The interrelation of "objects" and consciousness produces a meaning. According to Heschel, there is an objective content in indicative words but the response of the participant is essential to the formation of that content. Clearly this content has no natural objective nor any abstract status. It is a content born of correlation.

> There are two kinds of words; descriptive words which stand in a fixed relation to conventional and definite meanings, such as the concrete nouns, chair, table, or the terms of science; and indicative words which

stand in a fluid relation to ineffable meanings and, instead of describing, merely intimate something which we intuit but cannot fully comprehend. The content of words such as God, time, beauty, eternity cannot be faithfully imagined or reproduced in our minds. Still they convey a wealth of meaning to our sense of the ineffable. Their function is not to call up a definition in our minds but to introduce us to a reality which they signify. The function of descriptive words is to evoke an idea which we already possess in our minds, to evoke *preconceived meanings*. Indicative words have another function. What they call forth is not so much a memory but a response, ideas unheard of, meanings not fully realized before.[31]

The content of indicative words has no natural preconceived meaning. It can only be examined within a phenomenological reduction. Heschel's examples of descriptive words in the quote above, confirm his rejection of the natural attitude and its scientific validity. The prophetic act of perceiving and the object of perception are fundamental to Heschel's theory of language and his idea of the content of revelation. The correlation of object and content depends on the ability of the prophet to meet the transcendental aspect of reality and confirm it in his existence. The objective content of revelation is not an object "outside" the realm of man. It is an event in his life and according to Heschel, must be seen as a content that he supplies.

> By insisting upon the objective revelational character of the Bible, dogmatic theology has often lost sight of the profound and decisive share of man. The prophet is not a passive recipient, a recording instrument, affected from without without participation of heart and will, nor is he a person who acquires his vision by his own strength and labor. The prophet's personality is rather a unity of inspiration and experience, invasion and response. For every object outside him, there is a feeling inside him, for every event or revelation to him, there is a reaction by him; for every glimpse of truth he is granted there is a comprehension he must achieve. Even in the moment of the event he is, we are told, an active partner in the event. His response to what is disclosed to him turns revelation into a dialogue. In a sense, prophecy consists of a revelation of God and a *co-revelation of man*. The share of the prophet manifested itself not only in what he was able to give but also in what he was unable to receive.[32]

The religious language of the Bible is thoroughly responsive based on the interaction of God and man. The content of the Bible is grasped on a level of meaning which surpasses figurative and literal meaning. Heschel claims that words, in a responsive manner, act as clues to the meaning of the event from which they proceed. As such, responsive words have an ontological function. They are essential to the ontological presupposition which allows for preconceptual knowledge based on the phenomenological reduction (see Chapter Five).

The wind in the line quoted above is not a figure of speech. To take it *figuratively*, to regard it as referring to something else than a wind, is to misunderstand the poet's experience and intention. Yet, to take it literally in the same sense in which the meteorologist knows it is to cling to a level of meaning different than the level on which the poet sensed it. It is the wind on the metasymbolic level of meaning that the poet is referring to. Words used in this sense must neither be taken literally nor figuratively but *responsively*. To take a word literally means to reproduce in our mind an idea which the word denotes and with which it is definitely associated in our memory. It is apparent that only descriptive words can be taken literally. To take a descriptive word figuratively is to assume that the author is speaking double talk; saying one thing, he means another. It is apparent that only metaphoric expressions must be taken figuratively. Indicative words must be taken responsively. In order to understand them we must part with preconceived meanings; cliches are of no avail. They are not portraits but *clues*, serving us as guides, suggesting a line of thinking. This indeed is our situation in regard to a statement such as 'God spoke.' It refers to an idea that is not at home in the mind, and the only way to understand its meaning is by *responding* to it. We must adapt our minds to a meaning unheard of before. The word is but a clue; the real burden of understanding is upon the mind and soul of the reader.[33]

The noetic-noematic correlation which forms the basis of prophetic consciousness relies on an act of judgment based on "originally presentive intuitions."[34] It is the purpose of Heschel's use of language to preserve these intuitions. The ontological response required through the Heschelian use of language is based on his conception of the language of presence.[35]

Plato thinks of god *in the image of an idea;* the prophets think of God *in the image of personal presence.* To the prophets, God was not a Being of Whose existence they were convinced in the way in which a person is convinced of the truth of an idea. He was a Being Who is supremely real and staggeringly present. They could not use the language of *essence;* they had to use the language of *presence.* They did not try to depict Him; they tried to present Him, to make Him present. In such an effort only words of grandeur and intensity, not abstractions, can be of any avail.[36]

The words which result from revelation and determine the ontological status of the content of revelation are absolutely based in the noetic-noematic correlation that Heschel posits for prophecy. This is the only absolute comprehensible by man. Not God in His essence, but God in a relation of mutual significance to man, in a presentive intuition, creates the content of revelation.[37] Any attempt to isolate the content of revelation in Heschel's theology as a natural human product or construction or as an absolute object for God is unfaithful to the ideal phenomenological context and to the texts themselves.

> Thus the Bible is more than the word of God: it is the word of God *and* man; a record of both revelation and response; the drama of covenant between God and man. The canonization and preservation of the Bible are the work of Israel.[38]

There is still one outstanding question that needs treatment. Heschel recognizes the positive content of revelation in a phenomenological correlation. This content must be subjected to the same philosophical principles that form its structure or it will lose its authenticity. Since this content forms the essence of Heschel's theology his theological rhetoric must retain the principles incorporated in the content. But, not only must the principles be retained, a positive content must be theologically and not only phenomenologically ascertained.

> God does not reveal Himself; He only reveals His way. Judaism does not speak of God's self-revelation, but the revelation of His teaching for man. The Bible reflects God's revelation of His relation to history, rather than a revelation of His very self.[39]

It is clear that philosophically, there is no generic concept of content in Heschel's theology.[40] Revelation has no content except the particular content that is available in a noetic-noematic correlation in the consciousness of the individual prophet. The origin of the content is ineffably located in God. The phenomenological objectivity of the content of revelation depends on a response of the prophet. This phenomenology precludes a content that is absolutely fixed and describable. There can be no content of revelation without interpretation and interpretation is subjected to all the vicissitudes of time.[41] This is the meaning of Heschel's phrase, "As a report about revelation the Bible itself is *a midrash.*"[42] Revelation has a thoroughly dynamic structure that depends on the interpretive powers of the prophet and postprophetic man. The ideal content of revelation may possess identical meaning for different prophets but never the same expression.

> There is another aspect to the part played by the prophet. According to the Rabbis, 'The same idea is revealed to many prophets, but no two prophets use the same expression.' The fact that the four hundred prophets of King Ahab employed the same phrases was regarded as proof that they were not divinely inspired. When in the court of justice two people testifying to the same event use identical language, they are suspected of having conspired to bear false witness. The prophets bear witness to an event. The event is divine, but the formulation is done by the individual prophet. According to this conception, the idea is revealed; the expression is coined by the prophet. The expression

'the word of God' would not refer to the word as a sound or a combination of sounds....Out of the experience of the prophets came the words, words that try to interpret what they perceived. To this very day, these words make present what happened in the past. As the meaning and wonder of the event inspired the spiritual comprehension of the prophet, the meaning and wonder of the Biblical words continue to inspire the understanding of man.[43]

Theologically and phenomenologically the content of revelation is the idea revealed to the prophet. The function of "words" in the content of revelation is not to convey sounds or mystical visions.[44] As the result of the content of revelation, "words" indicate the ideas with which God inspired the prophet. These "words" cannot describe the content of revelation because that would deny the ineffable origin of the event.[45] These "words" are charges or instructions[46] which are completed by the interpretation and expression of the prophet.[47] Heschel never conceives of revelation as an appeal to man's conscience, even though conscience operates in the prophet's interpretation of the event. Conscience does not legislate the content of revelation.[48] Theologically, Heschel is basing this entire idea of revelation on the classical idea of mitzvah.[49] Phenomenologically he is providing the structure of the prophet's inspiration and postprophetic man's attachment to the content of that inspiration.[50] According to Heschel, the phenomenological structure of the event of revelation never generalizes or creates an abstraction of the event setting aside its content. It is the explicit purpose of Heschel's phenomenology to uncover the content of revelation without destroying its ineffable character nor reducing its uniqueness.[51]

> Thus, while the ineffable is a term of negation indicating a limitation of expression, its content is intensely affirmative, denoting an *allusiveness* to something meaningful, for which we possess no means of expression.[52]

Revelation for Heschel is fundamentally an event filled with positive content that undercuts fundamentalism (including naive empiricism and rationalism). According to Heschel, revelation is that one event in which rational and nonrational knowledge interact without destroying each other. Any other presentation of Heschel's idea of revelation ignores the profundity of his theological critique and ultimately lapses into a naive philosophical realism.

> In our encounter with the Bible we may take either a fundamentalist attitude which regards every word as literally valid, making no distinction between the eternal and the temporal, and allowing no place for personal or historic understanding, or for the voice of conscience. Or we may take a rationalist attitude which, taking science as the touchstone for religion, regards scripture as a poetic product or

myth, useful to men of an inferior civilization and therefore outdated at any later period of history. Philosophy of religion must carry on a battle on two fronts, trying to winnow false notions of the fundamentalist, and to dampen the over-confidence of the rationalists. The ultimate task is to lead us to a higher plane of knowledge and experience, to attachment through understanding.[53]

---

[1] *Ideas*, p. 311.

[2] *Ibid.*, p. 312.

[3] *Ibid.*, pp. 312-313.

[4] *Ibid.*, p. 313.

[5] This is clearly Heschel's point in the introduction to *Die Prophetie*, where he argues against a political, psychological or dogmatic theological interpretation of the content of the prophets lives and utterances.

[6] *The Prophets*, p. 360.

[7] *God in Search of Man*, p. 217.

[8] This would obviously involve Heschel's position with other problems. Heschel's idea of revelation would have no necessary link to the content of revelation in Jewish sources that preceded him. This regression would extend to all Jewish sources without exception and would ultimately involve Heschel in an absurdity. He would be using the events and acts of the prophets to explain his own idea of revelation without considering if they had any validity. I have demonstrated both internal and external evidence that shows how Heschel addressed this problem. It remains to be demonstrated, in the next chapter, how this affected Heschel's understanding of rabbinic theology and led to the thesis of *Torah Min Hashomayim*.

[9] These statements are collected in Chapter Two and completely justify this position.

[10] "Is it possible to define the content of such experiences? It is not a perception of a thing, of anything physical; nor is it always a disclosure of ideas hitherto unknown. It is primarily, it seems, an enhancement of the soul, a sharpening of one's spiritual sense, an endowment with a new sensibility. It is a discovery of what is in time, rather than anything in space." *God in Search of Man*, p. 142.

[11] *Ibid.*, pp. 178-183.

[12] *Ibid.*, pp. 178-183.

[13] *Ibid.*, p. 184.

[14] *Ibid.*, pp. 184-185.

[15] Gillman's attempt, "Toward a Theology for Conservative Judaism," *Conservative Judaism*, Vol. 37(1), Fall 1983, pp. 4-22, to present Heschel's view as a critique of verbal revelation does not capture the full force of Heschel's argument. Clearly, Heschel outrightly rejects the idea that God verbally communicates with man. But this is only part of Heschel's critique of the fundamentalist view of revelation. Heschel's critique is completed by his own attempt to supply the positive content of revelation, in the light of the rejection of any fundamental attitude whatsoever. Gillman's own pedagogical and

political inclinations force Heschel's critique into a mold that serves only part of Heschel's purpose. Ultimately, this leads Gillman to consider Heschel's position within the framework of theology as myth. Heschel distinguishes his phenomenological approach from that of myth-making (*Man Is Not Alone,* p. 114, and below, note 22). Another critic of Heschel's idea of revelation, E. Dorff, *Conservative Judaism: Our Ancestors to Our Descendants,* (New York: United Synagogue of America, 1977), pp. 114-115, places Heschel's idea of revelation into a context that simply does not fit. Amongst other things, Dorff ignores Heschel's existentialist position and the outright denial that God "dictates" his will and man simply writes it down. Dorff assumes that according to Heschel, "God spoke words" (p. 122), even though the prophets recorded what they understood (p. 123). This assumption completely misconceives Heschel's phenomenological explanation of the meaning of the statement "God spoke," (see *God in Search of Man,* p. 265). Dorff falls back on a literal explanation of the content of revelation, which Heschel emphatically denies. Since Dorff does not offer any argumentation, only his use of categories can help us locate the source of his error. Dorff, in criticizing and cataloguing different ideas of revelation in the Conservative movement does not use the category of the content of revelation. This absence has probably led him to conclude that the dictating of God's will is the nature of revelation according to Heschel. The nature of revelation, because of its content, is that of a correlation, which absolutely denies the dictation of God's will to man for Heschel (see note 10 above). Gillman's attempt (p. 24) to offer a textual reason for the discrepancy between his own and Dorff's view, is not validated by the evidence marshalled here. Every Heschelian text concerning revelation must be taken into consideration for a coherent view of the content of that idea. As has been demonstrated, no such text denies the basic correlation of the content of revelation.

[16] *God in Search of Man,* p. 177.

[17] "Are the words of Scripture coextensive and identical with the words of God? In the eyes of those who experience daily their inability to grasp fully the meaning of a Scriptural verse, such a question represents an attempt to compare the hardly known with the totally unknown." *Ibid.,* pp. 258-259.

[18] *Ibid.,* p. 265.

[19] *Ibid.,* p. 178.

[20] *Ibid.,* p. 211, "Revelation is not an act of interfering with the normal course of natural processes but the act of instilling a new creative moment into the course of history." This effects other Heschelian ideas as Rothschid points out. "The act of revelation – which is not to be construed as an interference with natural processes, but which is the ingression of a new creative moment into the course of history – supplies the key to creation, which is itself an act of primeval revelation." Rothschild, *Between God and Man,* p. 20.

[21] E. Kaplan in *Language and Reality in Abraham J. Heschel's Philosophy of Religion,* JAAR, XLI/1, (March, 1973), p. 103, also points out this incompatibility of content and expression. Kaplan incorrectly identifies the content of the Bible as "God's essential nature," which Heschel thoroughly denies (see the beginning of Chapter Seven).

22 *God in Search of Man,* pp. 257-258.

23 *Ibid.,* p. 180.

24 This point escapes the attention of Gillman in his presentation of the problem of revelation that Heschel faces, "Toward a Theology for Conservative Judaism," *Conservative Judaism,* Vol. 37(1), Fall 1983, pp. 4-22. The centrality of revelation and the theological critique of revelation that it implies for Heschel are correctly ascertained by Gillman. But, he fails to realize that the Tillichian solution of symbols that he proposes, is itself part of Heschel's critique. Heschel, in conjunction with the sources cited below rejecting symbolism, repudiates the ontology that supports them. Some of these positions have been noted in Chapter Three and will be ontologically formulated in the final chapter of this work. Gillman's interpretation of Torah as a midrash (p. 6), leads to his symbolic interpretation of revelation. "All of these positions affirm a decisive and active human role in the formulation of the content of revelation as we have it. Torah then is indeed a midrash, a human interpretation of some more remote content that is itself inherently beyond direct human apprehension. Whatever else it may be, it is also, then, a cultural document, reflecting the idiom of the societies and periods in which it was composed. Or to use a more contemporary formulation, it is an elaborate, complex myth (p. 6)." Gillman fails to distinguish between the prophetic and postprophetic mind. According to Heschel, the prophetic mind does not experience "some more remote content that is itself beyond human comprehension." The postprophetic mind experiences the content of revelation indirectly, but not as a remote content. The underlying asumption for Heschel is precisely that the content of revelation for the post-prophetic mind, although experienced indirectly, is not remote. It is present to man, just as the reality of God is present to man. Gillman's conclusion that the Torah is a cultural document, the priority of which he emphasizes in the centrality of revelation, cannot be extended to Heschel. To be sure, Heschel sees the Torah as a cultural document, that is, in its historical and communal context. But, the correlation of man and God in prophetic consciousness is its foremost significance for revelation, according to Heschel. Interpretation of the document is not made on the basis of its historical content but on the basis of its revealed content, which may or may not be subject to historical scrutiny. History may influence the development of interpretation but is not a necessary condition for interpretation even though the document itself is thoroughly historical. The authenticity of interpretation can never give up the revealed content of the document because it infuses the entire document since its inception, that is, in the event itself. Historical development is an accretion, a process and not an event, thereby minimizing its significance for prophetic inspiration (*God in Search of Man,* p. 209).

25 A. Heschel, *Man's Quest for God; Studies in Prayer and Symbolism,* (New York: Charles Scribner's Sons, 1954), p. 144.

26 A. Heschel, *Man's Quest for God; Studies in Prayer and Symbolism,* (New York: Charles Scribner's Sons, 1954), pp. 142-143.

27 *Man's Quest for God,* p. 144.

28 *The Prophets,* p. 364.

[29] *Ibid.*, p. 365.

[30] *God in Search of Man*, p. 178.

[31] *Ibid.*, pp. 181-182.

[32] *Ibid.*, pp. 259-260.

[33] *Ibid.*, p. 182.

[34] *Ideas*, p. 36.

[35] *The Prophets*, pp. 274-275.

[36] *Ibid.*, p. 275.

[37] "At Sinai God revealed His word, and Israel revealed the power to respond. Without the power to respond, without the fact that there was a people willing to accept, to hear, the divine command, Sinai would have been impossible. For Sinai consisted of both a divine proclamation and a human perception. It was a moment in which *God was not alone.*" *God in Search of Man*, p. 260.

[38] *Ibid.*, pp. 260-261.

[39] *Ibid.*, p. 261.

[40] "Revelation is not a voice crying in the wilderness, but an act of received communication. It is not simply an act of disclosing, but an act of disclosing *to* someone, the bestowal of a content, God addressing the prophet. There is no intransitive aimless revelation in prophecy. God's word is directed to man." *The Prophets*, p. 437.

[41] "Thus Judaism is based upon a minimum of revelation and a maximum of interpretation, upon the will of God and upon the understanding of Israel. For that understanding we are dependent upon Israel's unwritten tradition. The prophets' inspirations and the sages' interpretations are equally important." *God in Search of Man*, p. 274.

[42] *Ibid.*, p. 185.

[43] *Ibid.*, p. 265.

[44] "What is the ultimate nature of the sacred words which tradition preserves? These words are not made of paper but of life. The task is not to reproduce in sound what is preserved in graphic signs; the task is to resurrect its life, to feel its pulse, so that the life within the words should reproduce its kind within our lives. Indeed, there is a heritge of insight as there is a tradition of words and rituals. It is a heritage easily forfeited, easily forgotten." *The Insecurity of Freedom*, (New York: Schocken Books, 1972), pp. 118-119.

[45] *God in Search of Man*, p. 184.

[46] "His knowledge of man precedes man's knowledge of Him, while man's knowledge of Him comprehends only what God asks of man. This is the essential content of prophetic revelation." *Man Is Not Alone*, p. 129.

[47] "The reception of the word must be followed by the proclamation of the word. The prophet's role is that of a mediator; neither the author nor the final addressee, he stands between God and the people." *The Prophets*, p. 361.

[48] "Those who call upon us to rely on our inner voice fail to realize that there is more than one voice in us, that the power of selfishness may easily subdue the pangs of conscience. The conscience, moreover, is often celebrated for what is beyond its ability. The conscience is not a legislative power, capable of teaching us what we ought to do but rather a preventive agency; a brake, not a guide; a fence, not a way. It raises its voice after a wrong deed has been

committed, but often fails to give us direction in advance of our actions." *God in Search of Man,* p. 298.

49 The section on revelation, in *God in Search of Man,* is immediately followed with a statement on the function of mitzvot. "Knowledge of God is knowledge of living with God. Israel's religious existence consists of three inner attitudes: engagement to the living God to whom we are accountable; engagement to Torah where His voice is audible; and engagement to His concern as expressed in mitsvot (commandments)." *God in Search of Man,* p. 281.

50 "The Bible is an eternal expression of a continuous concern; God's cry for man; not a letter for one who sent out a message and remained indifferent to the attitude of the recipient. It is not a book to be read but a drama in which to participate; not a book about events but itself an event, the continuation of the event, while our being involved in it is the continuation of the response. The event will endure so long as the response will continue." *God in Search of Man,* p. 254.

51 "To convey these insights, man must use a language which is compatible with his sense of the ineffable, the terms of which do not pretend to describe, but to indicate; to point to, rather than to capture. These terms are not always imaginative; they are often paradoxical, radical or negative. The chief danger to philosophy of religion lies in the temptation to generalize what is essentially unique, to explicate what is intrinsically inexplicable, to adjust the uncommon to our common sense." *The Insecurity of Freedom,* p. 119. "The act of revelation is a mystery, while the record of revelation is a literary fact, phrased in the language of man." *God in Search of Man,* p. 258., and "We must neither reduce revelation to a matter of fact nor spiritualize the Bible and destroy its factual integrity." *God in Search of Man,* p. 259.

52 *Man Is Not Alone,* p. 22.

53 *God in Search of Man,* p. 272.

Chapter Nine

The Rabbinic Origin of Heschel's Idea of Revelation

At the center of Heschel's idea of revelation there is a content which is the product of his critique of fundamentalism and symbolism. The content of revelation is ideal in that it has an intellectual quality.[1] Heschel absolutely denies that symbols or words are the content of revelation. The prophet mediates ideas and gives them expression.[2] Therefore, the content of revelation, according to Heschel, is not coterminous nor coextensive with the words of the Bible. The Bible itself is at once both the product and the means of circumscribing the content of revelation. The main task of Heschel's theological critique is the upholding of the ineffable divine origin of the Torah.[3] Heschel's critique succeeds in doing this while denying the tenability of verbal revelation,[4] the Mosaic authorship of the Torah[5] and the identifying of the supposed Mosaic text with the one before us today.[6] Heschel's conception of the positive content of revelation is the bedrock of these critical positions. If revelation is a phenomenological fact, then it is available through the noetic-noematic correlation and is known through its content and not through any form of proof.[7] The centrality of Heschel's phenomenological presentation of the content of revelation is undeniable. This conception motivates every aspect of Heschel's theology. The apprehension of the content of revelation is the goal of phenomenological comprehension. All of the antecedents of faith gain integrity only in this context. This ideal content infuses any aspect of thought or deed in Heschel's presentation of prophecy and Judaism. Ultimately, the presentation of the ideal content of revelation through mitzvot, is the completion of revelation. The significance of the content of revelation for Heschel's theology cannot be understated and it does create a link to the past for Heschel that has not yet been examined.

The radical nature of Heschel's depth-theology, which investigates the act of believing and then the content of believing, seems to be in opposition to the vast body of rabbinic literature that interpreted and made the Bible a living text.[8] The emphasis in rabbinic literature is on the content of revelation as the focus for halachah. Rabbinic literature is not at all concerned with private moments of intuition based on a philosophical account of revelation. Seemingly, one must conclude, that Heschel's idea of revelation based on biblical prophecy is totally divorced from the substance of rabbinic literature and the fundamental development of Judaism's religious outlook.

The positive confirmation of the thesis stated above would effectively render Heschel's idea of revelation irrelevant for Judaism. His idea would be little more than a private suggestion about how the Bible *ought to have been interpreted*. It would have no consequence for a people and its civilization which have played an integral role in the exegesis of the text and events which have created and sustained them as a religious entity.[9]

It is in this context that Heschel's ideas about rabbinic Judaism's theology of revelation are significant. Heschel's idea of the content of revelation must have a rabbinic precedent or it has no authentic link to the texts and civilization from which it claims to have developed. The issues of verbal revelation, the Mosaic authorship of the Torah and the identification of the supposed Mosaic text with the text in our hands, while significant, are ancillary to Heschel's authenticity. If Heschel's idea of the content of revelation can be identified with a consistent rabbinic viewpoint, his conception of the conditions of its presentation (i.e. its verbal or nonverbal nature, its Mosaic authorship and an identical Mosaic and contemporary biblical text) do not affect the authenticity of his claims.

Heschel's own theological works, while incorporating rabbinic insights and views throughout all its aspects, do not attempt a construction of this rabbinic viewpoint. This is the task of *Torah Min Hashamayim Be-Aspaklaria Shel Ha-Dorot*. But, this major work in this area of rabbinics also makes no attempt to indicate a relation to depth-theology. Heschel seems to exclude the principles of rabbinic theology from his philosophical works and conversely, he seems to exclude the principles of depth-theology from his major work on rabbinic Judaism. What would seem like the best point of departure because of its thorough elaboration of revelation from a rabbinic point of view, *Torah Min Hashamayim*, is in fact the destination of this inquiry. Heschel's thesis in *Torah Min Hashamayim* is the basis and origin of his idea of revelation in depth-theology, but its significance and substance were not fully developed until after the publication of *God in Search of Man* in 1955. Therefore, Heschel's implicit remarks about rabbinic theology, in the context of his own theology, best indicate the direction in which he is proceeding.

The second section of *God in Search of Man,* "Revelation," begins with an enigmatic statement by Heschel.

> We have never been the same since the day on which the voice of God overwhelmed us at Sinai. It is for ever impossible for us to retreat into an age that predates the Sinaitic event. Something unprecedented happened. God revealed His name to us, and we are named after Him.[10]

Heschel, with the exception of this reference, "God revealed His name to us," never refers to the content of revelation in specific terms. It is his usual strategy to circumscribe the content of revelation using the noetic-noematic correlation, because the content of revelation can only be indicated and not described.[11] Heschel always relies on a negative description of revelation, except this one time.[12] He is always satisfied with a functional depiction of the content of revelation as has been demonstrated in Chapter Seven. This deviation from the established rabbinic practice, if not well-founded, not only makes Heschel's tie to rabbinic forms of thought tenuous, it contradicts his phenomenological thesis.

The first thing that should come to our attention is the fact that the name of God is ineffable. The one and only time Heschel refers to a specific content of revelation, it is ineffable. This is in complete agreement with Heschel's attempt to indicate the positive content of revelation without destroying the ineffable origin of the event.[13] Secondly, the one and only time Heschel refers to a specific content of revelation, it has a decidedly rabbinic overtone.

The Talmud has a discussion, in Makkot 23b and 24a, that quotes a homily of R. Simlai, which states that six hundred and thirteen mitzvot were communicated to Moses.

> R. Simlai when preaching said: Six hundred and thirteen precepts were communicated to Moses, three hundred and sixty-five negative precepts, corresponding to the number of solar days [in the year], and two hundred and forty-eight positive precepts, corresponding to the number of the members of man's body. Said R. Hamnuna: What is the [authentic] text for this? It is, *Moses commanded us* torah, *an inheritance of the congregation of Jacob,* 'torah' being in letter-value, equal to six hundred and eleven, '*I am*' and '*Thou shalt have no [other Gods]*' [not being reckoned, because] we heard from the mouth of the Might [Divine].[14]

This limitation of the content of public revelation, that Israel heard only two mitzvot from God and the rest from Moses, is based on another Talmud passage in Horayoth 8a.

> The school of Rabbi taught: Scripture says, *Which the Lord hath spoken unto Moses,* and it is also written, *That the Lord hath commanded you by the hand of Moses.* Now which is the commandment that was given in the words of the Holy One, blessed be He, and also by the hand of Moses? Surely it is that of Idolatry; for R. Ishmael has recited: [The words] *I* and *Thou shalt not have* were heard from the mouth of the Omnipotence.[15]

According to the opinion of R. Ishmael, the direct revelation of God to Israel at Sinai, consisted of the first and second commandments of the decalogue, which are ineffable. They refer directly to God who cannot be conceived of objectively. The passage from *God in Search of Man* quoted above, while not a direct quote of this rabbinic source, paraphrases and further limits the intention of R. Ishmael. Heschel's conception of revelation and its content, is based on the ineffability of these two commandments which have no direct objects. God, as the subject of the first commandment and the indirect object of the second commandment, does not receive the action of these verbs. Moreover, God cannot be seen as an object alongside of other objects. Consequently, even though the prohibited behavior is understood, the content of these commandments cannot be described through the use of natural language because God retains His ineffable status throughout them. Yet, these two are the commandments without which revelation in all its particularity, could not function. The content of these two commandments is ineffable. Hence, the ideal content of these commandments motivates and guarantees the validity of the entire relationship between God and Israel in Heschel's theology. Without these commandments and the event to which they point, there are no grounds for a correlation of God and man and no grounds for any positive content of revelation.

In his discussion of the meaning of obeying the will of God, in *Man's Quest for God,* Heschel indirectly adopts the position of R. Ishmael, described above. In criticising the misleading idea that either all or none of the law is observed, Heschel points to a rabbinic idea of revelation as a defense of his position.[16]

> Second is the assumption that every iota of the law was revealed to Moses at Sinai. This is an unwarranted extension of the rabbinic concept of revelation. 'Could Moses have learned the whole Torah? Of the Torah it says, *Its measure is longer than the earth, and broader than the sea* (Job 11:9); could, then, Moses have learned it in forty days? No it was only the principles thereof *(kelalim)* which God taught Moses' (Exodus Rabba 41:6).[17]

While this passage does not indicate the ineffablility of revelation, it supports the positive ideal content of revelation explicitly. These two references to the rabbinic concept of revelation and its content, point to Heschel's latent dependence on a rabbinic idea of revelation. The two references Heschel uses for the support of his idea of revelation are attributed to the school of R. Ishmael. He clearly uses them because he thinks his idea of revelation is an authentic extension of a rabbinic position.

The priority of ideas is not significant here. Whether or not Heschel's idea precedes his cognizance of the rabbinic position or vice versa, is of little consequence. Heschel's desire to demonstrate that his idea of depth-theology and its content of revelation is an extension of a rabbinic idea is central. The appearance of two of the three volumes of *Torah Min Hashamayim* in 1962 and 1965, which catalogue the rabbinic attitudes toward revelation, after the completion of Heschel's own theological works,[18] indicate the seriousness of the question of authenticity faced by Heschel. *Torah Min Hashamayim*, which basically catalogues two attitudes toward revelation, is a response to the problem of authenticity. It is not merely a restatement of rabbinic ideas but of the integrity of the midrashic process itself. The radical character of depth-theology, which refuses to identify the content of revelation with the text of the Bible, has its precedent in rabbinic theology according to Heschel. In the light of this precedence, the issues of verbal revelation, the Mosaic authorship of the Torah and the identification of the supposed Mosaic text with the one before us today, are of secondary importance.[19] The relation between depth-theology and rabbinic Judaism's attitudes toward revelation is an ideal relation not accessible merely through a historical-philological study.[20] If Heschel cannot demonstrate a consistent rabbinic position that treats the content of revelation ineffably, the central issue of his own concept is anchorless in the face of rabbinic tradition.

Heschel's research in *Torah Min Hashamayim* is meant to provide the basis for his own idea of revelation and to demonstrate the complex treatment that revelation received at the hands of the rabbis of the talmudic and medieval eras. Of these two purposes, only the first can command our attention here. The consistency and complexity of the treatment of revelation that Heschel perceives throughout the entire corpus of Jewish philosophy, theology and mysticism is beyond the scope of this investigation. The seminal issue here, is the effect the rabbinic material had on Heschel's own thinking.[21]

The primary thesis of *Torah Min Hashamayim* centers on the differences of the schools of R. Akiva and R. Ishmael.

> The result of this for us, is that we should not speak of the aggadic works as if they are of one texture or cloth. Just as there were different

methods in halachic matters, there were different methods in matters
of beliefs and opinions. There are those who gave *plain expositions* on
the one hand and those who gave *astonishing expositions* on the other
hand. The contrasts are many and their reasons are deep. In this book,
I shall try to prove that these contrasts are based on two ways of
thinking, and because of them the school of R. Ishmael and the school
of R. Akiva disagree.[22]

According to Heschel's analysis, the school of R. Ishmael is interested
in explaining the plain sense of the biblical text while the school of R.
Akiva treats the words of the text with astonishment because it
perceives its esoteric meaning, without concern for its logical
character.[23] Heschel's attempt to distinguish the consistent use of
certain hermeneutical devices by each of these respective schools is not
new in the history of Jewish scholarship. Previously, at least four
serious rabbinic scholars have catalogued the various hermeneutical
devices used consistently by these rabbis and their disciples.[24] The
conclusions of these scholars are almost identical. Each of them directs
attention to the consistent use of certain interpretive and legal devices
within the schools of R. Akiva and R. Ishmael, and none of them posits
a trend that indicates a doctrine or method separating the two schools
of thought.[25] Each of these scholars is satisfied with the conclusion
that the different positions concerning hermeneutical devices have no
ideal correlation. Indeed, if one were to judge the references of many of
the sayings of these rabbis without analyzing their content, one could
very well come to the same conclusion.

As we saw above, Heschel's limitation of the content of revelation
to the ineffable and its ideal correlations, was based on his use of R.
Ishmael's strategy. This would seem to lead to the conclusion that
Heschel only supports R. Ishmael and always rejects the position of R.
Akiva. It must be kept in mind that the favoring of one interpretation
over another is not always identical with favoring one strategy over
another. It should then come as no surprise that Heschel, who bases his
idea of revelation on a premise of R. Ishmael's, uses a characteristic of
R. Akiva's to explain the nature of the idea.

> In the teaching of R. Akiva, who dealt with the story of the chariot and
> entered the 'garden', a relation of feeling is joined with God. Not only
> did He redeem Israel from Egypt, 'As it were, He also redeemed
> Himself'. He teaches that the participation of The Holy One, Blessed
> Be He, with the life of Israel is not simply a matter of paying attention
> to them not simply the quality of mercy which emanates from the
> relation of mercy to His people. The suffering of compassion is a type
> of suffering from afar, the suffering of an onlooker, however the
> participation of the Holy One, Blessed Be He, is an identification, a
> matter that is part of His very nature, of His glory and essence, as it
> were He suffers with the suffering of His people. 'In every place Israel

is exiled the Presence is with them...and in the future when they return the Presence will be with them.' God is a participant in the suffering of His creatures, He is joined in a common destiny with His people, pained by its suffering, and redeemed in its redemption. In consequence of this method, that serves as a new form for the teaching of the prophets concerning THE DIVINE PATHOS, a profound revolution in religious thinking begins.[26]

The use that R. Akiva makes of this idea need not be similar to Heschel's.[27] But it is no doubt the origin of Heschel's idea of divine pathos, the object of revelation in depth-theology. This dependence on R. Akiva's idea of pathos does not exclude, in Heschel's eyes, the use of an idea of R. Ishmael's that determines the content of pathos or of revelation.

In the teaching of R. Ishmael there is a distant intellectual relationship to God. He [R. Ishmael] never speaks of the essence of the Holy One Blessed Be He, but only of his relationship to Israel. He, who tried to explain away the expressions that are inappropriate to the glory [of God], certainly would not maintain the idea of the salvation of God, neither in its content nor in its language. In his spirit these words of astonishment are said: 'And does He need the help of others?!' 'And does He need assistance?!' 'We need His glory.' The sages who did not accept the teaching of R. Akiva understood the relationship of The Holy One Blessed Be He, to Israel, as a moral relation; as it were, forced by the word and promise to our forefathers, and faithful to the covenant that He made with them. This relationship is based on will and moves to the outside. The first view stresses the divine pathos, a relationship which is dynamic view of occurrences. The second view stresses the covenant, a static relationship. The one is a matter of the soul, and the other is a matter of the will. The one stresses the spirit of the relationship of God to Israel in its own merit; the other one stresses the relationship of God to Israel in the merits of the forefathers.[28]

The position of R. Ishmael is based on a moral intention which never posits any meaning about the divine essence, but only sees meaning through the moral relationship of God and Israel itself. This point is also essential to Heschel's treatment of revelation. According to Heschel, revelation, as a transitive concern, is based on God's moral intention.[29] It is never based on God's self-existence.[30]

It is clear that Heschel, who, at certain points combines these competing ideas, does not see any implicit or explicit contradiction in them. If R. Akiva and R. Ishmael hold opposing views on such issues as poverty[31] and the acceptance of suffering,[32] to indicate but a few of their hundreds of opposing views, this does not present Heschel with a logical problem.[33] These ideas have no logical priority. They are part of an interpretive reaction to events based on intuition, in the light of a revealed text.[34] Their diametrical opposition indicates the paradox of existence to which there are no intellectual solutions because there are only personal problems.[35] Heschel's contention that R. Akiva and R. Ishmael respectively represent a transcendental and an immanent outlook, is based on a hermeneutical attitude toward reality.

> According to this the sages have two points of view. The first is the *transcendental outlook*, in which there is an intellectual method of penetrating the higher world and which seeks to understand the matters of the Torah through the heavenly prism. The second is the *immanent outlook*, which includes a modest and closed intellectual method, which is satisfied to understand the matters of the Torah through the prism of man's testimony in this world.[36]

It should be clear from this brief excursus, that the particular ideal content of revelation as seen in different legal or cultural points of view favored by either R. Akiva or R. Ishmael, while significant, is not the central issue. Heschel's attention is absorbed by the question of the content of rabbinic revelation per se. Any rabbinic strategy toward textual, historical and interpretive problems that supports Heschel's view of the nature of the content of revelation is given consideration in the two volumes of *Torah Min Hashamayim*. It is Heschel's contention that, historically, these attitudes have been systematically neglected. Of course, various exegetes, theologians and philosophers have treated these issues independently. But, it is his contention that previous to his own treatment of the rabbinic origin of this idea and its subsequent history, no one has seen it as a vital aspect of the religious tradition, as an ideal content. The history of the idea of revelation qua idea and not qua text is Heschel's concern.[37] In other words, the absolute chronology of texts demonstrating the idea, however desirable, is not absolutely necessary.

In Heschels's eyes, the distinction of ideas between R. Akiva and R. Ishmael is based squarely on their perceptions of the content of revelation.

> R. Ishmael does not hesitate to say, that there are things in the Torah Moses said on his own behalf, and that Moses heard things from the mouth of The Almighty of which he transmitted only the intention and not the exact language. And just as the Holy One, Blessed Be He, gave the prophet room to demonstrate his capacity, to be a partner in the act of prophecy, He also gave the sages room to demonstrate their capacity, to interpret according to the thirteen principles [of R. Ishmael]. Thus, there was no need for everything to be written in the Torah.[38]

R. Akiva's idea of the content of revelation is directly opposed to R. Ishmael's. According to Heschel, their ideas circumscribing the content of revelation are mutually exclusive because they require a logical judgment based on historical analysis and the categories of time and space.[39]

> In opposition to this, R. Akiva thinks, that the expansion of the Torah does not depend on the intellectual faculty of man. There is no thing which is not hinted at in the Torah; There is no law whose basis is impossible to find in Scripture. The laws are embedded in the Torah and hinted at in its letters. And the power and value of the proof that arises from the revealing of the secrets of the text is greater than that which arises from the rule of the inference drawn from a minor to a major premise.[40]

According to R. Ishmael, the Torah speaks in the language of man.[41] For Heschel this means that the Torah, as the record of revelation, may have been written down without the benefit of a direct relation to the event of prophetic inspiration and its writing may have occurred over a long period of time.[42] R. Akiva's position concerning the nature of revelation and its content, rejected by Heschel, holds the point of view opposite to R. Ishmael.

> In the school of R. Akiva they thought that everything was in the hands of heaven. The Torah in all its specificity was given from on high, and the prophet is only an instrument that receives the inspiration.[43]

Heschel's comparison of the transcendence of R. Akiva and the immanence of R. Ishmael is described by comparing the hundreds of interpretive and legal issues that he gathers. The ideal nature of all these issues points to one issue of depth-theology that is common to each of them. The nature of revelation, while not the sole motivating factor, is the fulcrum of the theological debate of these rabbinic schools. According to R. Akiva, revelation and its content are specified by God alone in a direct way to Moses who wrote it down word for word in its entirety and in a chronological order in the Torah.[44] According to R. Ishmael, revelation is an event in which the prophet plays a reciprocal role.[45] The content of revelation was not given at one time to one person[46] nor was it written down chronologically[47] in its entirety by one person.[48] The content of revelation has a divine and a human ideal character in accord with the view of R. Ishmael.[49] This agreement of Heschel with the view of R. Ishmael concerning the content of revelation, is focused on the expression, "Thus says the Lord," which also forms the basis of Heschel's treatment of the expression in *God in Search of Man*.[50]

> This difficult enigma will be solved for us when we see that the whole matter depends on a dispute of the Tannaim. According to the method of the school of R. Ishmael, every place Moses used the words 'this is the word' he transmitted the words of the Lord without addition

or deficit, or change in style. And if he used the expression, 'Thus says the Lord,' he did not transmit the word of the Lord precisely, rather he means to say: this is the will of God. According to this method, Moses was capable of changing the language of God, and of transmitting only the intention....In the school of R. Akiva they did not explain the expression 'Thus says the Lord' in this manner. [It was explained as 'this is the word'].[51]

In other words, the intention of God initiates the content of revelation and does not necessarily communicate the words which we consider to be the result of that event of revelation. While it is the expressed purpose of Heschel to demonstrate impartially the schools of thought of R. Akiva and R. Ishmael concerning their beliefs and doctrines about the nature of revelation, and how this affected commentators who followed them, Heschel clearly and consistently follows the lead of R. Ishmael on the most critical point. R. Ishmael's idea of the content of revelation guarantees the basis of Heschel's own idea and guarantees its authenticity in the light of rabbinic tradition. According to Heschel's idea of depth-theology, the content of revelation is never coterminous or coextensive with the words of the biblical text. The content of revelation has both religious and philosophical roots in Heschel's thought. But, from his position vis-à-vis the authenticity of rabbinic Judaism, Heschel's presentation of an expanded rabbinic concept underlies his desire to give a phenomenological account of the content of religious knowledge. The phenomenological treatment of religious ideas and texts, in Heschel's eyes, in no way misconstrues their content and is the only methodology which allows that content to be seen in its desired context. Moreover, it is the sole means that postprophetic man has in recovering the meaning of the biblical text, through the rabbinic tradition.

---

[1] *God in Search of Man*, p. 265.

[2] *Ibid*.

[3] *Ibid*., p. 247.

[4] "The Bible contains not only words of the prophets, but also words that came from non-prophetic lips. While it claims to convey words of inspiration, it also contains words of human search and concern. There is in the Bible God's word to man, but there is also man's word to Him and about Him; not only God's disclosure but man's insight. Prophetic experience is far removed from the reach of modern man. But the prophets were human, too; prophetic experiences were single moments in their lives beyond which lay the encounter with good and evil, light and darkness, life and death, love and hatred – issues which are as real today as they were three thousand years ago. These

perceptions reflect human, not only prophetic thinking." *God in Search of Man*, p. 26. See also *Ibid.*, p. 265.

[5] *Ibid.*, pp. 257-258.

[6] *Ibid.*, pp. 179-180, 220. Gillman, p. 5.

[7] This is the entire force of Heschel's argument in *God in Search of Man*, pp. 218-278. It is typified in the following statement, "The way to perceive the presence of God in the words of the Bible is not by inquiring whether the ideas they designate are in perfect agreement with the achievements of our reason or the common sense of man. Such agreement, granted that it could be established, would, indeed, prove that the Bible is the product of common sense or that the spirit in which it originated has nothing more to say than what reason is able to proclaim. What we must ask is whether there is any thing in the Bible that is beyond the reach of reason, beyond the scope of common sense; whether its teaching is compatible with our sense of the ineffable, with the idea of unity, helping us to go beyond reason without denying reason, helping man to go beyond himself without losing himself. This is the distinction of the Bible: on the highest level of radical amazement, where all expression ends, it gives us the word. Revelation is an issue that must be decided on the level of the ineffable." *Ibid.*, p. 250.

[8] This is clearly the impetus of M. Fox's criticism of Heschel's view in "Heschel, Intuition, and the Halakhah," *Tradition*, Vol., III, No. 1, Fall 1960, pp. 5-15. Heschel's direction, according to Fox, places too much emphasis on an exalted barely attainable intuition and not on the acts of piety which are accessible to every Jew. "In summary, our difference with Professor Heschel on this point is one of direction. He seems to suggest in many places that intuition is the way to faith. We are arguing that faith must precede intuition. This view seems more consistent with post-exilic Jewish tradition which saw the age of prophecy as ended, and a more realistic approach to the religious dilemma of the contemporary Jew." (pp. 10-11.)

[9] This is in fact what Heschel himself suggests in the inscription to *Torah Min Hashamayim* (Vol. II). "What is the central teaching on which the lives of the people Israel depend on? *The Torah is from Heaven*. There is no Torah except from Heaven, and there is no heaven except from the Torah. If heaven is cancelled from the Torah, only poetic words remain; if Torah is cancelled from Heaven, only the firmament remains. The assembly of Israel is given to the Torah, and The Torah is given to Israel. The Torah and Israel are like a flame of an ember. If Israel is cancelled from the Torah, only suspended letters remain; if the Torah is taken away from Israel, only dying embers remain. What is the central teaching that the grasping of the Torah depends on? *The Torah is not in Heaven*. One does not pay attention to a heavenly voice; a sage is superior to a prophet. 'When The Holy One, Blessed be He, gave the Torah to Israel, He only gave it to them as wheat from which fine flour is to be extracted, as flax to make clothes.' 'If the Torah was given in pieces there would be no place to stand firmly.' 'The Torah was given for the sages to interpret and expound.' 'If there are no sages there is no Torah.' Small mindedness brings the exile of the Torah with it."

[10] *God in Search of Man*, p. 167.

[11] *Ibid.*, pp. 181-182.

[12] "Revelation can only be described *via negationis;* we can only say what it is not. Perhaps the oldest example of negative theology was applied to the understanding of revelation...(I Kings 19:11-12)." *God in Search of Man*, p. 186.

[13] *Man Is Not Alone*, p. 22.

[14] Soncino ed., Nezikin, Vol. 4, p. 169.

[15] *Ibid.*, p. 55.

[16] *Man's Quest for God*, pp. 100-101.

[17] *Ibid.*, p. 101.

[18] I am including *Man Is Not Alone, The Sabbath, God in Search of Man* and *Man's Quest for God* in this group because they are based on his phenomenological method of inquiry. I am excluding *A Passion For Truth*, because it does not reflect his philosophical concerns. No doubt the material therein influenced Heschel's thinking, but not methodologically.

[19] "The principle of the Mosaic authorship of the Pentateuch rests upon two premises: One, that Moses was a prophet, that is, inspired by God, the recipient of divine revelation; two, that Moses wrote the Pentateuch. The first premise refers to a mystery which we can neither imagine nor define; the second premise refers to an act that can be described in categories of time and space. Theology would stress the second premise; depth-theology would stress the first premise." *The Insecurity of Freedom*, p. 118. See also, *God in Search of Man*, p. 258.

[20] E. Urbach, in *The Sages – Their Concepts and Beliefs*, (Jerusalem: 1975) Vol. I, p. 20 and Vol. II, p. 695 note 20, attempts to dismiss Heschel's purpose in *Torah Min Hashamayim* by pointing to its lack of emphasis on the historical-philological method. He accuses Heschel of adumbrating his own theology in the study. Urbach's claim that Heschel is giving a purely "historical account of religious ideas" is not substantiated by any of Heschel's statements. Heschel is giving a theological account of ideas of revelation and is trying to show how they develop in a midrashic framework. Heschel is solely interested in the ideas that underlie midrashic and legal texts. Heschel's methodology stands in direct contrast to Urbach's. Urbach's own attempt to give an historical account of religious ideas is more than suspect. The ideas, which Urbach introduces at the outset of each chapter, are never analyzed nor is their meaning presented in a philosophical manner. Urbach ultimately presents a philological-historical account of significant rabbinic texts but not of ideas.

[21] Gillman (p. 12) correctly identifies the fact that Heschel's critique of revelation in *God in Search of Man* used the material published seven to ten years later in *Torah Min Hashamayim*. But, Gillman only emphasizes the criticism of the literalist position and not the symbolic one. "In retrospect, Heschel's critique of the literalist position in *God in Search of Man*, clearly nurses from the material that he was to study in this later work [*Torah Min Hashamayim*]." Again, this indicates the incomplete attention that is given by Gillman to Heschel's theological critique and to his idea of the content of revelation.

[22] *Torah Min Hashamayim Be-Aspaklaria Shel Ha-Dorot* [Hebrew] (The Theology of Ancient Judaism), (New York: Soncino Press, 1962), Vol. I, p. XXXVI.

[23] *Ibid.*, Vol. I, p. XLI.

[24] *Torah Min Hashamayim*, Vol. II, p. 157. See J.N. Epstein, *Introduction to Tannaitic Literature* [Hebrew], (Jerusalem: 1957), pp. 521-536. W. Bacher, *The Aggadot of the Tannaim* [Hebrew], (Jerusalem: 1922), Vol. I, Part 2, pp. 1-80. I.H. Weiss, *Dor Dor ve-Doreshav* [Hebrew], (Jerusalem: 1954), Vol. II, Bk. 8, Chap. 11, pp. 91-106. D. Hoffman, "An Examination of Tannaitic Midrashim," [Hebrew], *Mesilot le-Torat ha-Tanna'im, ed.* A.S. Rabinowitz, (Tel Aviv: 1928), pp. 5-12.

[25] *Torah Min Hashamayim*, Vol. I, p. 10.

[26] *Ibid.*, Vol. I, p. XLIV.

[27] *Ibid.*, Vol. I, p. XLIV.

[28] *Ibid.*, Vol. I, p. XLIV

[29] "In ascribing a transitive concern to God, we employ neither an anthropomorphic nor an anthropopathic concept but an idea that we should like to characterize as an *anthropopneumatism (anthropo + pneuma)*. We ascribe to Him not a psychic but a spiritual characteristic, not an emotional but a moral attitude." *Man Is Not Alone*, p. 144.

[30] "The prophet reflects, not on heavenly or hallowed mysteries, but on the perplexities and ambiguities of history. He never discloses the life of the beyond, but always speaks of an appearance, God as turned toward man. The anthropotropic moment is the object of his experience; God in His eternal self-existence, never." *The Prophets*, p. 485.

[31] A. Heschel, *A Passion For Truth*, (New York: Farrar, Straus and Giroux,1973), p. 175. The fact that these two references on poverty and suffering were taken from Heschel's last work to be published and the work which seems most distant from the premise of this work, supports the contention of this chapter. Heschel's rabbinic theology sets the conditions for his idea of revelation. Heschel's use of these two references in *A Passion For Truth* demonstrates the priority of the paradox of existence as it was presented by the rabbis of antiquity, and then adopted by the Kotzker Rebbe. There is no doubt of the influence that Heschel's involvement and study of Hasidism had on his idea of depth-theology. Similarly there is no doubt that it's force is secondary to that of rabbinic Judaism.

[32] A. Heschel, *A Passion For Truth*, p. 268.

[33] "Man, in the ancient period, was used to seeing everything through a prism. In his eyes no part of reality is self-enclosed and shut. Each thing is a reflecting light. Reality rests on harmony and the relation of reciprocity." *Torah Min Hashamayim*, Vol., I, p. LV.

[34] "What leads R. Ishmael to the point of view, that Moses did not always transmit the word of the Lord exactly? I think that this point of view did not originate in an abstract inquiry into the nature of prophecy, but in the effort to apprehend the simple meaning of the Scriptures." *Torah Min Hashamayim*, Vol. II, p. 149.

It should be clear that Heschel's combination of R. Akiva's transcendence and R. Ishmael's immanence in his own depth-theology has a purely phenomenological purpose. Heschel has contended that the phenomenological method is the only one which lets religious ideas and religious texts speak for themselves because it does not impose meaning on them. Urbach's claim (*The Sages* p. 695, note 20), that Heschel tries to adumbrate his own theology in *Torah Min Hashamayim*, does not put the idea of transcendence and immanence into this phenomenological context. Heschel's attempt to detach himself from such a contention is exactly the reason he chose the phenomenological method. Whether the Rabbis were aware of these philosophical issues is not significant. They were surely unaware of Urbach's historical-philological method as well. The significant issue is, how can a modern, equipped with philosophical, historical and philological tools, begin to examine the meaning of rabbinic statements qua meaning. To this question Heschel gives a consistent, unambiguous answer.

[35] *God in Search of Man*, pp. 4 and 111.

[36] *Torah Min Hashamayim*, p. LV.

[37] This is the error of Urbach's interpretation of Heschel's study of rabbinic literature. The chronology of texts and ideas per se does not motivate Heschel. Obviously, Heschel would not consciously ignore the precedence of texts and the attribution of ideas to Rabbis in their proper chronological order. No critic has made this charge. D. Shapiro, "A New View on the Systems of Rabbis Akiva and Ishmael" [Hebrew], Hadoar, Vol. 44, No. 36, (Sept. 27, 1963), pp. 769-772, lists disagreements he has with Heschel's interpretations and attributions of texts to either R. Akiva or R. Ishmael. There are problems with his criticisms that need to be examined just as Heschel's attributions of these texts need to be examined. This is certainly a task that requires its own separate treatment.

On the other hand, almost every critic has misunderstood the history of the ideas that Heschel is developing. They are organic, intuitive concepts whose deductive character is meaningless (Lauer's description of Husserl best describes this, *The Triumph of Subjectivity*, p. 146, "Thus, when Husserl speaks of *active genesis* or original constitution and of passive genesis or motivation he is speaking of determinable laws of subjective development. Unlike the common conception of the law, however, Husserl's conception never implies *causality;* rather, an observable constancy of operation makes possible an intuition of an a priori necessity in operation – since the operation is intentional and not physical, causality is simply meaningless). For example, while R. Akiva represents the transcendental approach and R. Ishmael the immanent approach, they are not totally exclusive. R. Akiva may use an idea that incorporates something immanent without contradicting his basic attitude toward the transcendental nature of the biblical text. Consequently, the substance of Heschel's analysis is intended as statements about the history of meaning and not primarily as reconstructions of texts or formal inferences of these texts.

[38] *Torah Min Hashamayim*, p. XLIX.

[39] "The principle of the Mosaic authorship of the Pentateuch rests upon two premises: One, that Moses was a prophet, that is, inspired by God, the recipient of divine revelation; two, that Moses wrote the Pentateuch. The first premise refers to a mystery which we can neither imagine nor define; the second premise refers to an act that can be described in categories of time and space. Theology would stress the second premise; depth-theology would stress the

first premise." *The Insecurity of Freedom*, p. 118. See also, *God in Search of Man*, p. 258.

[40] *Torah Min Hashamayim*, Vol. I, p. L.

[41] *Ibid.*

[42] *God in Search of Man*, p. 258.

[43] *Torah Min Hashamayim*, p. LIV.

[44] *Ibid.*, Vol. I, p. 199.

[45] *Ibid.*, Vol. II, pp. 272-279.

[46] *Ibid.*, Vol. II, p. 198, p. 248 and p. 253.

[47] *Ibid.*, Vol., II, p. 199.

[48] *Ibid.*, Vol. II, pp. 357-406.

[49] *Ibid.*, Vol. II, p. 123.

[50] *God in Search of Man*, pp. 176-183.

[51] *Torah Min Hashamayim*, Vol. II, pp. 146-147.

Chapter Ten

The Unity of the Method and the Idea of Revelation: The Consistency of Depth-Theology and Theology

Heschel's phenomenological treatment of revelation requires that all substantive questions must be contained in the act of believing and not vice versa.[1] The noetic-noematic correlation of revelation must be consistently applied to each and every aspect of the content of revelation or Heschel may be accused of placing substantive issues prior to functional issues. According to Heschel's idea of revelation, these aspects are the result of the event of revelation. If Heschel's method and ideal structure did not complement one another, his methodological concerns would ultimately be irrelevant and his idea of pathos, the object of his method, would lead him to an internal inconsistency.[2]

If depth-theology (the act of believing) and theology (the content of belief) cannot achieve any consistency then the purpose of depth-theology is unfulfilled.[3] The question that needs urgent attention is whether depth-theology can satisfy its own conditions and incorporate the concrete ritual and moral practices of theology. There are two ways to proceed to examine the conditions stated above that could possibly fulfill Heschel's functional concerns. The first alternative would require the examination of Heschel's treatment of each particular result of the content of revelation. In theological terms that would mean that each mitzvah to which Heschel refers, would have to be investigated in the light of its phenomenological structure. If each structure were found to constitute a noetic-noematic correlation then one might conclude that Heschel has consistently united his methodological and ideal concerns, or to be more precise, his depth-theology and his theology. The second alternative is to locate and examine the consistency of the primary form of the noetic-noematic correlation in depth-theology as it applies to revelation. If this primary form of the noetic-noematic correlation proves to be consistent and can be applied to concrete situations, then depth-theology and theology can tolerate and even demand each other's aims and purposes.

The second approach is the most desirable for two reasons, one practical and one theoretical. The first alternative would require an immense undertaking which would not necessarily yield the desired conditions. If the phenomenological structure of each content of revelation were available and had been discussed by Heschel, which is itself doubtful, it would be impossible to conclude from the sum of the parts, that the whole is *necessarily* fulfilling its purpose. Secondly, the primary form of the noetic-noematic correlation in depth-theology necessarily supplies each resulting correlation with its primary identity. It alone is the bedrock upon which each other aspect of depth-theology rests and is the only way in which to proceed in examining the problem and achieving a satisfactory conclusion.

What is the primary form the noetic-noematic correlation takes in depth-theology? The dialogical nature of revelation, as yet left unexamined, is based on a primary consideration for Heschel.[4] Revelation is an event of God and man. God and man are reciprocal subjects. Their relationship disintegrates if it is moved onto an objective plane[5] and man's self-consciousness ultimately becomes an impossibility.[6] Heschel never wavers from the concept of God's subjectivity. It seems that his concept of situational thinking elaborated at the beginning of *God in Search of Man* demands the same consistency for man. Man's concern, i.e. his subjective participation and situational thinking, are absolutely distinguished from the conceptual thinker's outlook.[7] It seems, prima facie, that the dialogical nature of depth-theology requires the constant subjective involvement of man in revelation. The primary noetic-noematic structure of the divine-human relationship is subject to subject, that is "I" directed to "I."[8]

At least one of Heschel's critics has indicated that Heschel does not follow this position absolutely. Friedman, in an essay encompassing all of Heschel's thought, brings this to our attention.

> If Heschel were to use the language of I and Thou, he would speak, like the Protestant theologian Emil Brunner, of a 'Thou-I' relationship in which the initiative is entirely on the side of God. 'In view of the gulf which yawns between divine infinitude and the limitations of the human situation,' writes Heschel, 'a divine-human understanding is ultimately contingent upon an awareness of divine anticipation and expectation.' In his concluding on 'The Dialectic of the Divine-Human Encounter,' Heschel describes the 'twofold mutual initiative' as one in which 'the subject-man-becomes object, and the object-God-becomes subject.' This problem is not one of inconsistent terminology. There seems to be a still unworked-through unclarity in the relation between Heschel's divine pathos, in which 'the primary factor is our being seen

and known by Him,' and the dialogical structure of the prophetic relationship which he stresses in *God in Search of Man* and *The Prophets*....The mark of authenticity of the prophet, writes Heschel, is that God is not his experience, but he is 'an experience of God.' With this we are once again thrown back to the problem of knowledge involved in man's being the subject who knows that it is not he but God who is the subject and he is the object! In *God in Search of Man*, Heschel says that what is important is not our certainty of the origin of the Bible in God but our awareness of the presence of God in the Bible. In *The Prophets*, however, he says that the validity and distinction of the prophet's message lies in its origin in God. The prophet's 'certainty of being inspired by God,' writes Heschel, is based on 'the source of his experience' in God. Having an experience is indeed not central to the prophet, but neither can his 'certainty' of the source be objectified into an independent knowledge apart from the relationship with God. Nor does Heschel wish to see this certainty objectified in this way....Heschel himself said to me that he has pointed to the centrality of the prophet's certainty of being inspired by God not as a dogma but in the sense of Jeremiah's, 'Of a truth the Lord has sent me,' hence as a consciousness of a call.[9]

The reference by Heschel, to man as an object of God permeates all of Heschel's writings.[10] Heschel's reference to man as an object of God and concurrently his reference to man's consciousness of being an object of God, point to the same phenomenon which has its origin in another Heschelian idea. God, the supreme Subject,[11] is all personal.[12] Thus, it follows that the prophet's consciousness, as an object of God's concern, is infused with the personality of God. This is an ideal phenomenological objectivity consistent with Heschel's reliance on the noetic-noematic correlation.[13] Heschel never implies that the objectivity, which fills the consciousness of the prophet, is at all impersonal. If anything, Heschel is implying that there is no act of consciousness available that is more personal from the standpoint of ethos or pathos.[14]

> He is encountered not as a universal, general, pure Being, but always in a particular mode of being, as personal God to personal man, in a specific pathos that comes with a demand in a concrete situation.[15]

Clearly Heschel conceives of two mutually reciprocal structures in the relationship of God and man. There is a subject-subject and a subject-object structure. Ideally, revelation is the product of the cooperation of these structures. To view these structures as absolutely separable is to introduce an internal inconsistency into Heschel's phenomenology that does not exist. Moreover, to view these structures as leading to an impersonal objective response in the consciousness of the prophet to a divine initiative is completely baseless.[16]

> For biblical theology these ideas are as basic as the ideas of being and becoming are for classical metaphysics. They mark the difference between pagan and prophetic experience. There, experience is experiencing being; here, existence is experiencing concern. It is living in the perpetual awareness of being perceived, apprehended, noted by God, of being an object of the divine Subject. This is the most precious insight: to sense God's participation in existence; to experience oneself as a divine secret (see Ps. 139:17-18).[17]

The inseparability of these structures and their ultimate grasp of divine personality in human consciousness is the mechanism which allows the method and content of revelation to coexist. The transcendent attentiveness available in these phenomenological structures defines the limits of prophetic understanding by allowing the prophet to comprehend and give expression to God's directedness to man.[18]

The inseparability of these two structures also solves another problem of understanding Heschel's strategy of depth-theology. These dual structures may be seen as problematic because for Heschel, the antecedents of faith and faith itself are ideally inseparable.[19] It would seem that this dependence creates a severe problem for Heschel. If there are no independent grounds for believing in the realness of the living God, then Heschel's description of intuition begs the question.[20] The argument against Heschel's strategy goes as follows; if there is no set of genuine intuitions then no one intuition can be given credence. Since Heschel's idea of depth-theology is firmly rooted in the preconceptual and presymbolic, as opposed to the doctrinal and creedal elements of religion, there would seem to be no way out of this dilemma for Heschel.

But, this line of reasoning ignores the weight of the noematic aspect of consciousness and its correlation to noetic elements. It also places too much weight on the phenomenological idea of intuition. Obviously, an act of faithfulness or memory need not, as antecedents of faith, lead to genuine faith. A genuine or true experience of faith, is that event in which the noetic and noematic aspects can and do achieve correlation. It is the responsibility of the individual, in the ideal and in the real sense, to complete the event. More than any other facet of revelation, it is this phenomenological aspect which prevents the literalization of Heschel's idea of the content of revelation. From the point of view of Heschel's idea of corevelation, there is no completed noetic-noematic correlation which presents itself to man. The objectivity of the event must be matched with the rules that govern its subjectivity.[21] The prophet must achieve a sense of revelation as he is involved in the event. This is parallel to the intellectual challenge presented to the philosopher of religion who undertakes an understanding of the content of the prophetic act. He must unfold the phenomenological structure of revelation as he apprehends the realness of God in awe and wonder. Within this context, it is possible for the method and the content of revelation to coexist because they are rooted in the same act of consciousness even though they indicate different aspects of that act.

While Heschel's idea of revelation may easily be misconstrued because of its apparent lack of unity, another more profound problem is present because of Heschel's own dependence on a Husserlian idea. How is the objective nature of revelation to be construed if the content of revelation cannot be positively defined but only indicated? Unfortunately most of Heschel's critics, without realizing the source of this difficulty, have adopted either of two positions on this issue. Many critics have held the idea that there is no objective value or validity to Heschel's claims for revelation at all.[22] Another type of critic has pointed to Heschel's objective talk about revelation and criticized it for being impersonal.[23] The case has been made in this work, that, according to Heschel the method of revelation is apprehended as a phenomenological fact and that its objectivity is derived from this phenomenological description. Is this the case for the content of revelation as well? If it is not the case, then the unity of method and content posited above lapses into incongruity and Heschel's idea of depth-theology collapses from within. The difficulty of settling this issue is complex because Heschel uses language which, on the surface, is not always consistent with the objective phenomenological quality of his methodology. With no seeming justification, Heschel introduces an idea of perception into his discussion of the content of revelation, that is absent from his discussion of the method of revelation.

> The word of God in itself is like a burning flame, and the Torah that we received is merely a part of the coal to which the flame is attached. And yet, even in this form it would have remained beyond our comprehension as long as we are mortals. The word had to descend further and to assume the form of darkness ('arafel) in order to become perceptible to man. Out of the experience of the prophets came the words, words that try to interpret what they perceived. To this very day, these words make present what happened in the past. As the meaning and wonder of the event inspired the spiritual comprehension of the prophet, the meaning and wonder of the Biblical words continue to inspire the understanding of man.[24]

The source of this idea of perception is not explained in any of Heschel's works and obviously introduces a new concept of objectivity. Therefore, the attempt to locate the source of this problem must begin with an examination of the Husserlian ideas that Heschel adopts. This ambiguity of the objectivity of the methodology and content of prophetic consciousness arises because of Heschel's uncritical adaption of the noetic-noematic correlation and Husserl's ambiguous use of the noema. As Husserl conceived the noema, it was responsible for the mind's directedness towards objects. As such it had to have three components. The noema had to refer to, describe and synthesize a particular object outside the mind.[25] The noema also supplies a set of rules which determine the predicates that can apply to the same object.[26] The problem with the perceptual noema and its task does not arise if one tries to understand Husserl's proposed set of synonyms that explain the noema. As one critic states, "Thus all would readily agree that the perceptual noema is the intentional correlate of perceptual consciousness: it is neither a (real) physical object, nor a (reell) momentary state of consciousness, but rather a meaning, an ideal entity correlated with every act of perception, whether the object intended in that act exists or not."[27] The description of the noema in Chapter Four was rendered in these terms but not as an oversight. The general explanation of the noema had to be given in terms agreeable to his critics. The problematic nature of the noema and the real effect it has on Heschel's claims about revelation could only be grasped simultaneously at this juncture. The objectivity of Husserl's noema creates a parallel problem for Heschel's structure of the event of revelation.

When Husserl's noema is explained in independent terms it takes on either of two meanings[28] that systematically "run through the whole constellation of noema terminology."[29] The major exponents of these views are Dagfinn Follesdal[30] and Aron Gurwitsch.[31] Follesdal interprets the noema as a concept and Gurwitsch sees it as a precept. According to Follesdal's interpretation, the noema is an abstract entity,[32] "in virtue of which the act of perception is directed toward its object."[33] It is a meaning or an intentional entity not viewed from a perspective. Consequently, "the noema itself is never sensuously given but is 'entertained' in a special act of reflection called the phenomenological reduction."[34]

Gurwitsch's interpretation leads to an opposite result. According to him, "the perceptual noema is a concrete sensuous appearance, through which the object of perception is presented."[35] In Gurwitsch's own words, "We interpret the perceptual noema...as a Gestalt-contexture whose constituents are what is given in a direct sense experience."[36] Dreyfus points out that strictly speaking, according to Gurwitsch, the noema is not perceived like a physical object, but it is perceptually given and "can be thematized in a special act of attending to the perceptual object."[37]

The fact that both Follesdal and Gurwitsch can marshal texts to support their disparate views, doesn't prove or disprove their positions, but illustrates the concerns that Husserl showed about the noema. As Solomon notes, the noema of perception and the noema of judgments both occupy Husserl's attention in *Ideas*, even though most attention is given to the noema of judgments.[38] The conclusion, that the noema has both perceptual and conceptual characteristics is well founded. The attempt to limit the explanation of the noema, to either one or other of the views does not do justice to Husserl's texts or to the noema itself.[39] Whether or not the noema can ultimately sustain these two components does not mitigate their presence in the doctrine or that Husserl fully intended them both.[40]

This entire discussion of the two senses of interpreting the noema has a direct bearing on the understanding of Heschel's idea of revelation. The two structures Heschel uses, the subject-subject and the subject-object structures, use two types of language to describe the act of revelation as it refers to its content. Heschel's language concerning the method of revelation is always ideal. But, there is an ambiguity of language involving the content of revelation. Quite often Heschel explicitly refers to revelation and its content as ideal. Sometimes, as noted above, his language is perceptual and has led critics to assume Heschel believed in the literal idea of revelation. The texts are indisputably ambiguous, but Heschel's intention is not. The ambiguity never enters Heschel's methodological statements and it is the methodological statements that confer meaning on the statements concerning content. The language of perception is assimilated into few of the statements of content primarily because of Heschel's unfamiliarity with the complexity of the noematic doctrine. Yet, this outright simplification of the use of Husserl's doctrine does not change the meaning of Heschel's idea of revelation because Heschel has always given priority to its methodological character. Heschel's intention here also has a positive role. Heschel, while thoroughly denying the literalness of the content of revelation, never denies that the event literally and concretely took place.[41] Revelation is surely the most concrete or literal event that can take place according to Heschel's understanding of human existence.[42] The language of perception is portraying this reality graphically and nothing more.

Furthermore, the object of the subject-object phenomenological structure is never a mere object in the depersonalized sense. It is never an objective thing, that is incapable of intention. Even when Heschel does attribute objective impersonal language to this structure it is always limited to God's point of view.

> Man knows the word of revelation, but not the self-revelation of God. He experiences no vision of God's essence, only a vision of appearance. A subject of pathos, God Himself is not pathos. His insight always contains, together with the *subjectum relationis, a fundamentum* and a *terminus relationis*. The ground of the relation is moral, and from God's point of view, objective and impersonal. The goal of the relation is man. The divine pathos is transitive.[43]

From our point of view, borrowing from Husserl's method, the objective grasp of the subject is based on the cogitationes of the ego. There is no hint of depersonalized substance in this structure according to either Husserl or Heschel, but only of "change seen as the *flow of cogitationes* and that identity be seen as the *continuity* of this same flow."[44] The object which is constituted in Husserl's correlation and imported into Heschel's structure of revelation is the particular subject with certain actualities and possibilities. Although the ego is characterized by its continuous flow it has a sense of permanence and identity.[45] It is in this sense that "the world ceases to be abstraction; it is not just any world, but the world of this concrete subject. To speak of a world at all is to speak of a constant subjective identity, which is the concrete ego."[46] Man, the subject of the first Heschelian structure becomes regarded as the concrete object in his second structure, but only from God's point of view. As the object of divine concern, man's self-conscious value and intentional worth cannot be disregarded. Heschel is unambiguous about this value while maintaining its objective status.

> In prophetic thinking, man is the object of God's vision, concern, and understanding. It is man's vision, concern, and understanding for God that is the goal.[47]

This internal discrepancy of the structure of revelation and of the nature of intentionality caused by it, cannot be resolved intellectually. Man as subject and object, however depersonalized by God, ultimately maintains his personality in God. The fact that man cannot resolve this incongruity does not render the structure meaningless or insignificant, nor does it render Heschel's claims irrational. It merely points to the inherent limits of any act of human consciousness and its attending ontological commitment.[48]

> The Prophets stress not only the discrepancy of God and man, but also the relationship of reciprocity, consisting of God's engagement to man, not only of man's commitment to God. The disparity between God and the world is overcome in God, not in man.[49]

Finally, this leads us to an obvious departure by Heschel from Husserl's doctrine. The difference between Husserl's depiction of self-constitution as it is presented in the "Fourth Cartesian Meditation" and as it is used by Heschel is not in structure. Heschel's idea of revelation incorporates Husserl's idea of objective constitution but from a divine perspective. Husserl is not interested in that perspective at all. According to Heschel's phenomenological structure, man possesses his own intentionality but he is also the intentional object of God. Man, in relation to God, is constituted as this object just as he employs his own self-constitution, through "determinable laws of subjective development."[50] Since this is not a physical operation but an intentional one, the laws of causality are meaningless[51] and the intentionality of God overwhelms the intentionality of man without denying it altogether.[52]

---

[1] See Chapter Seven.

[2] See Chapter Seven.

[3] "Correspondingly, the study of religion has two major tasks to perform. One, to understand what it means to believe; to analyze *the act of believing*; to ask what it is that necessitates our believing in God. Two, to explain and to examine *the content of believing*; to analyze that which we believe in. The first is concerned with *the problem of faith*, with concrete situations; the second with *the problem of creed*, with conceptual relations." *God in Search of Man*, p. 6.

[4] "The divine pathos is like a bridge over the abyss that separates man from God. It implies that the relationship between man and God is not dialectic, characterized by opposition and tension. Man in his essence is not the antithesis of the divine, although in his actual existence he may be rebellious and defiant. The fact that the attitudes of man may affect the life of God, that God stands in an intimate relationship to the world, implies a certain analogy between Creator and creature. The prophets stress not only the discrepancy of God and man, but also the relationship of reciprocity, consisting of God's engagement to man, not only of man's commitment to God. The disparity between God and the world is overcome in God, not in man." *The Prophets*, p. 229.

[5] *God in Search of Man*, p. 127.

[6] This is true both for the relationship and for man considered from his own perspective. "To think of God is not to find Him as an object in our minds, but to find ourselves in Him." *Man Is Not Alone*, p. 127. See also *God in Search of Man*, pp. 159-160. "It is easy to raise verbally the question: Who is the subject of which my self is the object? But to be keenly sensitive to its meaning is something which surpasses our power of comprehension. It is, in fact, impossible to comprehend logically its implications. For in asking the question, I am always aware of the fact that it is I who asks the question. But as soon as I know myself as an 'I', as a subject, I am not capable any more of grasping the

content of the question, in which I am posited as an object. Thus, on the level of self-consciousness there is no way to face the issue, to ask the absolute question." *Man Is Not Alone*, p. 48.

[7] "What we face is not only a problem which is apart from ourselves but a situation of which we are a part and in which we are totally involved. To understand the problem we must explore the situation. The attitude of the conceptual thinker is one of detachment: the subject facing an independent object; the attitude of the situational thinker is one of concern: the subject realizing that he is involved in a situation that is in need of understanding." *God in Search of Man*, p. 5.

[8] "In prophetic inspiration, on the other hand, the knowledge and presence of Him who imparts the message is the central, staggering fact of awareness. There is a certainty of having experienced the impingement of a personal Being, of another I; not an idea coming from nowhere or from a nameless source, but always a communication reaching him from the most powerful subject of all, confronting the prophet, who is responsive and often participates in the act. Structurally, it may be described as a *subject-subject-relationship."* *The Prophets*, p. 389.

[9] M. Friedman, "Abraham Heschel Among Contemporary Philosophers: From Divine Pathos to Prophetic Action," *Philosophy Today*, Winter 1974, p. 298. The references by Heschel to man as an "object" of God are too numerous to list. They are to be found continually throughout his entire writings. It is not Friedman's intention to indicate these positions systematically, but to demonstrate that an internal epistemological problem exists for Heschel. In the Hebrew version of this essay, "Divine Need and Human Wonder," Friedman questions this incompatibility further. But, in neither essay, does Friedman posit that this is possibly a result of Heschel's phenomenological position. It should be minimally clear to Friedman that Heschel is not talking about man as a depersonalized object of God. The phenomenological status of objective terms in Heschel's theology, including man as an object of God, was ascertained in Chapter Five of this work. The significance of man as an object of God is what requires examination in this chapter because it stands at the center of the divine-human encounter in Heschel's eyes.

[10] Some of the many references to this idea may be found in the following places; *God in Search of Man*, pp. 85 and 158, *Man Is Not Alone*, pp. 126, 128, *Who Is Man?*, p. 74, *The Prophets*, pp. 308, 309, 366, 389, 419, 485, 487, and 488.

[11] *The Prophets*, p. 486.

[12] *Ibid.*, pp. 486-487.

[13] Merkle's analysis of God's personality in conjunction with the prophetic consciousness (p. 103), misses this point entirely. Merkle explains only one side of the correlation, its subject-subject aspect. God's personality, encountered as a Supreme Subject, is objectified in the consciousness of the prophet as part of a dynamic correlation. Without this objectification by the prophet, as the object of God, Heschel realizes that religious knowledge will remain undifferentiated from any other psychological representation and cannot claim validity in any form.

14 "God's pathos was not thought of as a sort of fever of the mind which, disregarding the standards of justice, culminates in irrational and irresponsible action. There is justice in all His ways, the Bible insists again and again. There is no dichotomy of pathos and ethos, of motive and norm. They do not exist side by side, opposing each other; they involve and presuppose each other. It is because God is the source of justice that His pathos is ethical; and it is because God is absolutely personal – devoid of anything impersonal – that this ethos is full of pathos." *The Prophets*, p. 225.

15 *Ibid.*, p. 486.

16 "There is no indication in the prophets' reports of their experiences of that emptying of consciousness which is the typical preparation for ecstasy, of a loss of self-consciousness or of a suspension of mental power during the reception of revelation. Unlike mystical insight, which takes place in 'the abyss of the mind,' in 'the ground of consciousness,' prophetic illumination seems to take place in the full light of the mind, in the very center of consciousness. There is no collapse of consciousness, no oblivion of the world's foolishness. The prophet's will does not faint; his mind does not become a mist." *Ibid.*, p. 359.

17 *Ibid.*, p. 483.

18 "Yet even here we must not think that we reach God's essence. Transcendent attentiveness merely defines the limits of the prophet's understanding of God. God in Himself, His Being, is a problem for metaphysics. The theme and claim of prophetic theology is God's concern for man, and man's relevance to God. Only one aspect of His Being, His directedness to man, is known to man. This, then, is the ultimate category of prophetic theology: involvement, attentiveness, concern. Prophetic religion may be defined, not as what man does with his ultimate concern, but rather *what man does with God's concern.*" *The Prophets*, pp. 483-484. Heschel, while indicating the how the method and content of revelation coexist, is also criticizing Tillich's doctrine of Being and ultimate concern (See *Systematic Theology*, Vol., I, pp. 211ff.).

19 "Faith comes out of awe, out of an awareness that we are exposed to His presence, out of anxiety to answer the challenge of God, out of an awareness of our being called upon. Religion consists of *God's question and man's answer.* The way to Faith is the way of faith. The way *to* God is a way *of* God. Unless God asks the question, all our inquiries are in vain." *God in Search of Man*, p. 137. "Jewish thought is disclosed in Jewish living. This, therefore is the way of religious existence. We do not explore first and decide afterwards whether to accept the Jewish way of living. We must accept in order to be able to explore. At the beginning is the commitment, the supreme aquiescence. In our response to His will we perceive His presence in our deeds." *God in Search of Man*, p. 282.

20 Fox, pp. 6-7.

21 "The great prophets had one feature in common: revelation came to them as a surprise, as a sudden burst. They were more startled *that* they heard, than *at what* they heard. Their perceptiveness came into being with revelation itself. It is revelation that makes man capable of receiving a revelation. He becomes expert with the experience." *God in Search of Man*, p. 219.

[22] This seems to be the position of Cohen, Fox, Petuchowski and Berkovits in their works cited in Chapter One.

[23] This is the position of Friedman noted above.

[24] *God in Search of Man*, p. 265.

[25] Dreyfus, p. 7.

[26] *Ibid.*, p. 8.

[27] *Ibid.*, p. 97.

[28] See R. Solomon, "Husserl's concept of the Noema," *Husserl: Expositions and Appraisals,* ed. F. Elliston and P. McCormick, (Notre Dame: University of Notre Dame Press, 1977), pp. 168-181, for a clear explanation of the differences of these positions.

[29] Dreyfus, p. 98.

[30] D. Follesdal, "Husserl's Notion of Noema," *Husserl, Intentionality and Cognitive Science,* ed. H. Dreyfus, (Cambridge: The M.I.T. Press, 1982), pp. 73-80.

[31] A. Gurwitsch, "The Phenomenology of Perception: Perceptual implications." In *An Invitation to Phenomenology,* ed. James Edie (Chicago: Quadrangle Books, 1965). Dreyfus outlines the historical development of this debate, and while he does not settle the debate on terms accessible to either Follesdal or Gurwitsch and their followers (note 12 p. 323), he seems to suggest that ultimately the idea of consciousness and phenomenology that follows Follesdal's view more accurately fits the phenomena (pp. 98-99).

[32] Dreyfus, p. 77.

[33] *Ibid.*, p. 74.

[34] *Ibid.*, p. 98.

[35] *Ibid.*, p. 98.

[36] Gurwitsch, p. 23.

[37] Dreyfus, p. 98.

[38] Solomon, p. 171.

[39] *Ibid.*, p. 176.

[40] Solomon works out a plausible explanation of how Husserl worked these components of the noema into his theory of intentionality (pp.177ff).

[41] "The problem concerning us most is whether revelation has ever taken place; whether there are any compelling reasons for accepting the Bible as an expression of the will of God. Our major aim is to find an answer to the question: Is revelation a fact? Did it actually take place? Such an answer will obviously depend on our ability to find evidence either to refute or to confirm the claim of the prophets." *God in Search of Man*, p. 218.

[42] *God in Search of Man*, pp. 180-181 and 239.

[43] *The Prophets*, p. 485.

[44] Lauer, *The Triumph of Subjectivity*, p. 145.

[45] *Ibid.*, p. 146.

[46] *Ibid.*, p. 146.

[47] *The Prophets*, p. 488.

[48] This limit of human consciousness is based on the prophet's insistence of God's subjectivity and involves a fundamental paradox which is part of every act of consciousness that apprehends God's pathos. "Prophetic thought is not

focused upon His absoluteness, as indeterminate being, but upon His 'subjective' being, upon His expression, pathos and relationship. The dichotomy of transcendence and immanence is an oversimplification. For God remains transcendent in His immanence, and related in His transcendence." *The Prophets*, p. 486.

[49] *The Prophets*, p. 229.

[50] Lauer, *The Triumph of Subjectivity*, p. 146.

[51] *Ibid.*, p. 146.

[52] "The structure of prophetic consciousness as ascertained in the analysis was disclosed as consisting, on the transcendent level, of pathos (content of inspiration) and event (form), and on the personal level, of sympathy (content of inner experience) and the sense of being overpowered (form of inner experience)." *The Prophets*, p. xix.

Chapter Eleven

Heschel's Ontology

The fundamental focus of this work has been the demonstration of the thesis that there is a recognizable act of consciousness in Heschel's description of biblical prophecy and that Heschel uses it as the basis for his idea of revelation. As such, the noetic-noematic correlation is that act of consciousness which gives depth-theology its philosophical integrity. This correlation entails a description of the phenomenological object and content of consciousness that has a definite effect on Heschel's idea of revelation. Consequently, the content of revelation according to Heschel is ideal. There is neither a literal nor a symbolic content of revelation which has objective status in any deductive sense. More important, the Bible itself may not be regarded as the revealed object of any such deductive philosophical program. Within the parameters of Heschel's philosophical program, the Bible is the record of the event of revelation but never identical with it.

Since no critic or follower of Heschel has heretofore examined these phenomenological principles that underlie Heschel's description of biblical prophecy and his own idea of revelation, the ontology of Heschel's thought has been completely neglected. Significantly, the assembling of Heschel's ontology, presents the same problem that surrounded his methodological and epistemological principles. To our regret, Heschel never gathers his ideas on a philosophical issue in one place to expound them systematically. He chooses to weave them throughout the theological ideas with which he deals. Consequently, his philosophical position was never made explicit so that it could come to the center of the stage. As a result it is most often ignored altogether. The primary task of reconstructing his ontology must begin in the same manner as the search for his methodology. Heschel's description of the ontology of biblical thinking is the first proper clue that could give us an insight into his own position.

Heschel's examination of biblical prophecy leads him to a significant conclusion at the beginning of his examination of the ideas surrounding prophecy.

> Biblical ontology does not separate being from doing. What *is*, acts. The God of Israel is a God who acts, a God of mighty deeds. The Bible does not say how He is, but how He acts. It speaks of His acts of pathos and of His acts in history; it is not as 'true being' that God is conceived, but as the *semper agens*. Here the basic category is action rather than immobility. Movement, creation of nature, acts within history rather than absolute transcendence and detachment from the events of history, are the attributes of the Supreme Being.[1]

According to Heschel, one cannot draw an absolute distinction for biblical ontology that separates theoretical from practical ontology. The category of being in the Bible is totally dependent on action and vice versa. There is no act of pure consciousness that intuits or understands being in prophetic consciousness.

Heschel's position vis-à-vis prophetic religion is clear in that he thoroughly rejects a prophetic ontology based on pure being. The clarity and firmness of Heschel's idea is based on another assumption. Being in biblical ontology, in contrast to many Greek notions, is changeable.

> The Eleatic premise that true being is unchangeable and that change implies corruption is valid only in regard to being as reflected in the mind. Being in reality, being as we encounter it, implies movement. If we think of being as something beyond and detached from beings, we may well arrive at an eleatic notion. An ontology, however, concerned with being as involved in all beings or as the source of all beings, will find it impossible to separate being from action or movement, and thus postulate a dynamic concept of divine Being.[2]

Thus far, according to Heschel's understanding of biblical prophecy, being, the source of everything, is changeable and known through its intentionality which cannot be separated from its essence. Since the prophets experience God's word and not what He is,[3] being is apprehended in relation and never in essence.

> Ontologically, the distinction between being and expression is rooted in the distinction between essence and relation. The theme of prophetic understanding is not the mystery of God's essence, but rather the mystery of His relation to man. The prophet does not speculate about God in Himself; in thinking about Him, the world is always present. His message does not seek to disclose or to impart new truth concerning the divine Being. What the prophet knows about God is His pathos, His relation to Israel and to mankind. God can be understood by man only in conjunction with the human situation. For of God we know only what He means and does in relation to man.[4]

There is one more seminal ontological factor that Heschel ascertains in his study of the prophets that influences the ontology of depth-theology. The two structures of human relationship to God that involve the prophet, the subject-subject and the subject-object, produce a corresponding ontology. The prophet relates to God not only dialogically but also dialectically.[5] Man, while never knowing the essence of God, is never totally removed from it.

> The divine pathos is like a bridge over the abyss that separates man from God. It implies that the relationship between man and God is not dialectic, characterized by opposition and tension. Man in his essence is not the antithesis of the divine, although in his actual existence he may be rebellious and defiant. The fact that the attitudes of man may affect the life of God, that God stands in an intimate relationship to the world, implies a certain analogy between Creator and creature. The prophets stress not only the discrepancy of God and man, but also the relationship of reciprocity, consisting of God's engagement to man, not only of man's commitment to God. The disparity between God and the world is overcome in God, not in man.[6]

The prophet stands in a discontinuous dialectical and in a reciprocal dialogical relationship to God.[7] The attempt to emphasize one side of the relationship without the other, ignores the crucial differences of man and God in prophetic religion. Being, as an ontological category, is apprehended as being-in-relation and as being-over-against. As a result of this ontological split, prophetic consciousness is open to the transcendence of divine pathos but cannot unify with it. At best, prophetic consciousness can become involved with the divine pathos. According to Heschel's understanding of prophetic religion, there is an ontological identification of God and man only on the existential level. Only in the act of turning toward one another does the ontological commitment of God and man achieve any recognition. There is no possible hypostasis of the commitment or of the event. Nor is there a possibility of conceptualizing, through the category of substance, a representation of the commitment. Pathos can only be apprehended in a functional mode.[8] Ontologically, only the egos of man and God inhere in their meeting because of their attentiveness to each other.

> A specific aspect of prophetic religion or of the religious phenomenon in general, as opposed to the purely psychological, lies in the fact of a mutual inherence of the 'I' and the object of religious experience, for an intention of man toward God produces a counteracting intention of God toward man. Here all mutual relations end, not in the original decision, but in a relationship which represents a counteraction. In turning toward God, man experiences God's turning toward him. Man's awareness of God is to be understood as God's awareness of man, man's knowledge of God is transcended in God's knowledge of man, the subject – man – becomes object, and the object – God – becomes subject. Not a reciprocal succession of acts, not a distinguishable alteration of sound and echo, but rather in every event

of the religious consciousness it is a question of a dual mutual operation, a twofold mutual initiative.[9]

The basic premises of the ontology of prophetic religion, as Heschel's inquiry has developed them, form the ground of the ontology of depth-theology. Discontinuity and reciprocity form the ground of man's relation to God in depth-theology. Reason, nature and history, the basic categories of being, are infused with the same polarity that constitutes revelation.[10] Within depth-theology, life is filled with discontinuity and reciprocity.

> A challenge is not the same as a clash, and divergence does not mean a conflict. It is part of the human condition to live in polarities. It is an implication of our belief in one God to be certain that ultimately reason and revelation are both derived from the same source.[11]

This polarity is no less apparent in Heschel's discussion of nature and it plays exactly the same role. Man, through awe and radical amazement must abide in the tension between God and nature as he must abide in the tension between reason and revelation.

> The world is not the all to the Bible, and so the all could never come to denote the world. Biblical man is not enchanted by the given. He realizes the alternative, namely the annihilation of the given. He is not enchanted by the order, because he has a vision of a new order. He is not lost to the here and now, nor to the beyond. He senses the non-given with the given, the past and future with the present...In a profound sense, the question: what is reality? what is the world to the Biblical man? is best answered by another question: what is the world to God? To him the subject matter of the question – the world – is too wondrous to be fully comprehended in relation to man. The world in its ultimate significance must be understood in relation to God, and the answer to the question is: all things are His servants.[12]

Nature is not a thing in itself,[13] nor does it supply an idea of sufficiency for its own rationalization.[14] Nature is an object that comes alive in relation to God.[15] The sublime in nature is "a silent allusion of things to a meaning greater than themselves."[16] As such, the sublime, as all Heschelian concepts that are accessible through nature, is based on a relation to God[17] and is therefore subject to the basic polarity of existence.[18] Without nature man cannot sense the presence of God, but with nature alone, man cannot respond to the transcendental meaning that fills his consciousness.[19] The ontological facticity of nature is a norm of human consciousness.[20] The discontinuous and reciprocal character of nature is the basic foundation of Heschel's ontological commitment to its reality and leads directly to the third of Heschel's ontological commitments.[21]

History, the third concept which fills out Heschel's ontology, reflects a basic polarity in the philosophy of Judaism. Heschel claims that Judaism is a religion of time, whose God spoke through events in history.[22] The particular events of the life of the Jewish people have an ontological and intentional role.[23] Yet, Heschel simultaneously claims that

> Judaism does not seek to subordinate philosophy to events, timeless verities to a particular history. It tries to point to a level of reality where the events are the manifestations of divine norms, where history is understood as the fulfillment of truth.[24]

The attempt to see this position merely as a statement of universalism and particularism does not do justice to its ontological character. History is not merely a process with no future.[25] The ontological commitment to sacred history presupposes exactly the opposite. There is no absolute break between past and present and between present and future. The past is the ontological presupposition of the present.

> It is, indeed, one of the peculiar features of human existence that the past does not altogether vanish, that some events of hoary antiquity may hold us in their spell to this very day. Events which are dead, things which are gone, can neither be sensed nor told. There is a liberation from what is definitely past. On the other hand, there are events which never become past. Sacred history may be described as an attempt to overcome the dividing line between past and present, as an attempt *to see the past in the present tense.*[26]

Similarly, the future may be seen as the ontological presupposition of the present.

> It was an act of transcending the present, history in reverse: thinking of the future in the present tense. It was a prophetic foresight, for to be a prophet is to be ahead of other people's time, to speak of the future in the present tense.[27]

The present, according to Heschel, has the ability to sustain an act of retention and of protention without having its integrity disturbed.[28] As such, history is not synonymous with time[29] but is an infusion of God's concern into the temporal realm. History is the ontological condition of God's concern in time.[30] If time did not have the ability to sustain the impetus of the past and the future, then the present, or any given moment, could not bear the inclusion of God's presence as an act of freedom.

> Jewish thinking, furthermore, claims that being is constituted (created) and maintained not only by necessity but by freedom, by God's free and personal concern for being. The divine concern is not a

theological afterthought but a fundamental category of ontology. Reality seems to be maintained by the necessity of its laws. Yet, when we inquire: why is necessity necessary? there is only one answer: the divine freedom, the divine concern.[31]

Reason, nature and history each have objective purposes in Heschel's ontology. They originate as an act of freedom in God and are recognizable through their polarities as applied to the mind and will of man.

What gives rise to faith is not a sentiment, a state of mind, an aspiration, but an everlasting fact in the universe, something which is prior to and independent of human knowledge and experience – *the holy dimension* of all existence. The objective side of religion is the spiritual side of the universe, the divine values invested in every being and exposed to the mind and will of man; an ontological relation. This is why the objective side of religion eludes psychological and sociological analysis.[32]

The ontological relation that Heschel specifies here is not a self-sufficient relation. It originates in God and in man. Aside from the phenomenological considerations that have been elaborated throughout this work, there is another aspect of the ontological relation that has not been investigated.

Heschel has made it clear that revelation is not a self-contained event. It is an open-ended event which cannot be analyzed sufficiently if its relation to the will of man is ignored. In another context, the moment of revelation was shown to be connected to its content, because of the ideal correlation that Heschel employed.[33] In this ontological context, the same text details the necessary aspect of revelation in connection to human action based on Heschel's ontological commitment.

And yet mere attachment to events does not fully express the essence of Jewish living. Event is a formal category, describing the fact of pure happening. However, to speak of a pure event, of an event in and by itself, is to speak of an artificial abstraction that exists nowhere except in the minds of some theologians. The moment of revelation must not be separated from the content or substance of revelation. Loyalty to the norms and thoughts conveyed in the event is as essential as the reality of the event. Acceptance was not complete, the fulfillment has not occurred. The decisive moment is yet to come. The event must be fulfilled, not only believed in. What was expected at Sinai comes about in the moment of a good deed. A commandment is a foresight, a deed is a fulfillment. The deed completes the event. Revelation is but a beginning, our deeds must continue, our lives must complete it.[34]

On an intellectual plane, reality for Heschel, is constituted through the noetic-noematic correlation. On the practical level we see that reality demands the input of human deeds. The unity of theory and practice or of depth-theology, which emphasizes intuition, and theology, which emphasizes creed, is located in the concept of mitzvah. According to Heschel, sacred deeds are actions which "make living compatible with our sense of the ineffable."[35] A sacred deed can integrate otherwise disparate elements, because it is based on intentionality.

> The presence of God demands more than the presence of mind. Kavanah is direction to God and requires the redirection of the whole person. It is the act of bringing together the scattered forces of the self; the participation of heart and soul, not only of will and mind; the integration of the soul with the theme of the mitzvah.[36]

While this solves some internal problems for Heschel's doctrine it presents a major obstacle in the way of understanding his concept of being.

Heschel's ontology, as has been demonstrated from the outset, contains no pure concept of being. The question, what is being? does not even present itself to Heschel because man is a constituted being whose personality is understood through the qualities required for being human.[37] There is only one positive statement that can be made about being and it is also made about revelation.[38] Being is ineffable.[39] Human action, generated in the human will and conditioned by human habits, completes the idea of being and the event of revelation and thereby contributes meaning to Heschel's ontological perspective. Being, while not synonymous with revelation is similar, in that it excludes literal or symbolic truth and is constituted through a response.[40] The question remains then, in what sense is Heschel's idea of being ontological, if contemplation is not central? While using the language of ontology,[41] Heschel seems to negate its purpose completely. Being and action, as in prophetic religion, are correlated. Heschel clearly does not posit a traditional ontology which relies on the conceptual analysis of being. Being qua being has no personal meaning within Heschel's phenomenological description of human being.[42]

The answer to this question is primarily found in *Who Is Man?* In that work, Heschel's attempt to examine the modes of being human lead him to posit a specific concept of being that is not fully discussed elsewhere.

> What follows is an attempt to describe some modes of being human which every reader as a human being will recognize and accept as essential. They represent a requiredness rather than a fabrication of the mind; not postulates of morality but fundamentals of human

existence. Failure in nurturing the essential sensibilities results in the decay of the humanity of the individual man.[43]

The requiredness of existence that Heschel mentions at the beginning of this essay is not explained until its completion. It is not a quality superadded to human existence which can then be deduced from human rationality.[44] Rather, requiredness complements the intuition of meaning that is available in consciousness through the noetic-noematic correlation.

> The sense of requiredness is not an afterthought; it is given with being human; not added to it. What is involved in authentic living is not only an intuition of meaning but a sensitivity to demand, not a purpose but an expectation. Sensitivity to demands is as inherent in being human as physiological functions are in human being.[45]

This idea of requiredness is a central aspect of Heschel's view of being because being is presented to man through a challenge and not through static intellectual categories. In language that parallels the famous dictum of Descartes, Heschel defines the basis of his ontology.

> Of one thing, however, I am sure. There is a challenge I can never evade, in moments of failure as in moments of achievement. Man is inescapably, essentially challenged on all levels of his existence. It is in his being challenged that he discovers himself as a human being. Do I exist as a human being? My answer is: I am commanded – therefore I am. There is a built-in sense of indebtedness in the consciousness of man, an awareness of owing gratitude, of being called upon at certain moments to reciprocate, to answer, to live in a way which is compatible with the grandeur and mystery of living.[46]

In keeping with his phenomenological program, Heschel reminds the reader that this intuition of indebtedness is a constituitive feature of being human and not a mere feeling.[47] Being qua created and not qua being establishes the fact that the "ought" of being precedes the "is" of being.[48] That is to say, man must first experience being, practically and ideally, as a demand and not as an object merely given to consciousness, which can be analytically depicted.[49]

This precedence given to the "ought," which is not only an epistemological category, but also a moral one as well,[50] defines the scope of Heschel's ontology. It is a deontological position, which is based on necessary moral obligations but not exclusively so.[51] For man, being is only available if he can intuit it as an imposition or an imperative. Man can only stand in a functional relation to being as presence.[52] Being is never substantial in Heschel's theology because of his phenomenological position. Heschel's presentation of this deontological position is difficult to dissect not only because of its parallel phenomenological structure, but because of its reliance on rabbinic doctrine. It is due to the profound complexity of Heschel's ideas that the elements which seem most disparate, his phenomenology and his rabbinic ideas, coalesce in his ontology. According to Heschel, to be is to obey.[53]

> Heidegger's rhetorical question, 'Has the Dasein, as such, ever freely decided and will it ever be able to decide as to whether to come into existence or not?' has been answered long ago: 'It is against your will that you are born, it is against your will that you live, and it is against your will that you are bound to give account....' The transcendence of human being is disclosed here as life imposed upon, as imposition to give account, as imposition of freedom. The transcendence of being is commandment, being here and now is obedience.[54]

This quote, left unidentified by Heschel, is based on the well-known statement from the Mishnah, Avot 4:22. Being, a divine imposition, is transcendentally available to man as commandment, specifically through mitzvot. The direct association by Heschel of his own deontological position with a rabbinic doctrine parallels the association of his idea of revelation with R. Ishmael's position. Underlying both of these positions is the act of consciousness described through its noetic-noematic correlation. The failure to uncover the noetic-noematic correlation as the act of consciousness grounding Heschel's deontological position presents a problem similar to that of the idea of revelation. Without a definite idea of the act of consciousness that grounds either Heschel's idea of revelation or his ontological commitment, the content of that idea remains unavailable. Due to Heschel's functionalism, the content of his ontology only becomes attainable when the act of consciousness is employed in the investigation itself. The mitzvot, the terminus ad quem of the investigation, supply the ideal and practical ends of knowledge which illustrate that content.

The dual role that the noetic-noematic correlation plays in Heschel's idea of revelation and in his ontology must in turn rely on another idea and experience that supports this bifurcation. This ultimate idea must be capable of penetrating each content of revelation and of transcending the natural situation of man. If this necessary ultimate idea cannot fulfill these functions, then Heschel's idea of revelation cannot claim to employ the noetic-noematic correlation consistently and according to Heschel, man will not be able, through his ontological commitment, to become an object of divine concern.

The idea that fulfills this pervasive and absolute function in Heschel's thinking is the idea of meaning. Meaning supplies the transcendental objectivity of God's concern and the response to any challenge, i.e. the objective content of revelation.

> Ultimate meaning as an idea is no answer to our anxiety. Humanity is more than an intellectual structure; it is a personal reality. The cry for meaning is a cry for ultimate relationship, for ultimate belonging. It is a cry in which all pretensions are abandoned. Are we alone in the wilderness of time, alone in the dreadfully marvelous universe, of which we are a part and where we feel forever like strangers? Is there a Presence to live by? A Presence worth living for, worth dying for? Is there a way of living in the Presence? Is there a way of living compatible with the Presence? As said above, the universe does not reveal its secret to us, and what it says is not expressed in the language of man. The ultimate meaning of man is not to be derived from ultimate being. Ultimate being is devoid of any relationship to particular beings, and unless meaning is related to me, I am not related to meaning. Man is in need of meaning, but if ultimate meaning is not in need of man, and he cannot relate himself to it, then ultimate meaning is meaningless to him. As a one-sided relationship, as a reaching-out or searching-for, the meeting of man and meaning would remain a goal beyond man's reach.[55]

This concept of meaning, while not a property, Platonic ideal or tautology derived from personhood,[56] is based in the same polarity as any other of Heschel's ontological concepts.[57] It is not an eternal idea but the implication of a relationship.[58] Consequently, man is impelled to go beyond the merely given.[59] According to Heschel, "Being is both presence and absence".[60] The mystery of being is not given in sheer being and is therefore dependent on meaning.[61] The existence of meaning beyond the mystery of being is the philosophical basis of revelation. This meaning, existing in a concealed manner, seeks to be revealed.[62] It is an intentional act of consciousness related to God.[63] As such, meaning is the transcendental basis of being and is accessible through the sense of the ineffable.[64]

> It is not by analogy or inference that we become aware of it. It is rather sensed as something immediately given, logically and psychologically prior to judgement, to the assimilation of subject matter to mental categories; a universal insight into an objective aspect of reality, of which all men are at all times capable; not the froth of ignorance but the climax of thought, indigenous to the climate that prevails at the summit of intellectual endeavor.[65]

Clearly, Heschel does not expect this concept of transcendence to be comprehended.[66] It is an experience that can be related to because of its phenomenological structure.[67] It can be apprehended because mystery is an ontological category that is not available to rational analysis.[68] The premise of transcendent meaning, available through awe and wonder,[69] nonetheless yields knowledge of presence because it is part of the subject-object structure of consciousness that Heschel specifies in revelation.

> Finite meaning is a thought we comprehend; infinite meaning is a thought that comprehends us; finite meaning we absorb; infinite meaning we encounter. Finite meaning has clarity; infinite meaning has depth. Finite meaning we comprehend with analytical reason; to infinite meaning we respond in awe. Infinite meaning is uncomfortable, not compatible with our categories. It is not to be grasped as though it were something in the world which appeared before us. Rather it is that in which the world appears to us. It is not an object – not a self-subsistent, timeless idea or value; it is a presence.[70]

Meaning, the core of Heschel's ontology, while deeply rooted in any intentional act of consciousness, cannot be adequately understood as such. Meaning is not only part of the subject-subject structure. The transcendence of meaning is existentially present in the subject-object structure as well. Meaning comes upon man without his choice. "Meaning insinuates itself into our existence. We cannot grab or conquer it, we can only be involved in it."[71] Yet, according to Heschel, it is the choice and loyal involvement of man with transcendence that inevitably completes the ontological reality presented to him.

> The mind is in search of rational coherence, the soul in quest of celebration. Knowledge is celebration. Truth is more than the equation of thing and thought. Truth transcends and unites both thing and thought. Truth is transcendence, its comprehension is loyalty.[72]

On this basis, Heschel's correlative deontology, can never achieve sufficiency without deeds. Man and God direct their concern toward each other in a specific situation. Human psychology and social reality only have meaning through deeds.[73] Heschel's rejection of the classic ontological question, what is being? in favor of his own question, why is being?[74] is based on an idea of practical relationships.[75] Contemplation, in any form, is not the foundation of this ontological position. Otherness is a category that arises through deeds. The deontological basis of this position is intimately connected to Heschel's phenomenological presentation of wonder and cannot be grasped without it. Wonder and actions are phenomenological facts. Once again the noetic-noematic correlation surfaces to provide the act of consciousness with an object. This connection of Heschel's idea of consciousness (wonder) and his deontology (actions) fulfills the final needs of Heschel's phenomenological methodology and demonstrates the deontological approach to a practical relationship.[76]

Not things but deeds are the source of our sad perplexities. Confronted with a world of things, man unloosens a tide of deeds. The fabulous fact of man's ability to act, *the wonder of doing,* is no less amazing than the marvel of being. Ontology inquires: what is *being?* What does it mean to be? The religious mind ponders; what is *doing?* What does it mean to do? What is the relation between the doer and the deed? between doing and being? Is there a purpose to fulfill, a task to carry out?[77]

---

[1] *The Prophets,* p. 264.

[2] *Ibid.,* p. 262.

[3] *Ibid.,* p. 484.

[4] *Ibid.,* pp. 484-485.

[5] This is the basis of Rothschild's polar concepts or Morris Cohen's scissor words. See Rothschild, "Introduction," p. 18.

[6] *The Prophets,* p. 229.

[7] This point is also made by Rotenstreich. The analysis he presents places the idea of correlation in the center of this framework where it belongs, but Rotenstreich rightly or wrongly emphasizes a Heschelian reaction to Hermann Cohen's and Martin Buber's dialectical and dialogical ideas of correlation. While Rotenstreich realizes the ontological significance of Heschel's position, he does not tie it completely to the dual structures that Heschel uses and Heschel's use of Husserl's noema. "The fact that Heschel employs the notion of pathos and attributes it to God does not annihilate the distance of God from man. And conversely, the fact that the prophetic consciousness entertains sympathy does not remove that consciousness from its correlative reference to God and does not bring about unification. The concept of correlation between man and God, the concept which is central to Hermann Cohen's interpretation of Judaism, is thus central for the phenomenological exploration of the prophetic consciousness. But the category of correlation remains within a rational frame of reference while the concepts of pathos and sympathy are deliberately meant to lodge the interpretation of religious interpretation of religious awareness in a transrational frame of reference. A similar wavering between the rational and the transrational nuances is visible in Heschel's employing of the concept of dialogue for the characterization of prophetic consciousness. Through the action and reaction of sympathy and pathos or pathos and sympathy, prayer and the prophetic response can be delineated as reactions to the divine word. Or else we find the prophetic act imbued with what is called 'subject structure', that is to say, the active self of the prophet is facing the subject of the inspiring God. Hence Heschel distinguishes between the dialectical aspect and the dialogical one: The dialectical aspect embraces the opposition and tension between components, while the dialogical structure constitutes the relation between God and man whereby the divine pathos is considered as the source of that dialogical structure. If we read this description correctly, the difference between the dialectical structure and the dialogical one is the following: The dialectical structure contains the distance and tension

between elements and thus is understood as based on the difference between a thesis and antithesis, while the dialogical structure is based primarily on the closeness between man and God, both from the end of man and from the end of God. Speaking in terms of two thinkers who interpreted religious consciousness, we may say that an attempt is made by Heschel to merge Hermann Cohen's notion of correlation with Buber's notion of dialogue. This has to be said, though at least one reader did not find in Heschel any reference to Buber's *Ich und Du,* though indeed there are references to Buber's writings on the Bible." "On Prophetic Consciousness," pp. 192-193.

[8] See Chapter Seven.

[9] *The Prophets,* pp. 487-488.

[10]Clarke, in his treatment of polarity and revelation, does not give it an ontological foundation. He limits the concept to three aspects of revelation (p. 134), which, however accurate, does not address the larger issue of Heschel's ontological commitment in relation to phenomenological claims about revelation (pp. 98-99).

[11] *God in Search of Man,* p. 19.

[12] *Ibid.,* p. 94.

[13] *Ibid.,* p. 97.

[14] *Who Is Man?,* p. 91.

[15] *God in Search of Man,* p. 97.

[16] *Ibid.,* p. 39.

[17] *Ibid.,* p. 40.

[18] "In Jewish thinking, the problem of being can never be treated in isolation but only in relation to God. The supreme categories in such [an] ontology are not being and becoming but law and love (justice and compassion, order and pathos). Being, as well as all beings, stands in a polarity of divine justice and divine compassion." *Ibid.,* p. 412

[19] *Man Is Not Alone,* p. 236.

[20]"The objection may be voiced that a psychological reaction is no evidence for an ontological fact, and we can never infer an object itself from a feeling a person has about it. The feeling of awe may often be the result of a misunderstanding of an ordinary fact; one may be overawed by an artificial spectacle or a display of evil power. That objection is, of course, valid. Yet what we infer from is not the actual feeling of awe but the intellectual certainty that in the face of nature's grandeur and mystery we must respond with awe; what we infer from is not a psychological state but a fundamental norm of human consciousness, a *categorical imperative.* Indeed, the validity and requiredness of awe enjoy a degree of certainty that is not even surpassed by the axiomatic certainty of geometry. We do not sense the mystery because we feel a need for it, just as we do not notice the ocean or the sky because we have a desire to see them. The sense of mystery is not a product of our will. It may be suppressed by the will but it is not generated by it. The mystery is not the product of a need, it is a fact." *Man Is Not Alone,* p. 27.

[21] "An event is a happening that cannot be reduced to a part of a process. It is something that we can neither predict nor fully explain. To speak of events is to imply that there are happenings *in the world* that are beyond the reach of our

explanations. What the consciousness of events implies, the belief in revelation claims explicitly, namely, that a voice of God *enters the world* which pleads with man to do His will. What do we mean by 'the world'? If we mean an ultimate, closed, fixed and self-sufficient system of phenomena behaving in accord with the laws known to us, then such a concept would exclude the possibility of admitting any super-mundane intervention or penetration by a voice not accounted for by these laws. Indeed, if the world as described by natural science is regarded as the ultimate, then there is no sense in searching for the Divine which is by definition the ultimate. How could there be one ultimate within the other? The claim of the Bible is absurd, unless we are ready to comprehend that the world as scrutinized and depicted by science is but a thin surface of the profoundly unknown. Order is only one of the aspects of nature; its reality is a mystery given but not known. Countless relations that determine our life in history are neither known nor predictable. What history does with the laws of nature cannot be expressed by a law of nature....Revelation is not an act of interfering with the normal course of natural processes but the act of instilling a new creative moment into the course of history. The chain of causality and of discursive reasoning, in which things and thoughts are fettered, is fixed in the space of endless possibilities like the tongue hanging in a silent bell. It is as if all the universe were fixed to a single point. In revelation the bell rings, and words vibrate through the world." *God in Search of Man,* pp. 210-211.

[22] *God in Search of Man,* p. 200.

[23]"We cannot, on the other hand, analyze man as a being only here and now. Not only here, because his situation is intentional with the situation of other men scattered far and wide all over the world. Not only now, because his total existence is, in a sense, a summation of past generations, a distillation of experiences and thoughts of his ancestors." *Who Is Man?,* p. 99.

[24] *God in Search of Man,* p. 204.

[25] *Ibid.,* p. 211.

[26] *Ibid.,* pp. 211-212.

[27] *Ibid.,* p. 216.

[28]"Judaism claims that time is exceedingly relevant. Elusive as it may be, it is pregnant with the seeds of eternity. Significant to God and decisive for the destiny of man are the things that happen in time, in history. Biblical history is the triumph of time over space. Israel did not grow into being through a series of accidents. Nature itself did not evolve out of a process, by necessity; it was called into being by an event, an act of God. History is the supreme witness for God." *Ibid.,* p. 206.

[29] Merkle, p. 264, note 8.

[30] "Man is being called upon, challenged and solaced. God is in search of man, and life is something that requires an answer. History is above all a question, a fathoming, a probing, a testing. The primary topic, then, of biblical thinking is not man's knowledge of God but rather man's being known by God, man's being an object of divine knowledge and concern. This is why the great puzzle was: Why should God, the Creator of heaven and earth, be concerned with man? Why should the deeds of puny man be relevant enough to affect the life

of God? 'Can a man be profitable to God? Or can he that is wise be profitable unto Him? Is it any advantage to the Almighty, that thou art righteous? Or is it gain to Him, that thou makest thy ways blameless?' Job 22:2-3. God takes man seriously. He enters into a direct relationship with man, namely, a covenant, to which not only man but also God is committed. In his ultimate confrontation and crisis the biblical man knows not only God's eternal mercy and justice but also God's commitment to man. Upon this sublime fact rests the meaning of history and the glory of human destiny." *Who Is Man?* pp. 74-75.

[31] *God in Search of Man*, pp. 412-413.

[32] *Man Is Not Alone*, p. 237.

[33] See Chapter Eight.

[34] *God in Search of Man*, p. 217.

[35] *Ibid.*, p. 350.

[36] *Ibid.*, p. 316.

[37] *Who Is Man?*, p. 107.

[38] See Chapters Eight and Nine.

[39] *Who Is Man?*, p. 87.

[40] "The loss of the sense of significant being is due to the loss of the commandment of being. Being is obedience, a response. 'Thou art' precedes 'I am.' I am because I am called upon to be." *Who Is Man?*, p. 98. See Chapter Eight for Heschel's rejection of the literal or symbolic interpretation of revelation in favor of a responsive interpretation.

[41] This is apparent throughout *Who Is Man?* and is especially prominent in pp. 66-72. This problem is also alluded to by Heschel in *God in Search of Man*, p. 289, from another viewpoint. "The Bible speaks of man as having been created in the likeness of God, establishing the principle of *an analogy of being*. In his very being, man has something in common with God. Beyond the analogy, the Bible teaches the principle of *an analogy in acts*. Man may act in the likeness of God. It is in this likeness of acts – 'to walk in His ways' – that is the link by which man may come close to God. To live in such likeness is the essence of imitation of the Divine."

[42] *Who Is Man?*, p. 71.

[43] *Ibid.*, p. 31.

[44] *Ibid.*, p. 106.

[45] *Ibid.*, p. 106.

[46] *Ibid.*, p. 111.

[47] *Ibid.*, p. 108.

[48] *Ibid.*, pp. 97 and 108.

[49] *Ibid.*, p. 109.

[50] "Knowing is not due to coming upon something, naming and explaining it. Knowing is due to something forcing itself upon us. Thought is a response to being rather than an invention. The world does not lie prostrate, waiting to be given order and coherence by the generosity of the human mind. Things are evocative. When conceits are silent and all words stand still, the world speaks. We must learn to burn the cliches to clear the air for hearing. Conceptual cliches are counterfeit; preconceived notions are misfits. Knowledge involves

love, care for the things we seek to know, longing, being-drawn-to, being overwhelmed." *Who Is Man?*, p. 109.

[51] For a moral explanation of this deontological position, see S. Spero, *Morality, Halakhah and the Jewish Tradition*, (KTAV: New York, 1983), pp. 83-85.

[52] "Being human is a most precarious condition. It is not a substance but a presence, a whisper calling in the wilderness." *Who Is Man?*, p. 100.

[53] *Ibid.*, p. 97.

[54] *Ibid.*, p. 97.

[55] *Ibid.*, p. 73.

[56] *Ibid.*, p. 72-73.

[57] *Ibid.*, pp. 76-77.

[58] "Ultimate meaning is not grasped once and for all in the form of a timeless idea, acquired once and for all, securely preserved in conviction. It is not simply given. It comes upon us as an intimation that comes and goes." *Ibid.*, p. 79.

[59] *Ibid.*, p. 76.

[60] *Ibid.*, p. 90.

[61] *Ibid.*, pp. 76-77.

[62] "Being is a mystery, being is concealment, but there is meaning beyond the mystery. The meaning beyond the mystery seeks to come to expression. The destiny of human being is to articulate what is concealed. The divine seeks to be disclosed in the human." *Ibid.*, p. 77

[63] "The mystery is not a synonym for the unknown, but rather a term for a meaning which stands in relation to God." *Ibid.*, p. 77

[64] *Ibid.*, pp. 77.

[65] *Ibid.*, pp. 77.

[66] *Ibid.*, p. 79.

[67] *Ibid.*, p. 79.

[68] *God in Search of Man*, pp. 57-58.

[69] *Who Is Man?*, p. 79.

[70] *Ibid.*, p. 78.

[71] *Ibid.*, p. 104.

[72] *Ibid.*, pp. 117-118.

[73] *God in Search of Man*, p. 284.

[74] *Ibid.*, p. 92, "But what are the foundations of nature? To the Greeks who take the world for granted Nature, Order is the answer. To the Biblical mind in its radical amazement nature, order are not an answer but a problem: why is there order, being, at all?"

[75] J. N. Mohanty, *Phenomenology and Ontology*, (The Hague: Martinus Nijhoff, 1970), pp. 92-103.

[76] Wonder and action, the foundational deontological ideas, are not the only ideas constituted by polarity. According to Heschel the basic categories of Jewish thought and life contain inherent polarities that constitute their reality. *God in Search of Man*, pp. 336-346.

[77] *Ibid.*, p. 285.

Epilogue

In one important way Heschel's philosophy of Judaism is dissimilar to much that has preceded and followed it. The work of Abraham Heschel gives serious consideration to the broad range of problems that have been integral to the philosophical and theological traditions of western intellectual history. Heschel's depth-theology is an attempt to locate the proper theological concerns of modern Judaism amidst the methods of modern philosophy. Heschel's considerations run the entire length of the philosophy of religion, from Spinoza to the Logical Positivists and from the ancient Greeks to Hegel and Heidegger. While he does not, as usual scholarship would require, address these positions in a discursive manner, Heschel does confront their seminal claims in an unsystematic way.

The success or failure of Heschel to make this program apparent or for modern Jewish scholars or philosophers of religion to notice this program is no longer the crucial issue. His thought is clearly positioned in the tradition of continental European philosophy. It remains for those who think seriously about theological issues and Judaism, to describe Heschel's relationship to the thought of the great thinkers of modern philosophy, such as Kant and Heidegger for example, whom he sees as his interlocuters.

The excitement (if one dare use such a description of a philosopher of religion or a rabbinic figure) of Heschel's intellectualism is that his achievement is framed in terms of almost every conceivable facet of Judaism. Heschel's thought is replete with references to Kabbalism, Hasidism, Medieval philosophy and Rabbinic thought, to name but a few of the major trends in the last two thousand years of the history of Jewish ideas. Heschel's use of these sources indicates the immense amount of work to be done in understanding their contribution to his theology and in his contribution towards their significance.

At a time when the philosophy of religion is reclaiming its impressive past and pushing toward new and unforeseen horizons, the philosophy of Abraham Heschel stands as one of the greatest attempts of the modern and postmodern era, to present the ideas of Judaism in their entirety without diminishing their traditional context or their dynamic philosophical import. In this light, Heschel's thought will stand head and shoulders above much that preceded it and much that is destined to follow it.

Index